Musical Bows of Southern Africa

Musical Bows of Southern Africa

Edited by
Sazi Dlamini

BLOOMSBURY ACADEMIC
NEW YORK • LONDON • OXFORD • NEW DELHI • SYDNEY

BLOOMSBURY ACADEMIC
Bloomsbury Publishing Inc
1385 Broadway, New York, NY 10018, USA
50 Bedford Square, London, WC1B 3DP, UK
29 Earlsfort Terrace, Dublin 2, Ireland

BLOOMSBURY, BLOOMSBURY ACADEMIC and the Diana logo are
trademarks of Bloomsbury Publishing Plc

First published in the United States of America 2021
This paperback edition published in 2022

Copyright © Sazi Dlamini and contributors, 2021

Cover design by Louise Dugdale
Cover image © Maria Cristina Giampietri

All rights reserved. No part of this publication may be reproduced or
transmitted in any form or by any means, electronic or mechanical,
including photocopying, recording, or any information storage or retrieval
system, without prior permission in writing from the publishers.

Bloomsbury Publishing Inc does not have any control over, or responsibility for,
any third-party websites referred to or in this book. All internet addresses given in this
book were correct at the time of going to press. The author and publisher regret any
inconvenience caused if addresses have changed or sites have ceased to exist,
but can accept no responsibility for any such changes.

Whilst every effort has been made to locate copyright holders the publishers would be
grateful to hear from any person(s) not here acknowledged.

Library of Congress Cataloging-in-Publication Data
Names: Dlamini, Sazi, editor.
Title: Musical bows of southern Africa / edited by Sazi Dlamini.
Description: New York City : Bloomsbury Academic, 2020. |
Includes bibliographical references and index. |
Summary: "An overview of the theory and practice of musical bows in
Southern Africa with emphasis on contemporary practices"– Provided by publisher.
Identifiers: LCCN 2020036731 (print) | LCCN 2020036732 (ebook) | ISBN
9781501346743 (hardback) | ISBN 9781501346750 (epub) | ISBN
9781501346767 (pdf)
Subjects: LCSH: Musical bow–Africa, Southern. | Music–Social
aspects–Africa, Southern.
Classification: LCC ML1091 .M87 2020 (print) | LCC ML1091 (ebook) |
DDC 787.9/20968–dc23
LC record available at https://lccn.loc.gov/2020036731
LC ebook record available at https://lccn.loc.gov/2020036732

ISBN:	HB:	978-1-5013-4674-3
	PB:	978-1-5013-7032-8
	ePDF:	978-1-5013-4676-7
	eBook:	978-1-5013-4675-0

Typeset by Integra Software Services Pvt. Ltd.,

To find out more about our authors and books visit www.bloomsbury.com
and sign up for our newsletters.

Contents

List of Contributors		vi
Preface		vii
1	A brief introduction to musical bows in Southern Africa *Bernhard Bleibinger*	1
2	Chipendani (mouth bow): The origin of the Shona *mbira* harmonic system and of Andrew Tracey's 'basic *kalimba* core', with an appendix on the Venda *tshihwana* Klaus-Peter Brenner	37
3	Musical bows of Namibia *Dave Dargie*	83
4	*Umakhweyana* and *ugubhu* Zulu musical bows as *inkokha, imvingo, inkohlisa, uqwabe* and *isiqwemqwemana* Sazi Dlamini	113
5	The social dynamics of three Zimbabwean musical bows: The *chipendani, mukube* and ground-bow *Jennifer W. Kyker*	157
6	The *sitontolo* mouth bow of eSwatini: Embodiment, stories and music *Cara Stacey and Vusi Sibandze*	183
7	Musical bows of the amaXhosa *David Dargie*	203
8	Eastern Kalahari bow music *Jürgen Schöpf*	229
Contributor Biographies		253
Index		255

For audio and visual examples, see https://www.bloomsbury.com/us/musical-bows-of-southern-africa-9781501346743/.

Contributors

Bernhard Bleibinger is musicologist, anthropologist and historian. He is currently professor of music at the University of Fort Hare in South Africa.

Klaus-Peter Brenner is ethnomusicologist at the University of Göttingen, Germany. Several of his publications deal with Shona *chipendani* and *mbira* music of Zimbabwe.

Dave Dargie is Visiting Professor to the International Library of African Music at Rhodes University, Makhanda, South Africa. He is the author of *Xhosa Music – Its Techniques and Instruments*. His CD, DVD collection and handbooks are available from the International Library of African Music.

Sazi Dlamini is musicologist/ethnomusicologist and lecturer in music at the University of KwaZulu-Natal, Durban (South Africa).

Jennifer W. Kyker received her PhD from the University of Pennsylvania in 2011. She is currently Associate Professor of Ethnomusicology at the University of Rochester.

Cara Stacey is a South African musician and academic based in Johannesburg and Mbabane. Her research focuses on traditional instrument players in eSwatini.

Vusi Sibandze is a researcher, musician and visual artist based in Mbabane, eSwatini. He has a vast experience working with traditional instrument players for many years.

Jürgen Schöpf is an ethnomusicologist with special interests in organology, sound analysis, the relationship of speech and music, and soundscape research.

Preface

Musical bows are among the most commonly practised indigenous musical instruments in Africa. Their widespread occurrence in particularly south of the Sahara confirms historical convergences between early pastoral, agrarian and hunter-gatherer societies of the continent's diverse ethnic cultures.

A worldwide distribution implicates musical bows in processes of the earliest musical socialization of humankind and potentially map probable routes of a diasporic settlement of the inhabited world. Furthermore, the diversity of contexts for musical bow practices among far-flung global communities particularizes these instruments for the interdisciplinary role music occupies generally across the sciences, the humanities, the arts and nature.

The regional focus of the present volume on Southern Africa draws attention to the ubiquity of musical bow practices among some of the world's most marginal indigenous societies. Musical bows and their cultures of practice are not solely an African phenomenon, as Bernhard Bleibinger points out in the first chapter, 'A Brief Introduction to Musical Bows in Southern Africa'. Since their revelation for the earliest anthropological and ethno-organological studies – as sound generative and musical performance artefacts – the occurrence of musical bows in seemingly inexhaustible variety has long baffled their categorization. This is acknowledged in Bleibinger's focus on criteria for classification, including principles of sound production, playing techniques and theoretical relationships of Southern African musical bows to Western European conceptions of scale and melody.

In Chapter 2 – '*Chipendani* (Mouth Bow): The Origin of the Shona *Mbira* Harmonic System and of Andrew Tracey's "Basic *Kalimba* Core" With an Appendix on the Venda *Tshihwana*', Klaus-Peter Brenner details two systematic analyses attributing characteristic harmonic sensibilities of two ethno-geographically disparate mouth bows, namely *chipendani* (Shona) and *tshihwana* (Venda). Brenner's two organo-archaeological studies demonstrate the bases of complex traditional Shona *mbira* and the Venda *tshikona* harmonic systems in tonal organization patterns of *chipendani* (Shona) and *tshihwana* (Venda) mouth bows respectively. Both instruments share a basic organological construction of a single divided string with several other mouth bows in the southern African region. In this regard, Brenner's work bears far-reaching implications for music-theoretical studies of other braced mouth bows still found in use in the SADC region, including the Swati/Zulu *isiqomqomana/isithontolo*, the Ndau-Shangana/Chopi/Thonga *xipendani*, the Damara/*noukhas* and the Chopi *xipendani*, among others.

The volume includes two invaluable contributions from David Dargie: 'Musical Bows of Namibia' (Chapter 3) and 'Musical Bows of the AmaXhosa' (Chapter 7). Both studies are ethnocultural organological surveys of diverse types of musical bows in their respective regions – Namibia and South Africa's Eastern Cape province. They are further complimented in aspects of scholarly research collaboration and Dargie's unique decades long practising of ethnomusical missiological work among the Xhosa people, and a subsequent teaching professorship at the University of Fort Hare for several decades. The chapter on Namibian musical bows incorporates leading ethnomusicological documentary research by Drs Minette Mans, Emmanuelle Olivier and Hervé Rivière. In reflecting the author's deep-rooted experiences of living and working among Xhosa rural communities, the chapter on Xhosa musical is framed by an understanding of underlying historical, social and political contexts of the many repertoires analysed and discussed. As they inhere in centuries-old bow music repertoires, such Xhosa folk memories include those of great border wars against conquering white settlerhood, pestilences of disease and famine, migration, destitution, landscape and cultural heritage.

Chapter 4 focuses on the theoretical significances of indigenous terms bequeathed to present studies by pioneering research and scholarly knowledge of *ugubhu* and *umakhweyana*, the two relatively well-recognized, Zulu calabash-resonated musical bows. The chapter is underlied by a contention that the meanings of little-understood Zulu terms as *umakhweyana*, *imvingo*, *inkohlisa*, *uqwabe* and *isiqwemqwemana* among others, embed rooted conceptions and widely shared indigenous cultural knowledge about *ugubhu* and *umakhweyana* musical bows in particular.

Jennifer W. Kyker's contribution 'The Social Dynamics of Three Zimbabwean Musical Bows: The *Chipendani*, *Mukube*, and Ground-bow' (Chapter 5) draws attention to the social embedding of *chipendani*, *mukube* and the ground-bow in musical practices of Shona gendered rites of passage and ritual exchanges in the oral transmission of culture, material goods and indigenous spirituality. She concludes her chapter with a provocative proposal for a broader social consideration of musical bow practices beyond the mere self-delectative.

Cara Stacey and Vusi Sibandze, the co-authors of 'The *Sitontolo* Mouth Bow of eSwatini: Embodiment, Stories and Music' (Chapter 6), regard the rare occurrence in eSwatini (formerly Swaziland), of *isithontolo* as symptomatic of dwindling practices of the braced mouth bow in the south and south-easternmost SADC regions. Using both music notation and text transcriptions, their study demonstrates how *isithontolo* songs function in the mediation of individual social experience and subjective power positions of traditional musicians in eSwatini.

Chapter 7 – 'Musical Bows of the AmaXhosa' – benefits from Dave Dargie's protracted work with Xhosa communities of Ngqoko, a rural village east of Lady Frere in the Eastern Cape province of South Africa, where he was deployed as ethnomusicologist by the Roman Catholic church. Among his teachers and music collaborators were included practising custodians of diverse forms of Xhosa indigenous musical performance – singing, dance, oratory and various types of musical bows. Dargie's studies of the foremost surviving indigenous Xhosa musical instruments provide an invaluable resource for continuing performance practice and teaching of *uhadi, umrhubhe (umqangi), ikatari* and *inkinge* monoheterochords.

In 'Eastern Kalahari Bow Music' (Chapter 8), ethno-organologist Jürgen Schöpf engages with marginal practices of *N!oma* (mouth bow solo performance) and *N!oma jieu* (calabash-resonated musical bow ensemble performance) among minority cattle-post caretakers of the Eastern Kalahari in central Botswana. His experiences reveal close affinities between the regional people's musical bow performance traditions and wildlife, especially antelopes and other prey that are historically central to the survival of their disrupted hunter gatherer heritage.

In addition, the chapters are enhanced with extensive figures and digital media of audio and video recordings. Most of the footage has emanated from contributors' field research experiences and also includes historical material from private, institutional and archival collections of photographs, transcriptions, recorded demonstrations and bow song performances, musical bow theory and technique captured in sound and audiosual medium. The digital media accompanying this volume may be accessed at https://www.bloomsbury.com/us/musical-bows-of-southern-africa-9781501346743/.

I am greatly privileged in the responsibility of editing a monograph volume by several scholars whose research informs and advances our present knowledge about musical bows of Southern Africa. It is my hope that the present volume of *Musical Bows of Southern Africa* engenders interest in researchers, students, performing groups and individuals as well as other formations of popular and traditional culture whose practices have musical bow performance as their focus.

I would like to sincerely thank contributors to this volume for their patience, attention and diligence. I am also grateful to Ms Maria Cristina Giampietri for looking out for my health and well-being, and for her beautiful illustrations of Zulu musical bows.

The volume is dedicated to the memory of my friends and mentors, the composers Cde. Ndikho Xaba and Prof Jurgen Brauninger, who passed away in 2019.

Dr Sazi Dlamini, volume editor

1

A brief introduction to musical bows in Southern Africa

Bernhard Bleibinger

Abstract

Musical bows may appear simple and old-fashioned; yet, the playing techniques and the construction of these musical instruments are fascinating and complex. Besides that, there is a wide variety of musical bows in Southern Africa. This chapter will provide the reader with a brief introduction to different types of musical bows, their playing techniques (including basic principles concerning the amplification of overtones and the production of scales and melodies) and the problem of their classification. As explained in this chapter, the interest of researchers in this type of musical instrument and its players, and the presence of artists and companies specialized in traditional instruments on the internet show that musical bows haven't lost their fascinating aura.

Introduction

One may almost believe that musical bows are extinct instruments. When asked if there is still somebody in the village who can play musical bows, people often reply that there isn't anybody or that bows used to be played by girls and in the past only. However, when they are given a musical bow the very same persons may all of a sudden start playing it in the most amazing way.[1] Therefore, it rather seems as if bows have their own niche in village communities and, as I will show later, in modern urban societies.

Musical bows are fascinating instruments, for, as Dave Dargie used to say, they seem to be simple instruments on the one hand and are used to produce complex music on the other hand. I agree with him.[2] Dargie gained deep insights in overtone music, i.e. bow music and overtone singing, in the Eastern Cape Province of South Africa and its neighbouring countries during research he conducted in the 1970s, 1980s and 1990s. His first overview of musical bows of Southern Africa dates back to 1986 and was published by the African Institute in *Africa Insight* (Dargie 1986), a journal concerned with revealing the injustice of apartheid. Since then he has produced a series of articles and booklets on that topic.

In this chapter, I will summarize some main principles of musical bows. However, other chapters in this volume are concerned with regional specific bow types in better confined regions and therefore are rich in details. I will therefore only introduce principles of bow music (e.g. production of tones and scales) and a condensed overview of the different types of musical bows in Southern Africa, followed by some remarks concerning their classification. Drawings and a table indicating classifications, bow types, names of bows, ethnic groups and playing principles are included to assist the reader.

First, what is Southern Africa? The demarcation is a bit complicated not only because the term refers to borders established in the nineteenth and twentieth centuries (i.e. in a time of colonialism and the artificial construction of nation states). It is also complicated because today some of the Southern African countries can be referred to as Central or East African countries at the same time (be it for economic, political or other reasons). Broadly speaking the following countries belong to Southern Africa: Angola, Botswana, Eswatini (or Swaziland), Lesotho, Malawi, Mozambique, Namibia, South Africa, Zambia and Zimbabwe. Angola can also be referred to as Central African, and Malawi, Mozambique, Zambia and Zimbabwe as East African countries. In ethnographic literature, all of these appear as Southern African nations, and in all of them, one can find musical bows. Bows as major chordophone are occasionally mentioned as a distinguishing feature of music in Southern Africa (Kaemmer 1997: 702). Cultural traits are more important in the description of music of Southern Africa than borders of modern national states. Thus scholars such as John Kaemmer, by loosely adapting George Peter Murdock's model (1959), prefer to explain music in connection with their respective societies. Such societies include:

Khoisan people, i.e. Khoi and San;
Nguni peoples, such as Xhosa and Zulu;
Sotho peoples, such as the Sotho in Lesotho, the Tswana or Chwana in Botswana, and Pedi or Eastern Sotho in South Africa;

South-eastern African peoples in the Transvaal, southern Malawi, southern and central Mozambique and the region between the Limpopo and Zambezi rivers, such as the Venda, Chopi, Tsonga, the Sena and Nyungwe;

Middle Zambezi peoples, such as the Ila and Tonga, Lozi and Nkoya; Southwestern Bantu peoples in Namibia and Angola, such as the Ovimbundu, Ovambo, Nkhumbi and Herero (Kaemmer 1997).

Musical bows – sound production, scales and characteristics

Musical bows are not an entire African phenomenon, but can be found on other continents as well, as early publications on the distribution of this type of instrument show (Balfour 1902; Mason 1897). Nevertheless, there is a remarkable number of different sorts of musical bows which are still played or have been in use until recently in Africa, and specifically in sub-Saharan Africa. For that reason, we easily establish an imaginary connection between Africa and musical bows. Musical bows and other musical instruments are subject to migration, whereby ethnic groups other than the group of origin may adopt, incorporate and modify them. Because of that fact, we may find that the very same instrument may be known by different names in different regions. It may be hard and even impossible to trace the origin of a particular type of instrument [see for instance early descriptions mentioned by Dargie (1988: 41–3[3]); Mugglestone (1982[4]); and Schöpf (2008: 54–5)]. Thus, musical bows are evidence and product of transcultural encounters and processes. Some bows may even be modern creations or may have incorporated materials that have only been in existence since the twentieth century, if – as stated by Kirby ([1934] 1968: 215) – we think, for instance, of the Venda *tsijolo* or Sotho *sekatari*, or the Xhosa *ikatari*, which use a five-litre oil tin made of metal as resonator.

With reference to Southern Africa, several authors explain the before-mentioned processes of transmission of musical instruments and elements. According to current theories, immigrating Bantu-speaking people borrowed some bows and specific scales derived from at least two fundamentals from the Khoi and San, the indigenous people of Southern Africa, over the last 1,000 years. Yet besides that, a transfer of musical instruments and musical knowledge took place among Bantu-speaking groups during the eighteenth and nineteenth centuries.[5]

Musical bows in principle consist of a bent stick with a string attached to both ends. The string may be made of metal, sinew, hair or plant fibre, but nowadays

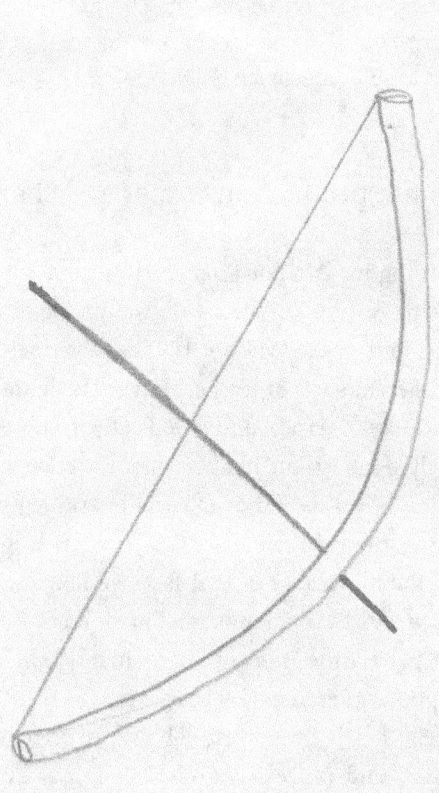

Figure 1.1 Unbraced bow in one piece (e.g. Xhosa *umrhubhe*). Drawing by author.

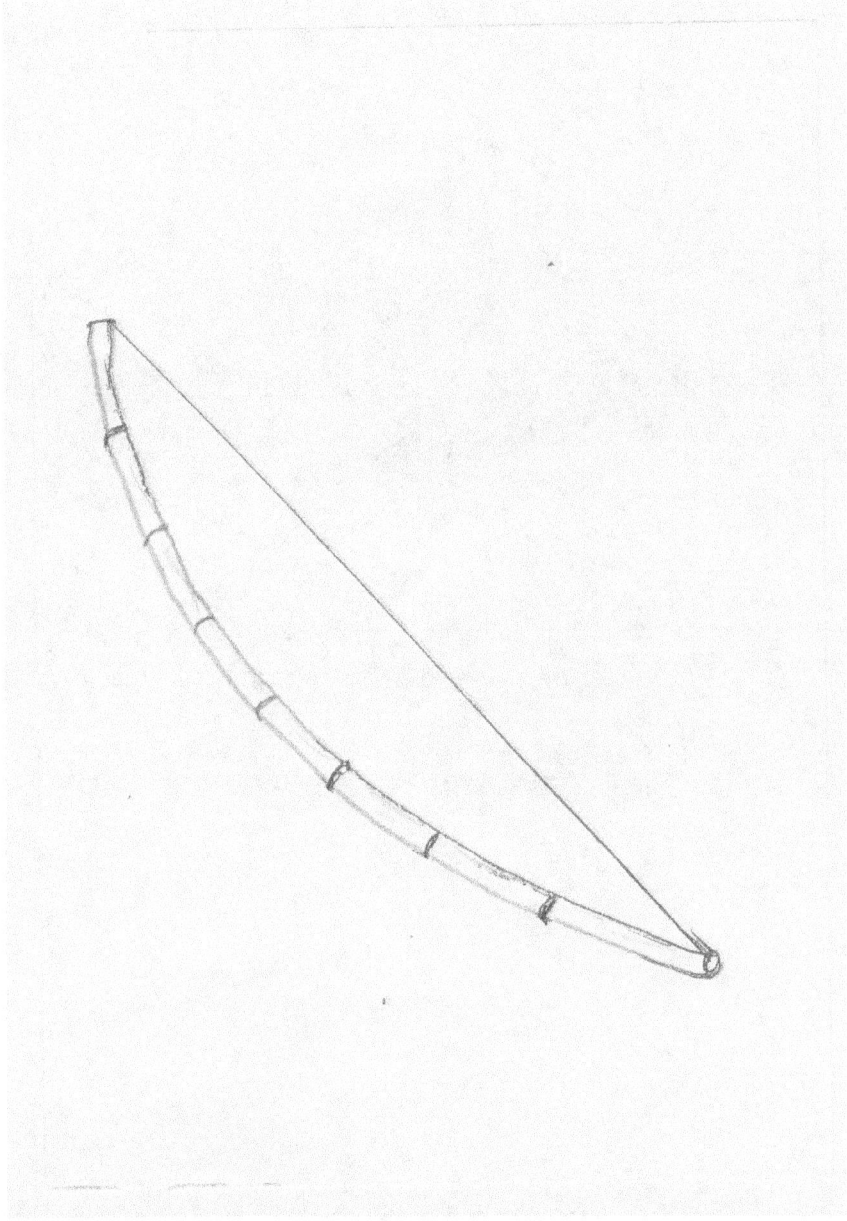

Figure 1.2 Unbraced bow made of river-reed (e.g. Xhosa *inkinge*). Drawing by author.

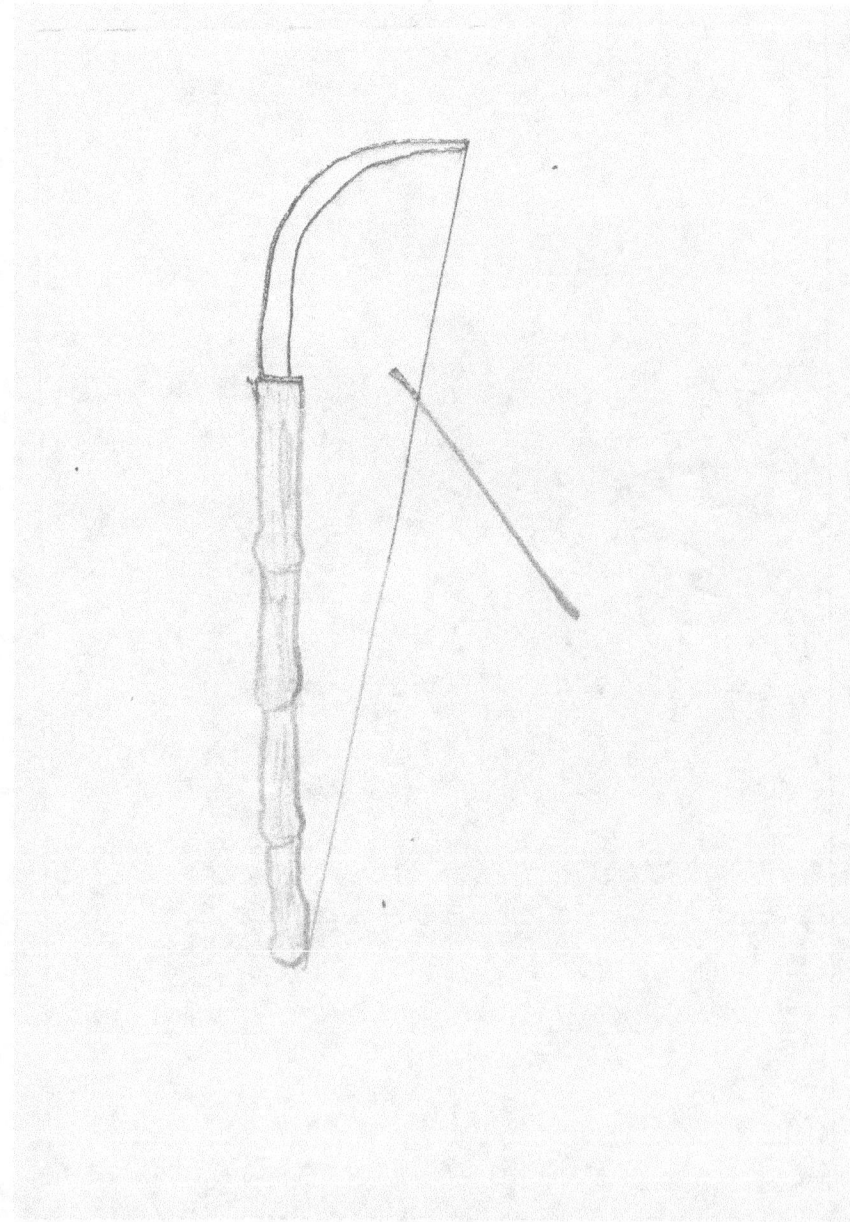

Figure 1.3 Unbraced bow in two pieces, e.g. Xhosa *inkinge*. Kirby ([1934] 1968: 239) also refers to it as *umrhubhe* among Xhosa and Zulu, and as *umqunge* among the Mpondo. Drawing by author.

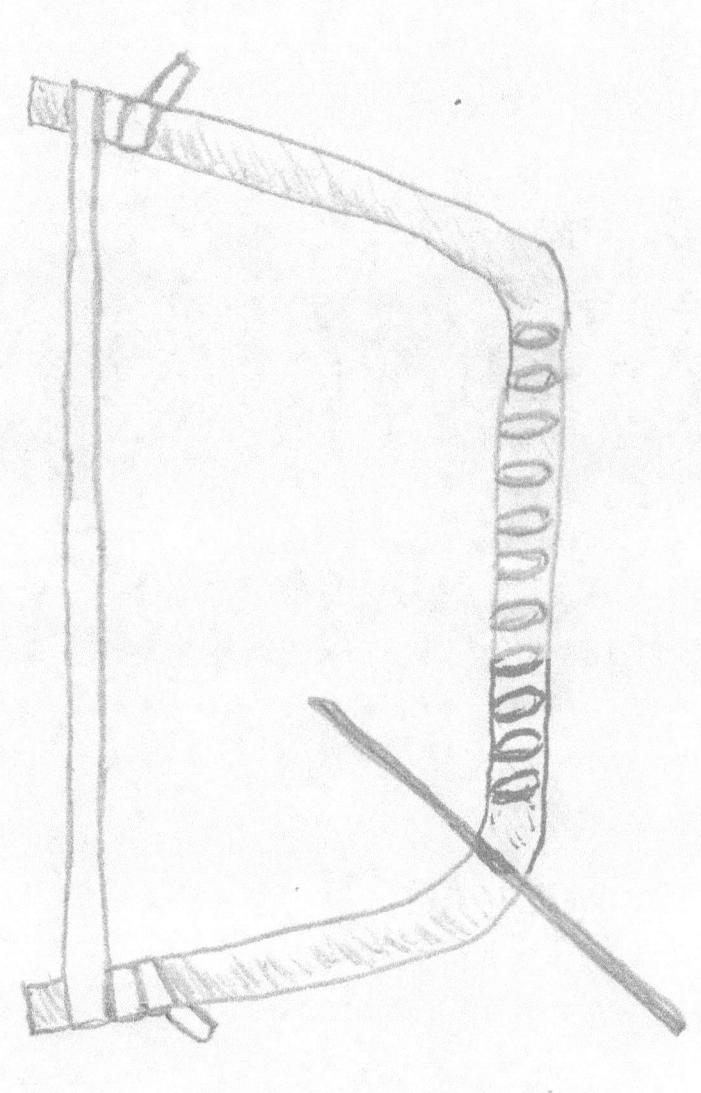

Figure 1.4 Unbraced bow, vibration/sound produced by scrapping a stick over notches in the bow (e.g. *xizambi* from Mozambique). Drawing by author.

Figure 1.5 Braced mouth bow with bracing loop around string and staff (e.g. Shona chipendani). Drawing by author.

Figure 1.6 Braced mouth bow with bracing loop tied to string (e.g. Shona chipendani). Drawing by author.

even fishing line is in use (Dargie 1986: 50). The vibration produced when plucking, tapping or bowing the string or notches on the bent stick – as in the case of the *xizambi* (Figure 1.4) from Mozambique – is amplified and specific harmonics emphasized; the amplification is done either with the help of the mouth cavity or a resonator. A resonator is basically a means which provides some sort of cavity, such as a calabash, native vessels, a tin, container or even a hole in the ground [see for instance Kruger (1985, 1989), Tessmann (1914) in Ziegler (2006: 283); or Djenda (1968) concerning the latter case]. In the case of the *lesiba*, a stringed wind instrument, vibration is produced by blowing at a feather quill attached to the string.

Bows can roughly be grouped as follows:

Mouth resonated bows

Mouth resonated bows are subdivided into unbraced bows such as the Xhosa umrhubhe (Figure 1.1) and braced bows similar to the Shona chipendani in Figure 1.5 and Figure 1.6 (which have an adjustable brace loop and brace loops attached to the string). These can again be subdivided into bows whose staff consists of one wooden piece (Figure 1.2) and bows that consist of two to three different pieces of wood and cane inserted into each other (Figure 1.3). Some authors use further subdivisions that refer to the way the bows are played.

Bows with an attached resonator

Another type of bow is that with an attached resonator. They can be unbraced (Figure 1.7), e.g. Xhosa *uhadi* or Zulu *ugubhu*, or braced (Figure 1.8), e.g. Zulu *umakhweyane* and Ovambo okamburumbumbwa or OvaZimba ombulumbumba (Figure 1.9). The attached resonators mostly consisted of calabashes; yet, other materials[6] can be used as well.

Bows without an attached resonator

Besides that, there are bows without an attached resonator. In this case, the bow is held against or put on top of a vessel that serves as resonator, e.g. a pot covered with a mat or membrane, such as the *lipuruboro* from the Kavango (Figure 1.10). Similar

Figure 1.7 Unbraced bow with attached resonator (e.g. Xhosa *uhadi* or Zulu *ugubhu*). Drawing by author.

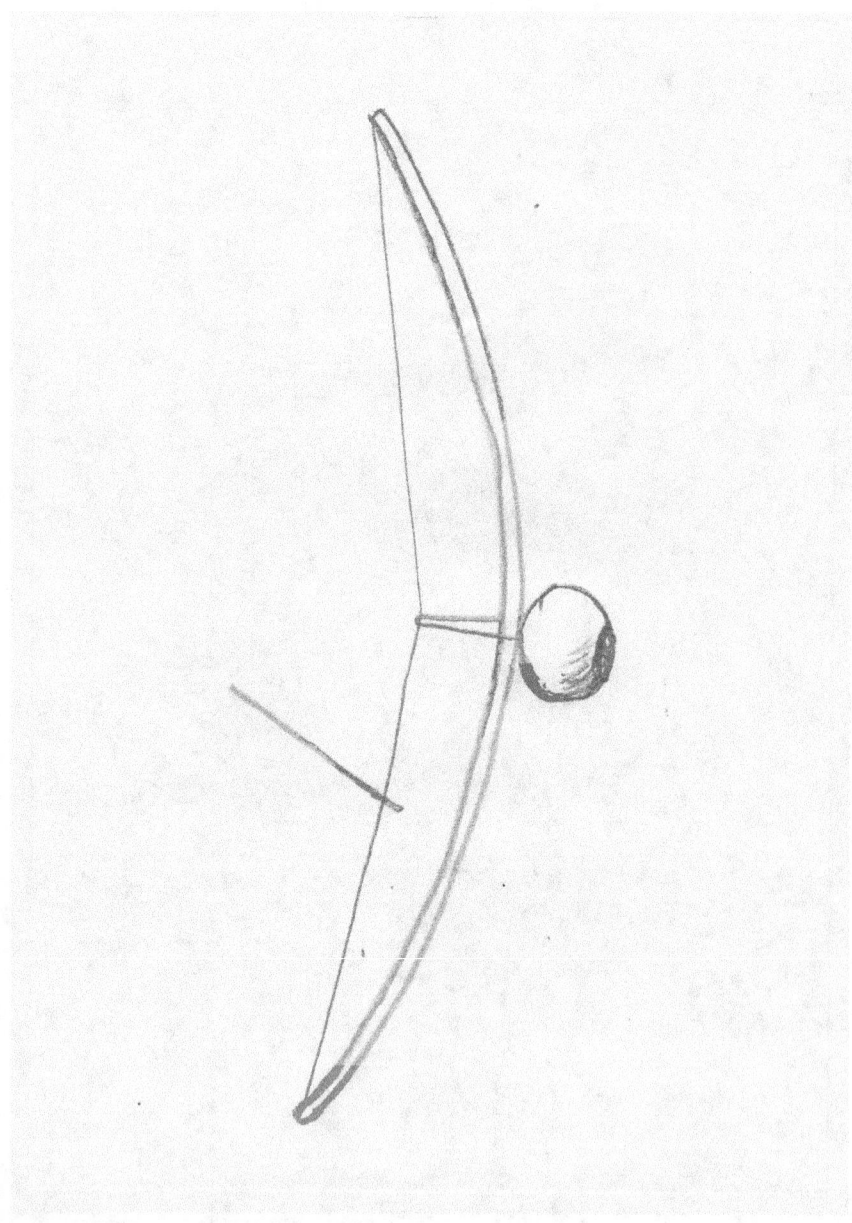

Figure 1.8 Braced bow (middle braced) with attached resonator (e.g. Zulu *umakhweyane*). Drawing by author.

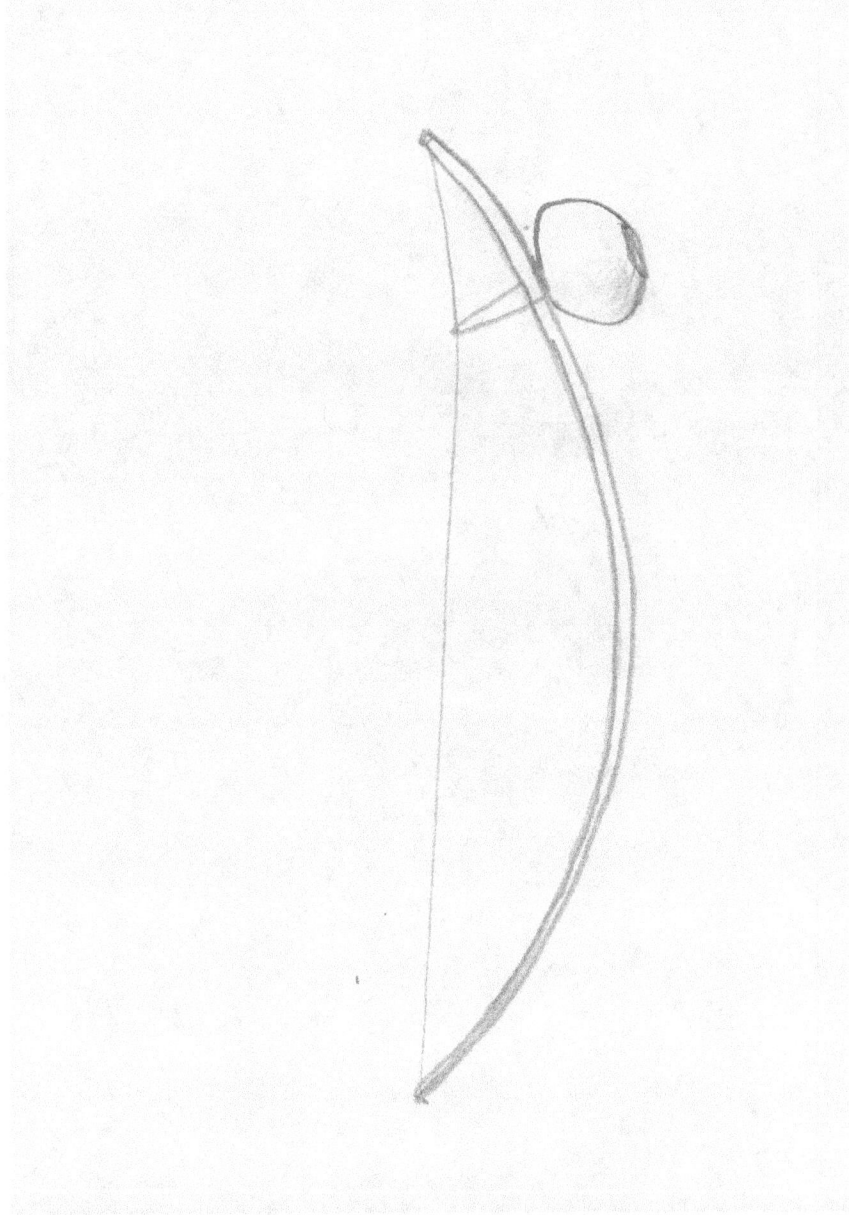

Figure 1.9 Braced bow (end braced) with attached resonator (e.g. Ovambo *okamburumbumbwa* or OvaZimba *ombulumbumba*[7]). Drawing by author.

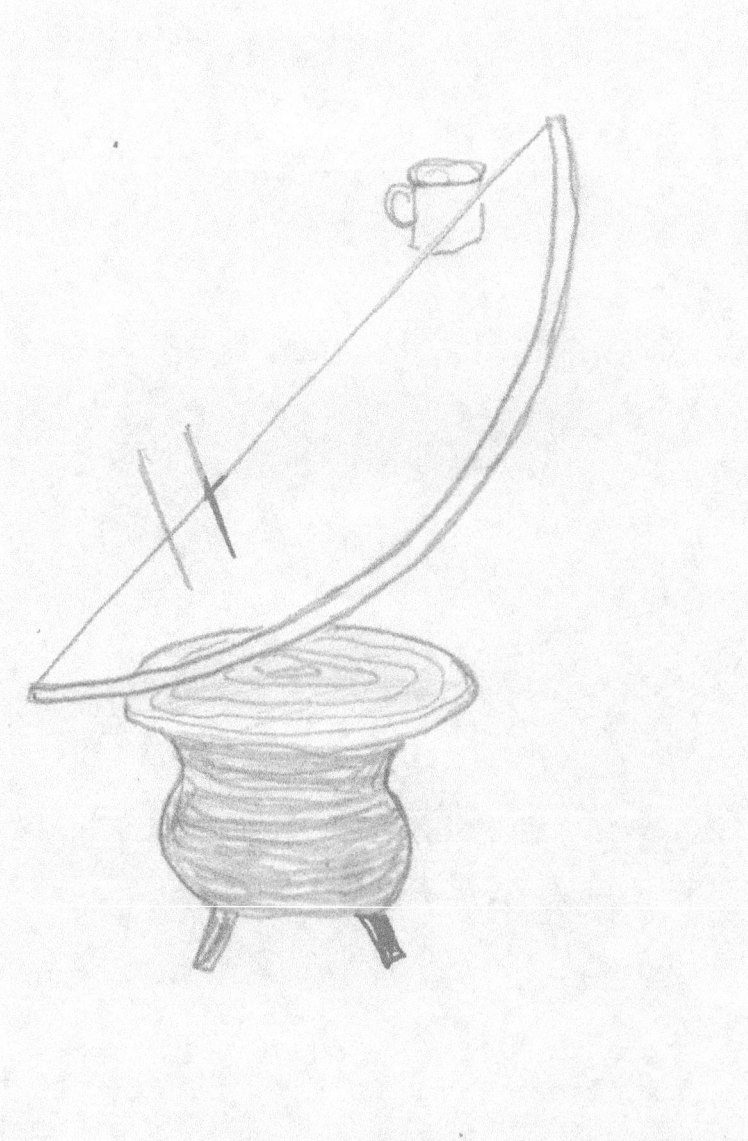

Figure 1.10 *Lipuruboro*, as found in the Kavango and mentioned by Dave Dargie (1986). Drawing by author.

instruments are known among the San and Damara from Namibia, where the resonator can be a vessel (e.g. a metal or plastic basin) turned upside down on which a hunting bow is placed. Hai//Om is one of the terms used for this instrument.[8]

Further musical bows which can/could be found in Southern Africa

Jaco Kruger (Kruger 1985: 11) mentions another type of chordophone known as ground-bow and classified as a ground harp, which could be found among the Venda and which most probably came from the Karanga in Zimbabwe (Figure 1.11). This bow consists of a bent sapling. One end of a rope is attached to the top part of the sapling and the other end to a resonator that is placed in a hole in the ground. By pulling the sapling towards the resonator, i.e. by varying the tension of the string, different tones can be produced. If a player only operates with two fundamentals, another rope that is bound around the sapling and the string can, as in the case of a braced bow, also divide the string into two sections (Figure 1.12).

Figure 1.11 Ground-bow <u>without</u> tension noose (e.g. Venda *galinga* or *kalinga*; also classified as ground harp (see Kruger 1985:11)). Drawing by author.

Figure 1.12 Ground-bow <u>with</u> tension noose (e.g. Venda *galinga* or *kalinga*; also classified as ground harp (see Kruger 1985:11)). Drawing by author.

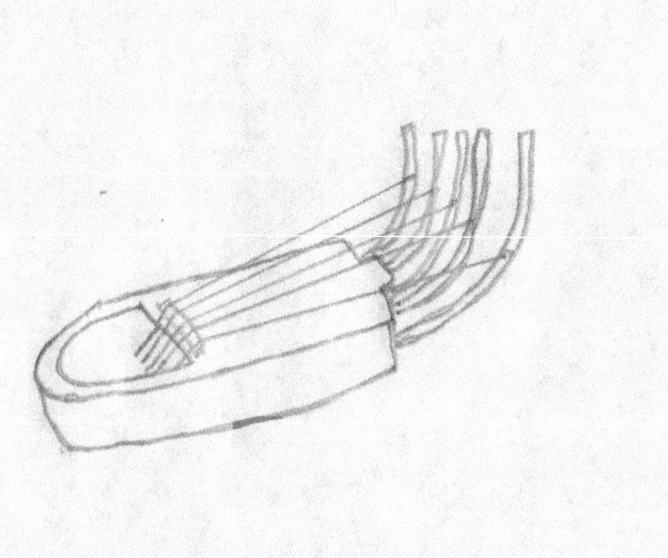

Figure 1.13 Multi-bow harp-type, or poliarc, which Dargie calls *Okuimba otjihumba* of the OvaZimba in Namibia.[9] Kirby describes similar instruments among the Damara (Kirby [1934] 1968: 243). Drawing by author.

A special case is that of the pluriarc which is also considered to be a multi-bow harp-type. It consists of a resonator with several bows inserted (Figure 1.13).

Examples of other, recent types of bows that use modern materials

Musical bows can be used to produce melodies, low and high tones or just rhythms. The technique of producing melodies by amplifying overtones is clearly explained by Dargie (1988: 50-1) and Kubik (1988: 39-76). On the unbraced mouth resonated Xhosa bow *umrhubhe* as well as the Xhosa musical bow with attached resonator *uhadi*, the player preferably amplifies the harmonics numbers 4, 5 and 6, i.e. the tones of a major chord. By shortening the string with the thumb of the left hand, the player may shift these tones one full tone up, which then leads to the tonal material necessary to produce the scale shown below (Figure 1.14).[10]

A number of tuning systems in Southern Africa are influenced by bow music. It might not be the case with scales derived from overtones over one fundamental, like that of the Wagogo in Tanzania[11] (Eastern Africa), but those whose tonal material is deduced from the overtones over two different fundamentals (Kubik 1988:47-8). In addition, the harmonics chosen to be amplified are crucial. In the case of the !Kung, as explained by Kubik, the harmonics 2, 3 and 4 are used which lead to a tetratonic system over two fundamentals. Besides that, the three tuning intervals applied, i.e. 200, 300 and 400 cents, lead to different tetratonic scales as well (Kubik 1988: 48-9).

Different fundamentals are not only produced by shortening the string via the thump, but by dividing strings as in the case of braced bows, e.g. the Zulu *umakhweyane* or the Shona *chipendani*.[12] One section of the vibrating string sounds higher than the other.

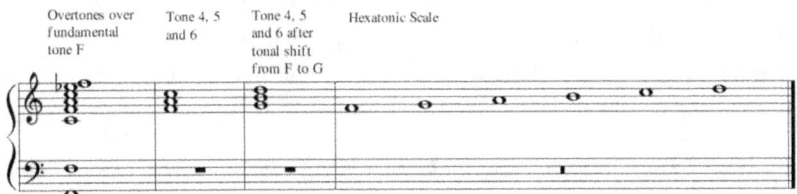

Figure 1.14 Xhosa Scale and Tonal Shift.

Types of bows in Southern Africa and (the problem of) their classification

Even though musical bows occasionally received attention in accounts of travellers and descriptions of collections in museums over the last centuries, it took time before a useful classification was developed. From the beginning of the twentieth century until today, several attempts have been undertaken to accommodate musical bows in general classifications of musical instruments or to establish specific classifications of musical bows.

In 1914 musical bows were listed in Hornbostel's and Sachs's *Systematik der Musikinstrumente. Ein Versuch*, in which geographical sites, where the instruments were found, were mentioned (e.g. in Africa and Oceania). In Hornbostel's and Sachs's system they appear under 3 *Chordophone*, 31 *Einfache Chordophone oder Zithern* (simple chordophones or zithers) and more specifically 3.11.1 *Musikbögen* (musical bows). Their system furthermore distinguishes bows with reference to the strings. In the case of idiochords, the string consists of the bark from the bow itself while heterochords have a string made of other material attached. Besides that, there may be bows with one or more strings, with or without *Fadenschlinge* (i.e. if bows are braced or unbraced; Rycroft calls it tension noose, some authors talk of loops), with or without resonator (or attached or unattached resonator) and bows with several staffs[13] (Hornbostel and Sachs 1999: 182-4; see also Hornbostel and Sachs 1961: 20-1). Kirby (1932), as stated by Rycroft (1982: 75), followed the main categories as established by Sachs (1929 and 1940), i.e.:

I. Bows with separate resonator
II. Bows with attached resonator, or gourd bows
III. Bows that depend upon the player's mouth for resonance, or mouth bows.

Yet Kirby added additional aspects concerning the function of harmonics, which only people who had access to players could have picked up. Unlike Kirby, Hornbostel and Sachs, we must keep in mind, had to work with recordings, instrument collections and documentations established by others. Kirby writes about his main categories:

> For, although to the superficial observer, most of these instruments appear to be capable of emitting, when played, only one or two sounds, a close examination of them reveals the fact that in every instance, as I have shown in the case of the

bow played by the Qung Bushman for Dr. Bleek, not only are the fundamental tones of the string heard by the performer, but also the harmonic sounds generated by those fundamentals. These harmonics are either

(1) Sounded together as a chord,
(2) Isolated for melodic purposes, or
(3) Used in conjunction with their fundamentals in order to produce elementary polyphony.

In all cases [...] a resonator is employed to amplify the sounds produced by the string, and such a resonator is sometimes a calabash or other hollow object, which may, or may not, be permanently attached to the instrument, and sometimes the mouth of the performer.

(Kirby [1934] 1968: 196)

Camp and Nettl apply another very similar condensed version of different bow types (1955: 65–80), and, by referring to Sachs (1913 and 1940), differentiate between the following bows:

Type I: Bows with separate resonators
Type II: Bows with resonators attached
Type III: Bows using the human mouth as resonator
Type IV: The *gora*

Just as in the case of Hornbostel's and Sachs's, Camp and Nettl pay attention to the production of sound and, as indicated in the title of their article,[14] their system lists more examples linked to the bow types in Africa. The above listed four types are furthermore subdivided:

Type I (Bows with separate resonators) into single and double bow
Type II (Resonators attached with Bows) into unbraced and braced
Type III (Bows using the human mouth as resonator) into unbraced (with the categories: hard wood stave; flat cane stave; stave of hollow river reed; stave of hollow river reed with rod inserted) and braced (with one-piece shaft; three-piece shaft; and friction).
No subdivision is provided for Type IV (*gora*).

The subdivisions for Types II and III refer to characteristics of the instrument's construction which have to do with the tuning interval and thus with the production of scales. Furthermore subdivisions, as outlined in brackets, pay attention to the material used and characteristics in the design and construction of the instrument (e.g. if it consists of several pieces or different materials). While Camp and Nettl followed Hornbostel and Sachs's model in their systematic approach, Dave Dargie applied main characteristics as outlined by them, but gave his classification a different structure. Besides that, he incorporated instruments that do not appear in the before-mentioned classification, for he could draw from rather modern or recent bow types he was exposed to during his research. His first classification consisting of five groups, as outlined in the 1980s (Dargie 1986: 42–52), was later extended to eleven types or groups.[15]

The groups mentioned in Dargie (1986) consisted of:

A1: musical bows with attached resonator and undivided string (Xhosa *uhadi* or Zulu *ugubhu*, Ovambo *okamburumbumbwa*)
A2: musical bows with attached resonator and divided string (Zulu *umakhweyane*, Swati *makhweyane*, Tsonga *xitende*)
B1: mouth resonated bows with undivided string (Xhosa *umrhubhe*, Zulu *umhubhe*, Xhosa *inkinge*, Zulu *umqangala*, Kavango *rugoma* and *kaworongongo*; in the latter case the player scratches a stick over notches in the wood of the bow)
B2: mouth resonated bows with divided string (Zulu *isiqomqomana*, Damara *noukhas*)
C: The *gora* type (Khoi *gora*, Sotho *lesiba*, Xhosa *ugwali*)
D: The fiddle types (mostly played over the shoulder, e.g. Zulu *isicelekeshe*, Sotho *sehankule*, Tswana *segankuru*, Damara *gorito*. Dargie also mentions the Xhosa *ikatari* in this connection)
E: Bows with unattached resonator (Dargie mentions here the *lipuruboro*, a bow that is held on top of a cooking pot on which a mat is placed. A second player holds a cup filled with mealies against the string).

Later Dargie revised his classification and used eleven types instead of five groups. Among the reasons for this readjustment are technical details such as:

(1) The difference between a brace loop and a brace tied to the bow besides which, instruments can be middle or end braced.
(2) Playing techniques (a string can be plucked, tapped or bowed, or notches in the wood of the bow can be scratched).
(3) Differences with reference to the construction of instruments (e.g. if we think in the *segankuru*, the *lipuruboro* and the *ikatari* which he defined as different types).

Table 1.1 Types and groups according to Camp and Nettl (1955), and Dargie (1986 and article in print).

Dargie revised and 1986 – Types (revised) and Groups (1986)	Camp and Nettl 1955 - Types	Resonator or not	Braced or not	Ethnic group – instruments' names (examples)	Playing techniques	Further comments
Type 1 Group BI	Type III (Bows using the human mouth as resonator)	No resonator	Unbraced mouth-resonated bow 1986: undivided string	Xhosa: umrhubhe, umqangi Zulu: umqangala Pondo: umqunge	Friction, percussion/tapping	Overtone melody. Player may additionally whistle.
Type 2 Group BII	Type III (Bows using the human mouth as resonator)	No resonator	Braced mouth-resonated bow with bracing loop 1986: mouth-resonated bows, divided string	Zulu: isiqomqomana Damara: noukhas Pedi: lekopo Shona: chipendani (see Brenner) Karanga: tshipendani	Plucking, tapping	The two sections of the string provide fundamentals.
Type 3 Group BII	Type III (Bows using the human mouth as resonator)	No resonator	Braced mouth-resonated bow with brace tied to string 1986: mouth-resonated bows, divided string	Damara: outa Sotho: setolotolo Venda: tshigwana Ndebele: isitontolo Zulu: isitontolo Thonga: isitontolo	Plucking	Both sections of string and bracing tie can be plucked.
Type 4 Group BI	Type III (Bows using the human mouth as resonator)	No resonator	Unbraced mouth-resonated bow. String is plucked (by fingers or plectrum)	Kavango: rugoma Xhosa: inkinge Zulu: umqangala Swazi: umqangala Sotho: lekope Thonga: umqangala Pedi: lekope	Plucking	Different fundamentals are created by shortening the string with tip of finger.

Table 1.1 Types and groups according to Camp and Nettl (1955), and Dargie (1986 and article in print). (*Continue*)

Dargie revised and 1986 – Types (revised) and Groups (1986)	Camp and Nettl 1955 - Types	Resonator or not	Braced or not	Ethnic group – instruments' names (examples)	Playing techniques	Further comments
				Venda: logube Chwana: lengope Korana: !gabus Chisena-speaking people in Malawi: nyakantangali (Malamusi 1996: 60)		
Type 5 Group BI	Type III (Bows using the human mouth as resonator)	No resonator	Unbraced mouth-resonated friction bow. Player scraps notches with a small stick.	Kavango: kaworongongo Shangana/Tsonga: xizambi Bushman: nxonxoro Venda: tshizambi Tonga: zambi Brought to Malawi by refugees and known there as nyakazeze (Malamusi 1996: 61) Mukhavele provides the following names for this instrument used in Namibia and Angola (Mukhavele 2017: 76): Namibia: Silozi: Kaholoholo Oshikwanyama: Okayaya Thimbukutshu: Kagrorongongo	Friction: notches in wood scraped with small stick	Small calabash rattles may be attached to the bow.

Table 1.1 Types and groups according to Camp and Nettl (1955), and Dargie (1986 and article in print). (Continue)

Dargie revised and 1986 – Types (revised) and Groups (1986)	Camp and Nettl 1955 – Types	Resonator or not	Braced or not	Ethnic group – instruments' names (examples)	Playing techniques	Further comments
				Otjizema: Elumba Sisambyu: Kagrorongongo Rukwangali: Kaorongongo Kxo: Rxonxoro Angola: Bangala: Lukungu Lunda: Lukungu Quioco: Lukungu Gangela: Kawayawaya Ambuela: Kawayawaya		
Type 6 Group AI	Type II (Resonators attached with bows)	Resonator attached	Musical bows with attached resonator	Xhosa: uhadi Zulu: ugubhu Chwana: segwana Swazi: ligubu Sotho: thomo	Tapping with reed or stick	Different overtones are amplified by opening and closing the calabash resonator against the breast.
Type 7 Group AII	Type II (Resonators attached with bows)	Resonator attached to bracing loop	Braced, i.e. middle braced with loop over the string	Tsonga: xitende Zulu: umakhweyane Swazi: umakhweyana Thonga: nkoka Venda: dende Pedi: sekgapa The instrument is also known as kalirangwe in southern Malawi (Malamusi 1996: 60)	Percussion: striking of both section of strings	Each section of the string provides a fundamental. By touching finger to string a third fundamental can be created.

Table 1.1 Types and groups according to Camp and Nettl (1955), and Dargie (1986 and article in print). (*Continue*)

Dargie revised and 1986 – Types (revised) and Groups (1986)	Camp and Nettl 1955 - Types	Resonator or not	Braced or not	Ethnic group – instruments' names (examples)	Playing techniques	Further comments
Type 8 Group AII	Type II (Resonators attached with bows)	Resonator attached to bracing loop	Braced, i.e. end braced	Ovambo: okamburumbumbwa	Percussion: striking of only long section of string	This sort of instrument came to Brazil from Angola and is known as berimbao
Type 9 Group E	Type I (Bows with separate resonators)	Resonator not attached	Bow, e.g. lipuruboro, is held onto a grass mat on top of resonator (e.g. cooking pot). Other instruments of this kind consist of a bow held on top of a resonator (e.g. a tin or a metal or plastic basin turned upside down).	Kavango: lipuruboro Korana: kha:s	In the case of the lipuruboro one player holds the bow onto the resonator, i.e. the mat on the pot, and a cup filled with seed onto the string. The string is beaten with two sticks by a second player	This group should be subdivided, as there is a variety of different bows without attached resonator to be found. Dargie mentions the lipuruboro, whilst Camp and Nettl Dargie on lipuruboro: 'Double idiophone, combined drum and rattle. This is not an overtone bow.'

Table 1.1 Types and groups according to Camp and Nettl (1955), and Dargie (1986 and article in print). (*Continue*)

Dargie revised and 1986 – Types (revised) and Groups (1986)	Camp and Nettl 1955 - Types	Resonator or not	Braced or not	Ethnic group – instruments' names (examples)	Playing techniques	Further comments
						The instrument shows characteristic features of chordophones (string), membranophones (mat as membrane on top of pot) and idiophones (rattle) and can therefore be considered as hybrid. The main source of sound is the string.
Type 10 Group D (fiddle type)		Resonator attached (mostly 5 litre oil tin)	Unbraced	Damara: gorito Sotho (S.): sehankule Sotho (N.): tsorwani Tswana: Segankuru, sekhankula, mamokhorong (Moitse 1994: 106 and Schöpf 2008: 55)	Friction: string is bowed with a small bow of hair or fibre	Overtones controlled by bowing movements and pressure.

Table 1.1 Types and groups according to Camp and Nettl (1955), and Dargie (1986 and article in print). (*Continue*)

Dargie revised and 1986 – Types (revised) and Groups (1986)	Camp and Nettl 1955 - Types	Resonator or not	Braced or not	Ethnic group – instruments' names (examples)	Playing techniques	Further comments
				Xhosa: isigankuri (see Rycroft 1966:94 and Schöpf 2008: 55). The instrument was seen among the amaPondo and most probably borrowed. Kirby lists instruments similar to the dirankure from Botswana (Kirby [1932] 1968: plate 59): Chwana: segankuru Zulu: ubhel'indhela Xhosa: uhadi (!)		'Boat'-shaped piece of wood instead of stick. One end of this piece of wood is put into the opening of a 5 litre oil can which serves as resonator. The dirankure from Botswana, which has a straight staff, falls under this group as well.
Type 11 Group D (fiddle type, played in front of player)		Resonator attached (mostly 5 litre oil tin)	Unbraced	Sotho (S.): sekatara Xhosa: ikatari Pondo: isankuni	Friction: string is bowed with a small bow of hair or fibre	One end of the bow is inserted into the opening of a 5 litre oil tin. The string is fixed to the other end and to the oil tin.

Table 1.1 Types and groups according to Camp and Nettl (1955), and Dargie (1986 and article in print). (*Continue*)

Dargie revised and 1986 – Types (revised) and Groups (1986)	Camp and Nettl 1955 - Types	Resonator or not	Braced or not	Ethnic group – instruments' names (examples)	Playing techniques	Further comments
Group C The gora type, i.e. the 'feather bow' (Mentioned in Dargie's recent article, but not listed under his last classification of bows)	Type IV	No resonator attached	Unbraced, mouth-resonated	Khoi: goraSotho: lesiba Xhosa: ugwali	An airstream that makes a feather quill between the bow and the string vibrates. The vibration of the quill and the string is then amplified via the mouth cavity of the player	The instrument combines features of aerophones and chordophones.
No type or group provided by DargieGround bows (also known as ground harp)	Not listed	Resonator either consists of calabash or modified container buried in ground or hole in ground covered with skin or sheet of other material	Unbraced/braced	Venda: kalinga, galinga (see Jaco Kruger 1989 and 1985: 11)	Played by striking string with a stick. Tension and therefore tones are changed by pulling the sapling towards the ground.	Tuning reference is the highest note.

Table 1.1 Types and groups according to Camp and Nettl (1955), and Dargie (1986 and article in print). *(Continue)*

Dargie revised and 1986 – Types (revised) and Groups (1986)	Camp and Nettl 1955 – Types	Resonator or not	Braced or not	Ethnic group – instruments' names (examples)	Playing techniques	Further comments
					String can also be divided by tension/tuning noose.	
No group provided by Dargie Pluriarc	Not listed	Several bows inserted in resonator	Unbraced	OvaZimba: Okuimba otjihumba (Dargie on musical bows in Namibia, forthcoming) According to Kirby ([1932] 1968: 243) also called Ovambo Guitar among the Damara	Plucking	

Apart from that, he differentiates via comments whether a bow is an overtone or not an overtone bow. Below is a table showing Dargie's groups and types, and the classification according to Camp and Nettl, with names of the instruments and the ethnic group in Southern Africa where they are or were played.

All of these classifications (Hornbostel and Sachs, Camp and Nettl, and Dargie) have in common that they link the different bow types and subgroups with ethnic groups. This is reasonable, if we keep in mind that nation states are a comparably late phenomenon in the history of Southern Africa and that people travel and cross borders. In his article on musical bows in Malawi, Moya Malamusi refers to this fact and describes bows that have originally come from Mozambique (Malamusi 1996: 60-6). It is quite common that authors who specifically focus on one or two bows either find those types of bows in other regions or among other tribes, or that they find evidence of transcultural transfer (see for instance Kruger 1989: 395 and 403; Dargie 1988: 24-8). Luca Mukhavele, for instance, provides an extensive list of different ethnic groups from Namibia and Angola that play bows related to the xizambi from Mozambique (Mukhavele 2017: 76). The fact that the last classification mentioned above dates from 2019 is an indicator that musical bows still stir the mind of researchers.

Recent events, projects and activities – a very brief South African outlook

A look at the variety of collections, projects and events connected with musical bows reveals that this kind of musical instrument has not lost its fascinating aura. Dargie's publications (Dargie 1988, 1995 and 2001 among others) and his collection of indigenous music with CDs and DVDs on bow music are a good example. Besides that we can find a number of entries in the internet, including video clips showing famous bow players, such as Madosini Manqina (2006), Mantombi Matotiyana (2019) and Van den Berg (2008) or Dizu Plaatjies (2014), as well as instructions on how to make your own musical bows by celebrities such as Johnny Clegg (Birgé 2013). The latter and Sipho Mchunu have used mouth bows in popular South African music since the 1970s; their album Universal Men (1979) by Juluka and specifically in the song 'Inkunzi Ayihlabi Ngokumisa' was an extraordinary endeavour, considering the political circumstances of that time. The appreciation of bow music as performed by the before-mentioned musicians is furthermore evident in academia in form of interviews with artists, e.g. Sazi Dlamini's interview with Madosini in the *Journal of the Musical Arts in Africa* (Dlamini 2004). In addition, a specific interest in researchers who have worked on bows, e.g. Brother Clement Sithole who was concerned with Zulu bows, can be observed (see Treffry-Goatley 2015).[16]

Two recent conferences on musical bows that took place in Durban[17] (24–27 February 2016 and, in connection with SASRIM, 29 August–1 September 2018) are proof of the ongoing research on this type of instrument. Both conferences attracted scholars and musicians from Africa, the Americas and Europe. They also provided space for performances and platforms for exchange of knowledge and skills between researchers and practitioners.[18]

Today indigenous musical instruments, including musical bows, have found their way into tertiary institutions and form part of their curricula. At the University of KwaZulu-Natal, Walter Sisulu University (Donsa 2008), Rhodes University and the University of Fort Hare (Bleibinger 2017; Dlamini 2017),[19] to mention just a few universities in South Africa, they are part of the course content or, as in the case of the University of Cape Town, of specific research projects.[20]

Musical bows are a useful tool to connect tertiary institutions with schools and communities, for they are very special instruments and can even be handled by children. Jonathan Ncozana (Figure 1.15), a former lecturer from the Music Department at the University of Fort Hare, for instance, modified bows for children at primary and secondary schools in Alice in the Eastern Cape. The staff was shortened to fit the size of the children, and since calabashes have become rare in the region, Ncozana uses plastic floaters[21] as resonators.

Today one can buy musical bows among other indigenous musical instruments from established enterprises, such as AMI[22] in Grahamstown. Another East London-based company, Qangi Qangi (https://web.facebook.com/QangiQangiMusic/), is specialized on musical bows. Run by Luyolo Lenga[23] and describing itself as record label, the company sells indigenous musical instruments, including bows, and offers workshops in bow making and playing. Also modern business models of this type help to keep indigenous instruments alive.

Considering the above-mentioned projects and developments in a comparably small region, one can see how musical bow enthusiasts are able to create a vibrant scene in which practice, research, conservation and transmission go hand in hand. It further shows that it needs people who keep cultural memory alive and who can provide information, be it by playing or by writing, like the contributors of this volume.

Figure 1.15 Jonathan Ncozana with *umakhweyane*. Photo: Bernhard Bleibinger.

Notes

1. Last time this happened to me was in 2016 in a village close to Engcobo. Fortunately, I had brought an *umrhubhe* with me.
2. Dave Dargie introduced me to musical bows in South Africa and showed me how to build them. I also need to mention Jonathan Ncozana, my African brother, with whom I had a constant exchange of ideas concerning the improvement of bows. He is currently involved in projects in schools and churches in Alice in the Eastern Cape Province in South Africa and designed a small braced bow made of recycled material (e.g. toilet floaters instead of calabashes as resonators) which is more suitable for children.
3. Dargie cites Liechtenstein, La Vaillant, Barrow and Campbell.
4. Mugglestone focuses on Kolb's description.
5. See for instance Kubik's work on !Kung and San heritage (Kubik 1975–76; Kubik 1988). John Kaemmer (1997: 700–21), citing Kubik's work, mentions those transitions too. Dargie refers to those processes as well with reference to the San and Xhosa (1988: 24–8); the cultural contact happened through intermarriage and partly through war.
6. Nowadays for instance tins.
7. Dave Dargie describes the instrument on the basis of material collected by Minette Mans and Emmanuelle Olivier in a forthcoming article titled 'Bows of Namibia'.
8. Ibid.
9. Ibid.
10. To try to produce overtones oneself, one would need a bow stick (e.g. of hazel nut wood) of approximately 60 cm in length and a diameter of *c.* 1.6 cm on the upper and *c.* 2.4 cm on the lower end. The stick must be peeled, bent and kept in shape with strings until dried out properly. Once dried, strings made of brass wire (*c.* 0.6 mm) or cello strings can be attached. The lower end of the bow is held by left hand of the player and the upper end rests on the right cheek of the player or in front of the mouth. The vibration produced when beating the string with a little stick can then be amplified in the mouth cavity.
11. Overtones can also be produced via specific vocal techniques.
12. As explained by Brenner, chipendani players may even produce four fundamentals (Brenner 1997: 22).
13. If we think of the poliarc.
14. 'The Musical Bow in Southern Africa'.
15. Dargie, Southern Africa's Remarkable Heritage of Musical Bows: Does It Have a Future?, in print.
16. Even though one must keep in mind that a number of academics who conduct research on musical bows are at the same time performers.

17 Both conferences were organized by Sazi Dlamini.
18 The same can be said about the international symposium of the study group Applied Ethnomusicology which was held in 2014 at the University of Fort Hare in East London, Alice and Hogsback where workshops on musical bow making and playing were organized for delegates.
19 At the University of Fort Hare it was compulsory until 2016.
20 A project on musical bows is currently run by Sylvia Bruinders from the University of Cape Town.
21 As used in the water tanks for toilets.
22 AMI, i.e. African Musical Instruments, was established by Andrew Tracey. Christian Carver is currently responsible for the production of musical instruments.
23 Luyolo Lenga is a former Fort Hare student.

References

Balfour, H. (1902), 'The Goura, a Stringed-wind Musical Instrument of the Bushmen and Hottentots', *The Journal of the Anthropological Institute of Great Britain and Ireland* 32 (January–June): 156–76.

Bleibinger, B. (2017), 'How to Tune Modernised Versions of a Traditional Musical Bow, the Umrhubhe, from the Eastern Cape', in S. Dlamini (ed.), *Proceedings of the First International Bow Music Conference – University of KwaZulu-Natal, 24–27 February 2016*, 86–93, Grahamstown/Rhodes University: International Library of African Music.

Brenner, Klaus-Peter. (1997), *Chipendani und Mbira. Musikinstrumente, nichtbegriffliche Mathematik und die Evolution der harmonischen Progressionen in Musik der Shona in Zimbabwe*, Abhandlungen der Akademie der Wissenschaften in Göttingen, Philologisch-Historische Klasse, 3rd Series, 221, with 2 companion audio CDs, Göttingen: Vandenhoeck and Ruprecht.

Camp, C.M. and Nettl, B. (1955), 'The Musical Bows in Southern Africa', *Anthropos*, Bd. 50 (H.1/3): 65–80.

Dargie, D. (1986), 'Musical Bows in Southern Africa', *Africa Insight* 16 (1): 42–52.

Dargie, D. (1988), *Xhosa Music. Its Techniques and Instruments: With a Collection of Songs*, Cape Town & Johannesburg: David Philip.

Dargie, D. (1995), *Make and Play Your Own Musical Bow. A First Guide to Making and Playing the umqangi Mouth Bow and the uhadi Calabash Bow of the Xhosa of South Africa, the People of Nelson Mandela*, Melusinenstrasse 13, Munich, Germany: Dargie.

Dargie, D. (2001), 'Magical Musical Bows', *Talking Drum*, September 2001: 4–12.

Dargie, D. n.d., 'Musical Bows of Namibia', in S. Dlamini (ed.), *Musical Bows of Southern Africa*, New York: Bloomsbury Academic.

Djenda, M. (1968), 'L'Arc-En-Terre Des Gbaya-Bokoto', *African Music* 4 (2): 44–6.

Dlamini, S. (2004), 'The Role of the Umrhubhe Bow as Transmitter of Cultural Knowledge among the AmaXhosa: An Interview with Latozi 'Madosini' Mpahleni', *Journal of the Musical Arts in Africa* 1 (1): 138-60.

Dlamini, Sazi. (ed.) (2017), *Conference Proceedings of the First International Bow Music Conference – University of KwaZulu-Natal, 24–27 February 2016*, Grahamstown/ Rhodes University: International Library of African Music.

Dontsa, L. (2008), 'From the Museum to the Music Classroom: Teaching the Umrhubhe as an Ensemble Instrument', *International Journal of Music Education* 26 (2): 177–90.

Hornbostel, E.M. von. and C. Sachs. (1999), 'Systematik der Musikinstrumente. Ein Versuch', in C. Kaden and E. Stockmann (eds.), *Erich Moritz von Hornbostel. Tonart und Ethos. Aufsätze zur Musikethnologie und Musikpsychologie* (=Taschenbücher zur Musikwissenschaft 117), 151–206, Wilhelmshaven: Florian Noetzel. First published in: *Zeitschrift für Ethnologie* 46 (1914): 553–90.

Hornbostel, E.M. von and C. Sachs. (1961), 'Classification of Musical Instruments: Translated from the Original German by Anthony Baines and Klaus P. Wachsmann', *The Galpin Society Journal* 14 (March): 3–29.

Juluka (Musical Group) (1979), *Universal Men*, [Music LP]. S.L. : CBS.

Kaemmer, J. (1997), 'Southern Africa: An Introduction', in R.M. Stone (ed.), *The Garland Encyclopedia of World Music Volume 1 – Africa*, 700–21, New York: Routledge. Available online: http://glnd.alexanderstreet.com/view/327232 (accessed 31 August 2012).

Kirby, P.R. (1932), 'The Recognition and Practical Use of the Harmonics of Stretched Strings by the Bantu of South Africa', *Bantu Studies* 6: 31–46. Kirby, P. R. ([1934] 1968), *The Musical Instruments of the Native Races of South Africa*, Johannesburg: Wits University Press.

Kruger, Jaco. (1985), 'The State of Venda Chordophones: 1983–1984', in *Papers Presented at the Fifth Symposium on Ethnomusicology, Faculty of Music, University of Cape Town*, 8–12, Grahamstown: International Library of African Music/Rhodes University.

Kruger, Jaco. (1989), 'Rediscovering the Venda Ground-Bow', *Ethnomusicology* 33 (3): 391–404.

Kubik, Gerhard. (1975/76), 'Musical Bows in South-Western Angola – 1965', *African Music* 5 (4): 98–104.

Kubik, Gerhard. (1988), 'Nsenga/Shona Harmonic Patterns and the San Heritage in Southern Africa', *Ethnomusicology* 32 (2): 39–76.

Malamusi, Moya. (1996), 'Stringed Instrument Traditions in Southern Malawi', in *African Music* 7 (3): 60–6.

Mason, O. (1897), 'Geographical Distribution of the Musical Bow', *American Anthropologist* 10 (11): 377–80.

Moitse, S. (1994), *The Ethnomusicology of the Basotho*, Roma: Institute of Southern-African Studies.

Mugglestone, E. (1982), 'The *Gora* and the Grand *Gom-Gom*: A Reappraisal of Kolb's Account of Khoikhoi Musical Bows', *African Music* 6 (2): 94–115.

Mukhavele, Luka. (2017), 'Music Bows from the South and Centre of Mozambique', in S. Dlamini (ed.), *Proceedings of the First international Bow Music Conference, University of KwaZulu-Natal*, 69–83, Grahamstown/Rhodes University: International Library of African Music.

Murdock, G. (1959), *Africa: Its Peoples and Their Culture History*, New York: McGraw-Hill.

Rycroft, David K. (1966), 'Friction Chordophones in South-eastern Africa', *The Galpin Society Journal* 19: 84–100.

Rycroft, David K. (1975/76), 'The Zulu Bow Songs of Princess Magogo', *African Music* 5 (4): 41–97.

Rycroft, David K. (1982), 'The Musical Bow in Southern Africa', *Papers Presented at the Second Symposium on Ethnomusicology, Music Department, Rhodes University*, 70–5, Grahamstown, Rhodes University: International Library of African Music.

Sachs, C. (1913), *Real-Lexicon der Musikinstrumente*, Berlin: Bard.

Sachs, C. (1929), *Geist und Werden der Musikinstrumente*, Berlin: Dietrich Reimer.

Sachs, C. (1940), *History of Musical Instruments*, New York: W. W. Norton.

Schöpf, J. (2008), 'The Serankure and Music in Tlôkweng, Botswana', in Max Peter Baumann (ed.), *Intercultural Music Studies 13*, Berlin: VWB – Verlag für Wissenschaft und Bildung.

Treffry-Goatley, A. (2015), *Brother Clement Sithole: A Musical Biography*, Knysna: Outcomes Publishing.

Tessmann, G. (1914), 'Ethnologisches Museum/Berliner Phonogramm-Archiv, Brief von G. Tessmann an Hornbostel von. 14.4.1914', in S. Ziegler (ed.), *Die Wachszylinder des Berliner Phonogramm-Archivs*, 116–283, Berlin: Ethnologisches Museum – Staatliche Museen zu Berlin – Preußischer Kulturbesitz.

Ziegler, S. (ed.) (2006), *Die Wachszylinder des Berliner Phonogramm-Archivs*, Berlin: Ethnologisches Museum – Staatliche Museen zu Berlin – Preußischer Kulturbesitz.

Online Audio-Visual Examples

Birgé, J. (2013), *Making of Musical Bows by Johnny Clegg*, filmed in Johannesburg (1993), Available online: https://www.youtube.com/watch?v=l_Xeg5Ox0hc (accessed 16 November 2019).

Manqina, M. (2006), URL: https://www.youtube.com/watch?v=Q9iIXnP1UBY (accessed 16 November 2019).

Matotiyana, M. (2019), *Songs of Greeting, Healing and Heritage*, Available online: https://www.youtube.com/watch?v=arvhqgt8t-A (accessed 16 November 2019).

Plaatjes, D. (2014), URL: https://www.youtube.com/watch?v=TNvG3Uc0nNI (accessed 16 November 2019).

Qangi Qangi LTD. URL: https://web.facebook.com/QangiQangiMusic/ (accessed 13 December 2019).

Van den Berg, R. (2008), *On the Couch with Mantombi Part 3*, URL: https://www.youtube.com/watch?v=Ft1y2eMwC-E (accessed 16 November 2019).

2

Chipendani (mouth bow): The origin of the Shona *mbira* harmonic system and of Andrew Tracey's 'basic *kalimba* core', with an appendix on the Venda *tshihwana*

Klaus-Peter Brenner

Abstract

An analysis of the Shona mouth bow *chipendani* is presented that comprises its construction, its unique acoustical properties, and the specific musical exploitation of the latter by means of its fifth-tuning and peculiar playing technique. The analysis brings to light a highly sophisticated organo-musical system whose acoustically crucial element is the 'one-dimensional string divider' or tuning thread. The hexatonic *chipendani* system of harmonic patterning generated on this basis turns out to be, in synchronic perspective, the structural core of the heptatonic Shona *mbira* system. This prompts the conclusion that it is, in diachronic perspective, its embryonic prototype as well as the origin of the hypothetic embryonic prototype of all present-day Shona *mbira* tuning plans, Andrew Tracey's 'basic *kalimba* core'. The appendix provides a comparative analysis of the closely related Venda *tshihwana* whose thirds-tuning leads from the same acoustic prerequisites to a completely different tonal-harmonic system resembling the Venda *tshikona* system.

In this chapter, I am going to present an outline of my analytical findings on the Shona mouth bow, the *chipendani*, based on my 1993 field research in Zimbabwe as well as on Hugh Tracey's 1949 and 1951 *chipendani* recordings. I shall moreover draw from my earlier and more comprehensive German publications on this topic (Brenner 1997: 17–64 and 375–400, 2004a, *cf* Dias 1986, Kauffman 1970, Kubik 1988a, Kyker 2007, 2015, 2017, 2018, Rutsate 2007,

H. Tracey 1991, H. Tracey et al. 2000, 2003). My main informants and teachers were the late Mr. Sydney Musarurwa Nyandoro (1949–2000, Zezuru dialect area, Mheremavende village, Mashayamombe chiefdom, Mhondoro Communal Land, Chegutu District, Mashonaland West Province, Zimbabwe) and the late Mr. Green Tamanikwa Mususa (1936–95, from Korekore dialect area, Mususa village, Dandawa chiefdom, Hurungwe District, Mashonaland West Province, Zimbabwe).

Other *chipendani* players whom I had the privilege to meet and record during a concert tour in Cologne/Germany in 1994 were the late Mr. Mondrek Muchena Hwata (1939–95, Zezuru dialect area, Harare/New Canaan township and Nyamweda chiefdom, Chegutu District, Mashonaland West Province, Zimbabwe) and Mr. Chaka Chawasarira (b. 1941, biographically rooted in both Zezuru and Korekore dialect areas, Zimbabwe), and, at the University of KwaZulu-Natal's 1st Bow Music Conference in Durban in 2016, Mr. Compound Muradzikwa (b. 1943, from Zezuru/Manyika dialect area, Buhera District, Manicaland Province, Zimbabwe) (*cf* again Kyker 2007, 2015, 2017, 2018) whose trip to South Africa had kindly been organized by Jennifer Kyker.

Organologically, the *chipendani* consists of a flattened bow stave[1] made of *mubedu* wood (bot. *ozoroa reticulata*), with a carved-out cylindrical handle in the middle and small lugs at the ends to which a thin wire[2] string is attached (Figure 2.2).

A tuning thread is knotted onto the string and draws it towards the stave to the right of the handle where its loose end is temporarily coiled around the stave, thereby bending the string in an obtuse angle and dividing it into a shorter segment to the right, and a longer one to the left (Figure 2.3). The desirable and acoustically most efficient string tension is moderate. The player holds the stave with the left hand in a horizontal or slightly inclined position with the string pointing outwards. The string is plucked by the left index finger, and either plucked or stopped by the right index or middle finger and thumb. By using his mouth cavity as an adjustable resonator, the player selectively amplifies harmonic partials at the convex back of the stave, somewhat to the right of the handle. Sometimes he proceeds to whistling from the side of his mouth. Occasionally, a secondary rattle made of bottle tops loosely attached to a piece of sheet metal and called *chijaka* (Figure 2.21) is bound to the left end of the stave.

Figure 2.1 Sydney Musarurwa Nyandoro playing *chipendani* at the evening kitchen fire in his house in Mhondoro in 1993. Photo: Klaus-Peter Brenner.

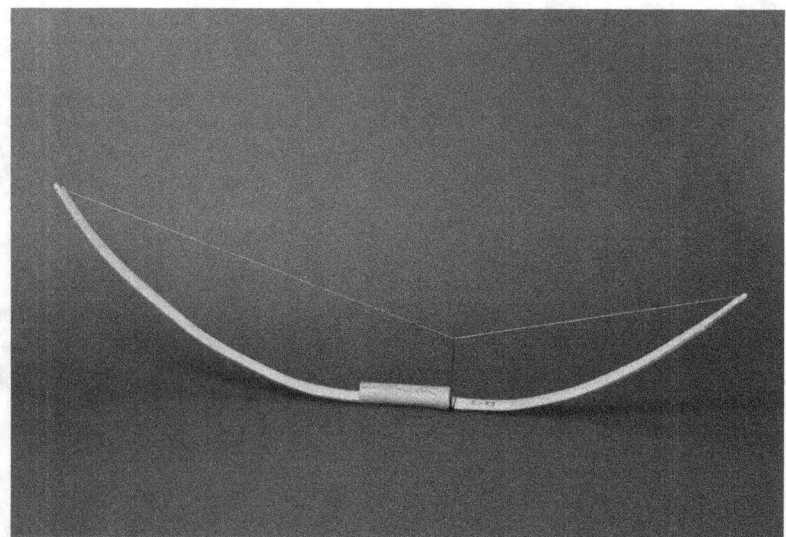

Figure 2.2 *Chipendani* made by John Hakurotwi Mude, Highfield, Harare, Zimbabwe, before 1995 (now: Georg-August-Universität Göttingen, Collection of Musical Instruments, inventory number L-89). Photo by Stephan Eckardt. Courtesy Stephan Eckardt.

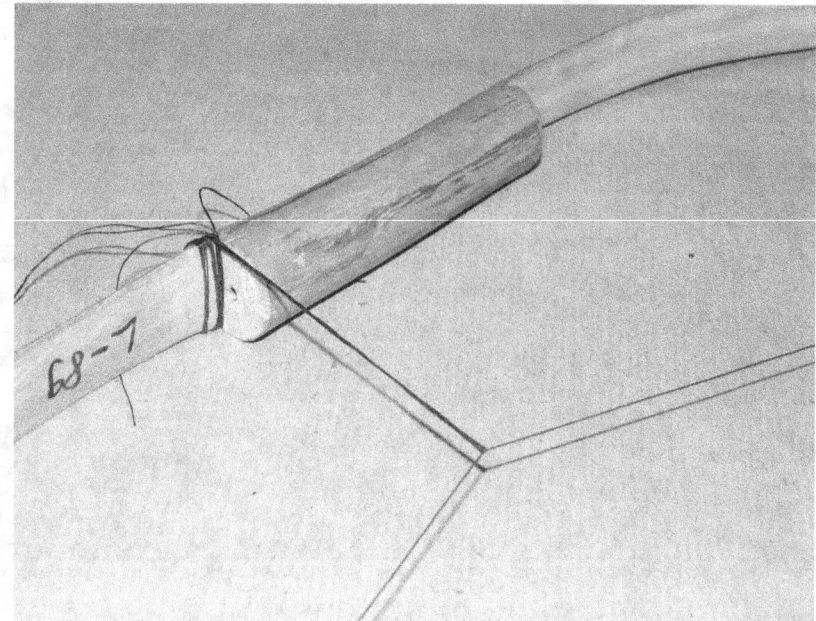

Figure 2.3 *Chipendani*: close-up of middle section with cylindrical handle and one-dimensional string-divider. Photo: Klaus-Peter Brenner.

These are my main points:

(1) An analysis of the organology, acoustics, playing technique and music of the *chipendani* (Brenner 1997, 2004a) brings to light an ingenious organo-musical system of admirable complexity and structural coherence. Its hallmark and fingerprint, as we shall see, are its unique and style-moulding tonal-harmonic system.

(2) A comparison of the latter with the system of harmonic patterning underlying Shona *mbira* (except *mbira dzaVaNdau*) music (Brenner 1997, 2013, 2015, 2019a, Grupe 1998, 2004, Jones 2019, Kauffman 1970, Kaemmer 1973, 1975, Kubik 1987, 1988b, A. Tracey 1961, 1970, 1989, 2015) uncovers a surprisingly close structural affinity: in fact, the *chipendani* harmonic system turns out to be, in synchronic perspective, the structural core of the Shona *mbira* harmonic system.

(3) This prompts the conclusion that the *chipendani* system is, in diachronic perspective, the embryonic prototype of the *mbira* system,[3] as well as

(4) the origin of the hypothetic embryonic prototype of all present-day Shona *mbira* tuning plans, i.e. Andrew Tracey's 'basic *kalimba* core' (A. Tracey 1972, 1974, 2013, *cf* Brenner 1997, Kubik 1998, 2002, Kubik et al. 2014, van Dijk 2019).

In the following, I am going to present some evidence for this theory. There are four physical laws that are exploited in the *chipendani* type of mouth bow. While the first three of these are shared with most other African musical bows, the fourth one is specific of the *chipendani* type of mouth bow (including its relatives such as the Venda *tshihwana*, the Zulu *isiqomqomana*, the Mbuti *kabarome* and others).

(1) The vibrational modes of an ideal string produce a column of harmonic partials whose frequencies are integer multiples of the fundamental.

(2) A bulb-shaped cavity or Helmholtz resonator is able to selectively amplify a specific frequency from a complex sound.

(3) A given ratio of vibrating string lengths corresponds to the reciprocal ratio of frequencies, hence to a specific interval.

(4) A string which is bent by a one-dimensional string-divider can vibrate in each of its two segments separately as well as it can vibrate as a whole. In this case, the third law applies to the ratio of all three involved string lengths and produces three acoustically interdependent fundamentals and their respective columns of harmonic partials (Brenner 1997, 2004a).

A two-dimensional string-divider or tuning loop (Figure 2.4) fixes – relative to the bow stave – the thread string-dividing point in all directions. For that reason, it allows the string to vibrate only separately in its two segments.

As opposed to this, a one-dimensional string-divider or tuning thread (Figure 2.5) additionally allows the bent string to vibrate as a whole, at least in an upward and downward movement. It still behaves that way when one of the segments is stopped by the player in order to shorten the vibrating length of the bent whole string.

How is this inconspicuous, but tricky device utilized in the Shona *chipendani* tradition?

The string is divided in such a way that the interval between the two segments is a pure fifth, which means that the second harmonic partial (and its octave equivalents) of the short segment coincides with the third harmonic partial (and its octave equivalents) of the long segment. In other words, the whole string is divided by 5, and the string length ratio 2:3:5 is established (Figure 2.6, top). Furthermore, the string is temporarily stopped at the short segment in such a way that another pure fifth is produced on top of the resulting whole string pitch,

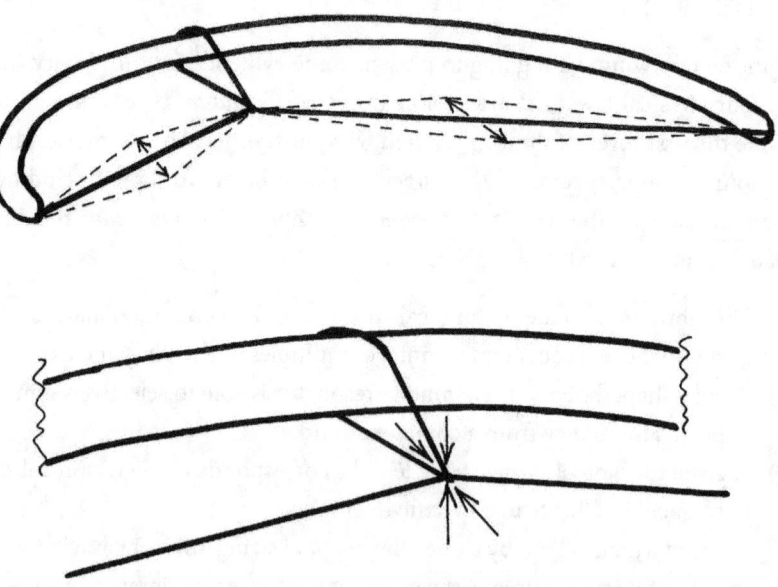

Figure 2.4 Two-dimensional string-divider (tuning loop). String segments vibrating separately. Illustrations: Klaus-Peter Brenner.

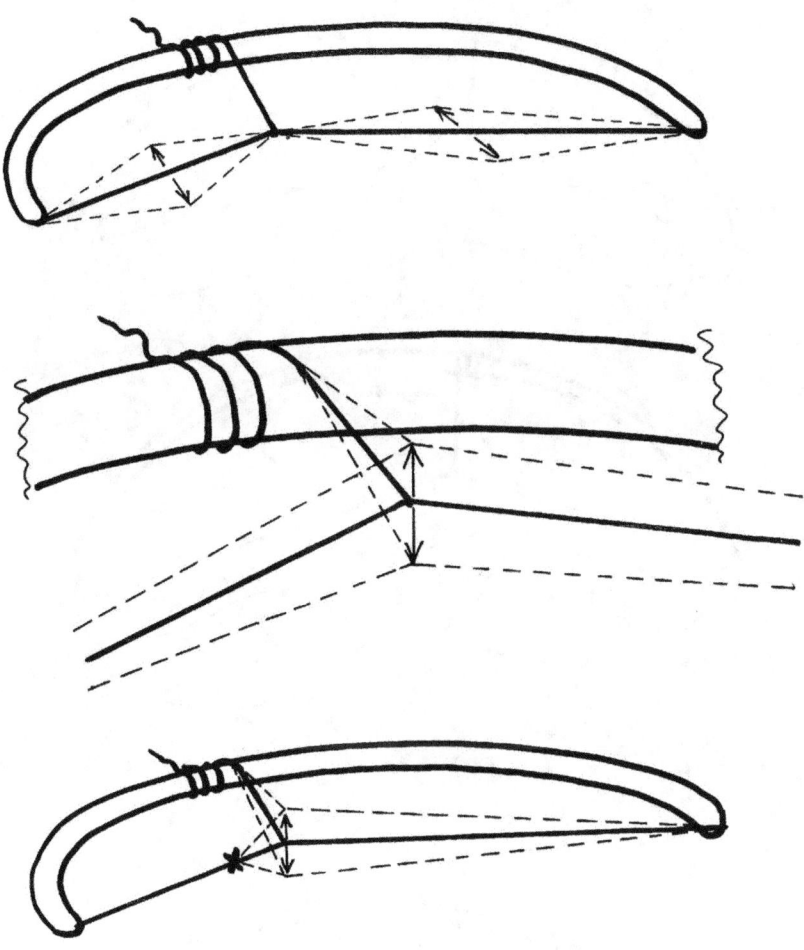

Figure 2.5 One-dimensional string divider (tuning). String segments vibrating separately (top), bent string vibrating as a whole (centre), stopped bent string vibrating as a whole (bottom). Illustrations: Klaus-Peter Brenner.

which means that the second harmonic partial (and its octave equivalents) of the stopped bent string coincides with the third harmonic partial (and its octave equivalents) of the whole bent string. In other words, the whole string is divided by 3, and the ratio 1:2:3 is established (Figure 2.6, centre).

The superposition of these two conflicting divisions can be expressed as one set by expanding both ratios to their smallest common denominator 15 (Figure 2.6, bottom):

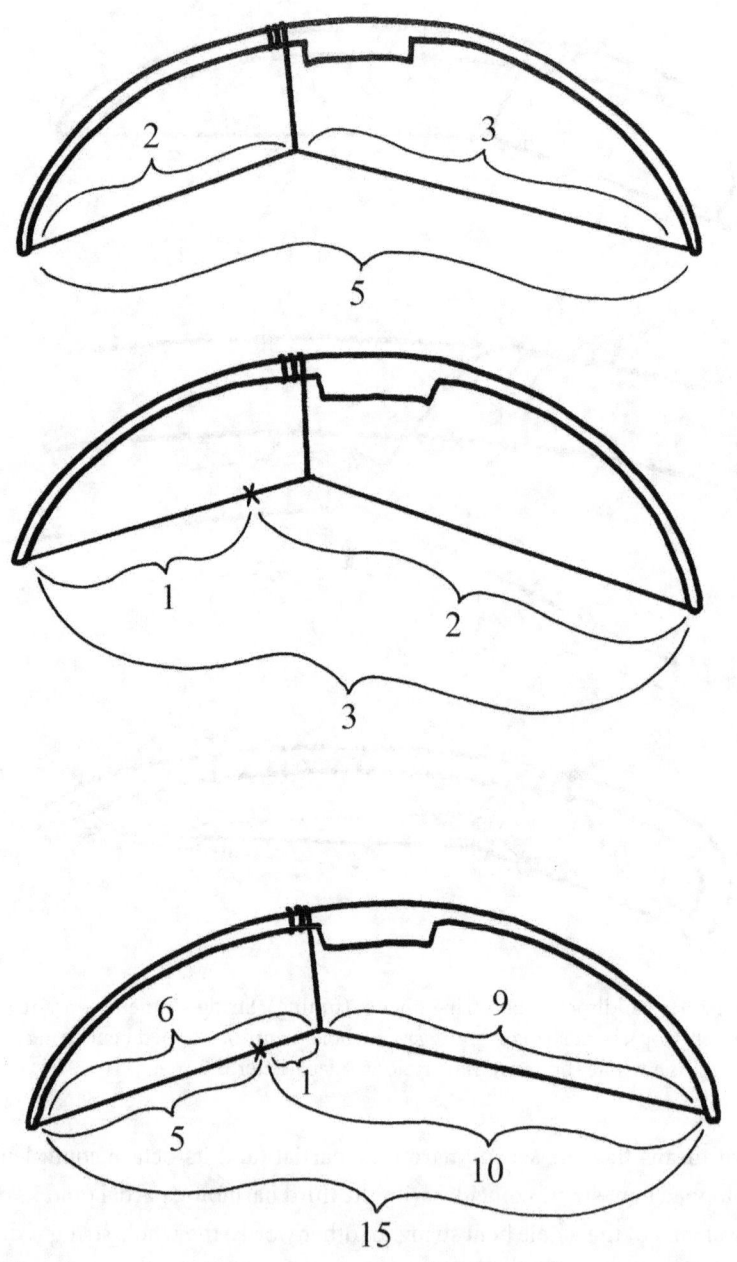

Figure 2.6 *Chipendani*: Ratios of vibrating string lengths. Division of whole string by 5 (top). Division of whole string by 3 (centre). Superposition of these conflicting divisions by expanding both ratios to their smallest common denominator (bottom). Illustration: Klaus-Peter Brenner.

2:3:5 = 6:9:15
1:2:3 = 5:10:15

Among these the four musically utilized string lengths are:

15:6:10:9 (but not 5)

From this set of string length ratios, we calculate the corresponding frequency ratios and hence the intervals between the four fundamentals (Figure 2.7, Audio 1). Expressed in relative pitch, these are:

F:a:c:d

Henceforth we also address them as:

Root I:II:III:IV

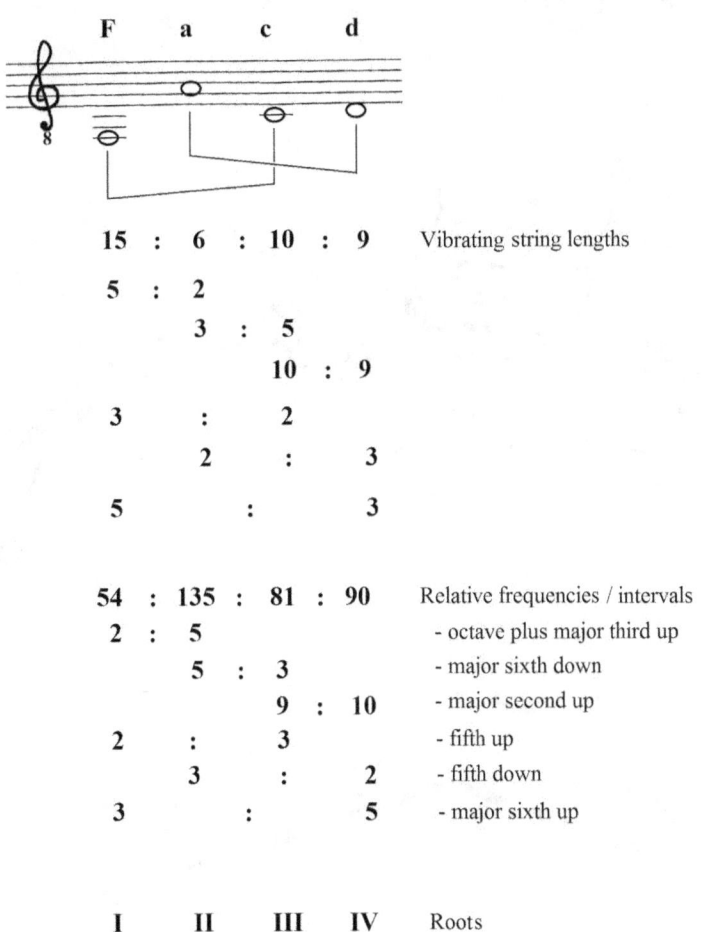

Figure 2.7 *Chipendani*: Intervals between fundamentals.

> → Audio 1. *Chipendani*: Fundamentals F, a, c, d. – Demonstration played by Klaus-Peter Brenner. Duration: 0'23".

Let us now turn to the playing technique. How are these four roots executed by the player?

Root I (Figures 2.8–2.10): The left index finger plucks the whole string close to the bending point in a downward movement. The relative string length 15 vibrates and produces the relative pitch F.

Root II (Figures 2.11–2.14): The right hand plucks the short segment in an outward movement by pinching and releasing it with either index finger and thumb, or middle finger and thumb. The relative string length 6 vibrates and produces the relative pitch a.

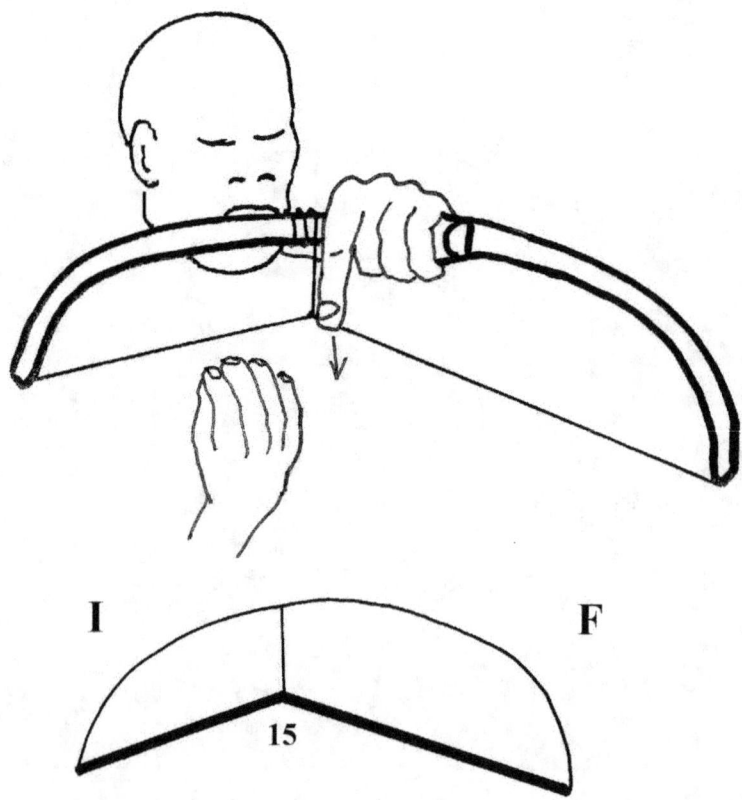

Figure 2.8 *Chipendani* playing technique. Root I: Left index finger plucks whole string close to the bending point in a downward movement. Illustration: Klaus-Peter Brenner.

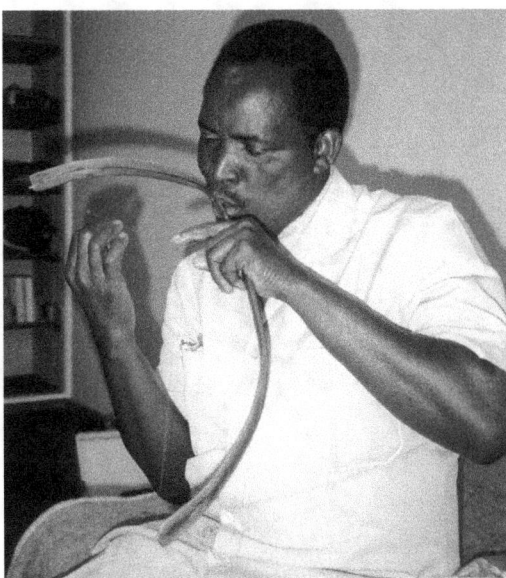

Figure 2.9 Green Tamanikwa Mususa 1993, playing root I. Photo: Klaus-Peter Brenner.

Figure 2.10 Sydney Musarurwa Nyandoro 1993, playing root I. Photo: Klaus-Peter Brenner.

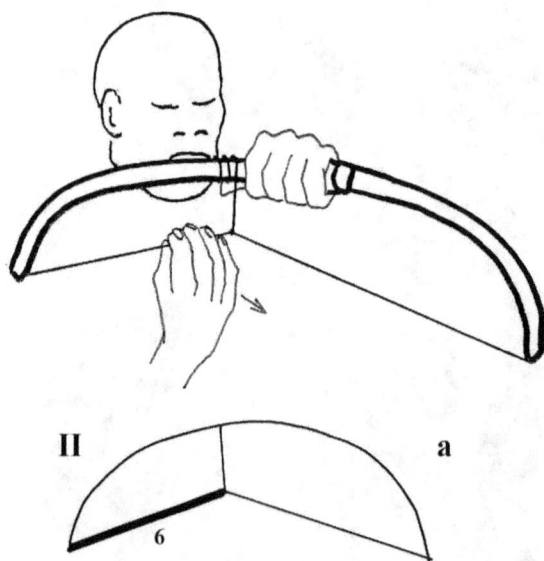

Figure 2.11 *Chipendani* playing technique. Root II: Right hand plucks short segment in an outward movement by pinching and releasing it with either index finger and thumb, or middle finger and thumb. Illustration: Klaus-Peter Brenner.

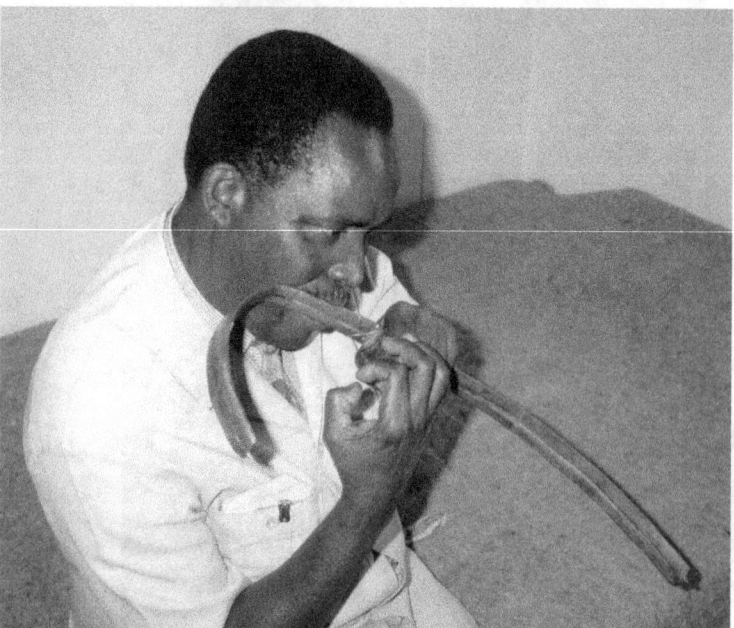

Figure 2.12 Green Tamanikwa Mususa 1993, playing root II (first perspective). Photo: Klaus-Peter Brenner.

Figure 2.13 Green Tamanikwa Mususa 1993, playing root II (second perspective). Photo: Klaus-Peter Brenner.

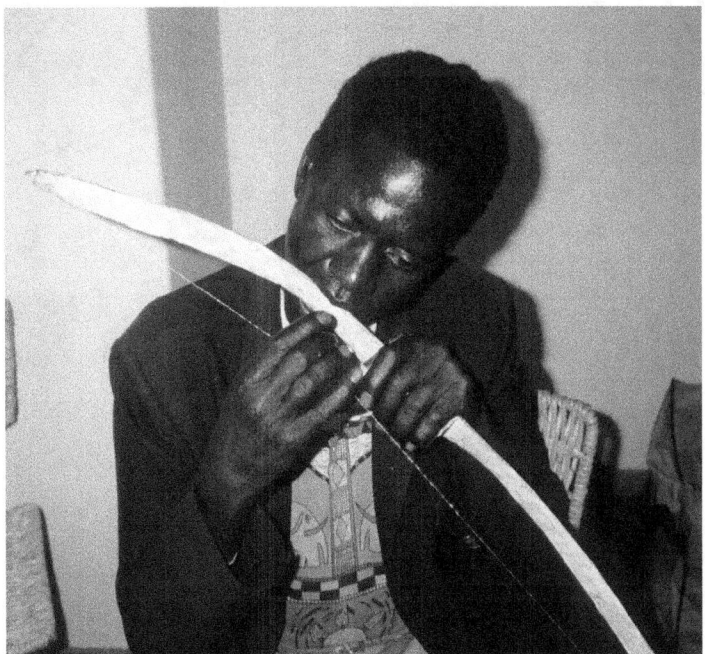

Figure 2.14 Sydney Musarurwa Nyandoro 1993, playing root II. Photo: Klaus-Peter Brenner.

Root III (Figures 2.15–2.17): The left index finger plucks the long segment close to the bending point in a downward movement, while the right hand stops the short segment by pinching it with either index finger and thumb, or middle finger and thumb. The relative string length 10 vibrates and produces the relative pitch c.

Root IV (Figures 2.18–2.21): The right hand plucks the long segment in an outward movement by pinching and releasing it with either index finger and thumb, or middle finger and thumb. The relative string length 9 vibrates and produces the relative pitch d.

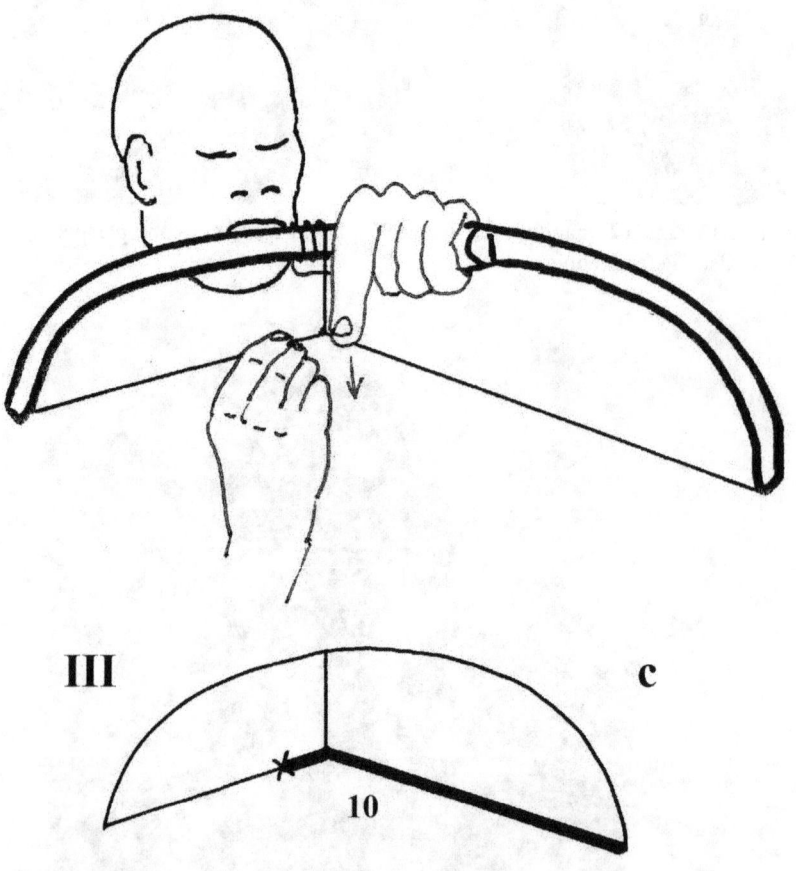

Figure 2.15 *Chipendani* playing technique. Root III: Left index finger plucks long segment close to the bending point in a downward movement, while right hand stops short segment by pinching it with either index finger and thumb, or middle finger and thumb. Illustration: Klaus-Peter Brenner.

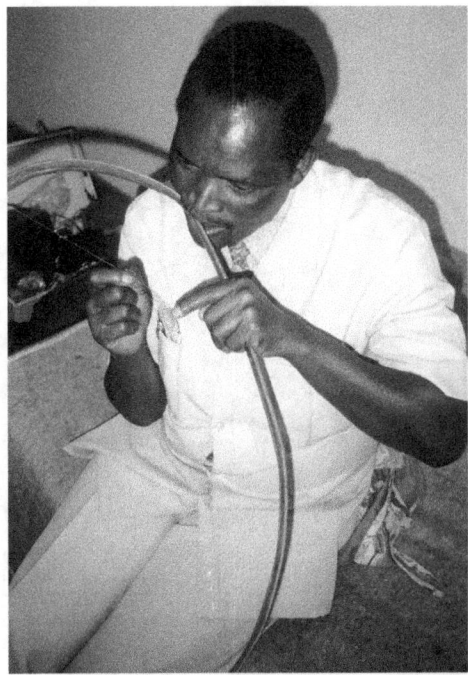

Figure 2.16 Green Tamanikwa Mususa 1993, playing root III. Photo: Klaus-Peter Brenner.

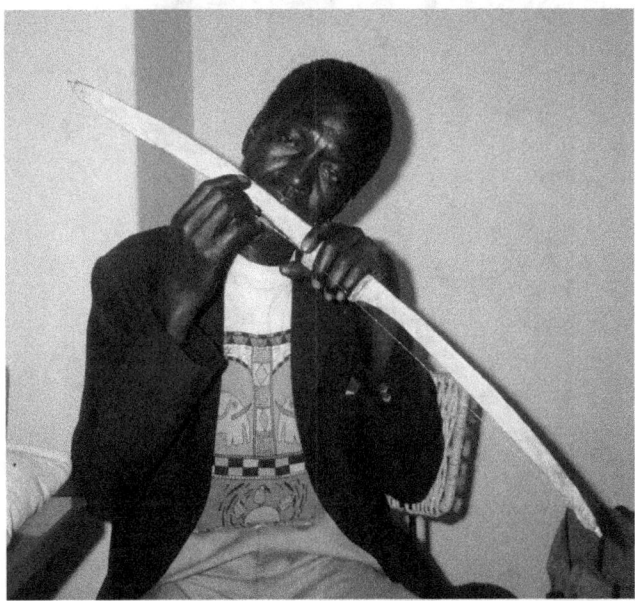

Figure 2.17 Sydney Musarurwa Nyandoro 1993, playing root III. Photo: Klaus-Peter Brenner.

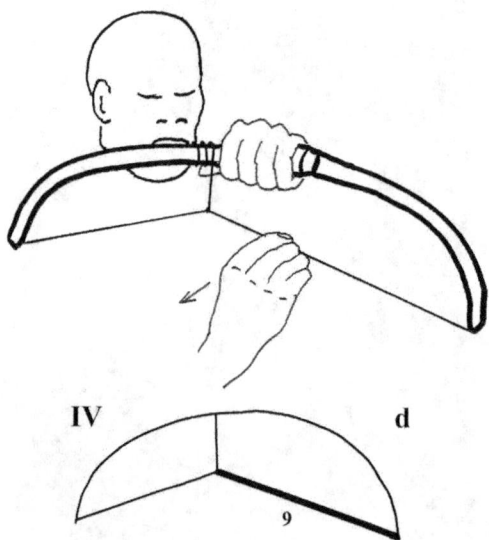

Figure 2.18 *Chipendani* playing technique. Root IV: Right hand plucks long segment in an outward movement by pinching and releasing it with either index finger and thumb, or middle finger and thumb. Illustration: Klaus-Peter Brenner.

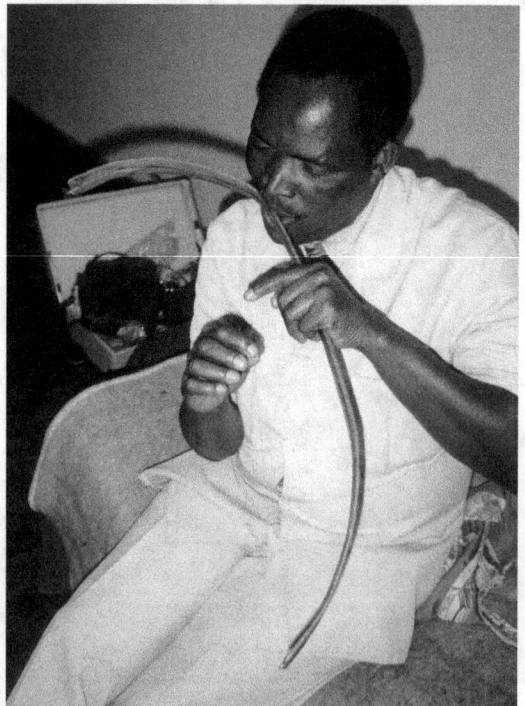

Figure 2.19 Green Tamanikwa Mususa 1993, playing root IV. Photo: Klaus-Peter Brenner.

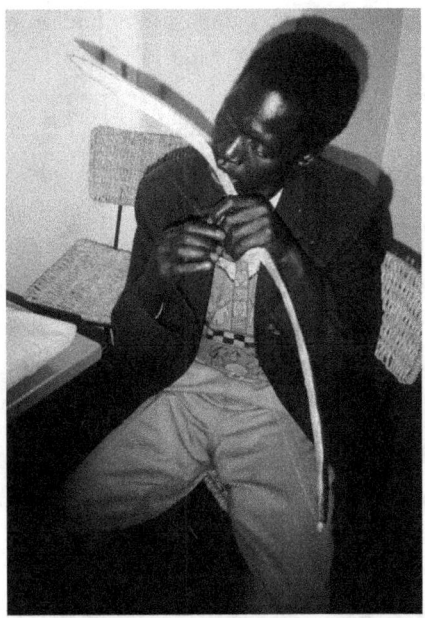

Figure 2.20 Sydney Musarurwa Nyandoro 1993, playing root IV (first perspective). Photo: Klaus-Peter Brenner.

Figure 2.21 Sydney Musarurwa Nyandoro 1993, playing root IV (second perspective). Note the secondary rattle *chijaka* temporarily attached to the bow in this case. Photo: Klaus-Peter Brenner.

Here is the synopsis of the hand positions and movements required to produce those four roots (Figure 2.22, Audio 1).

> → Audio 1 (second listening). *Chipendani*: Fundamentals F, a, c, d.

The characteristic tonal-harmonic system of *chipendani* music is based on the four – due to the one-dimensional string-divider acoustically interdependent (!) – fundamentals F, A, C and D, and the fifth dyads FC, AE, CG and DA, which are obtained by selectively mouth-filtering them from their respective columns of partials. The columnar representation of this tone material (Figure 2.23, Audio 2) shows that only those harmonic partials are selected which are octave equivalents of the first to third partials, i.e. of the fundamentals and their respective fifths. That's how the four dyads FC, AE, CG and DA come about.

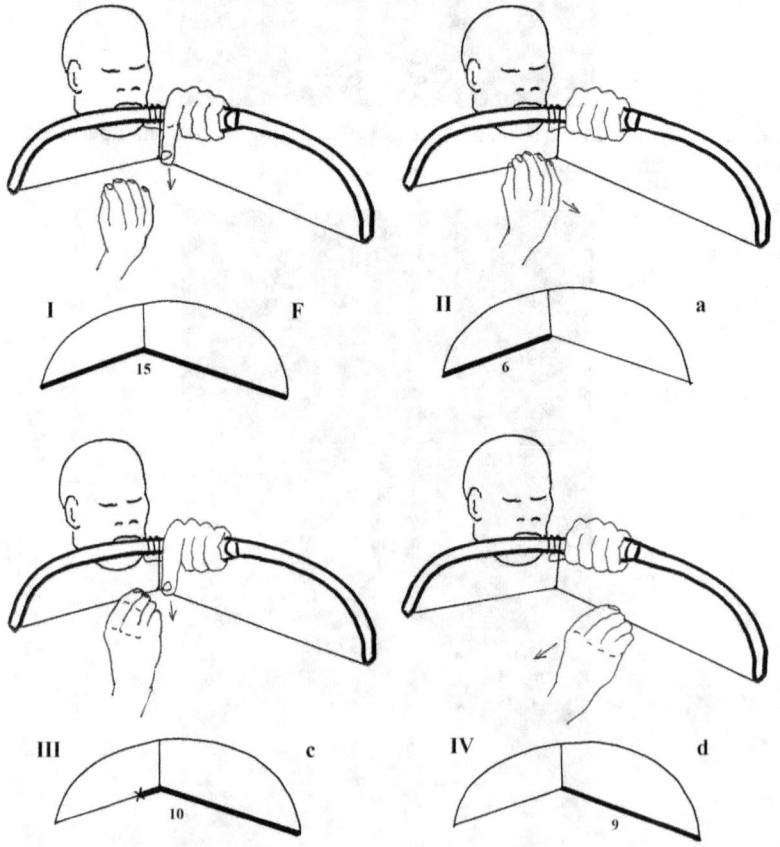

Figure 2.22 *Chipendani* playing technique. Synopsis of the four roots. Illustration: Klaus-Peter Brenner.

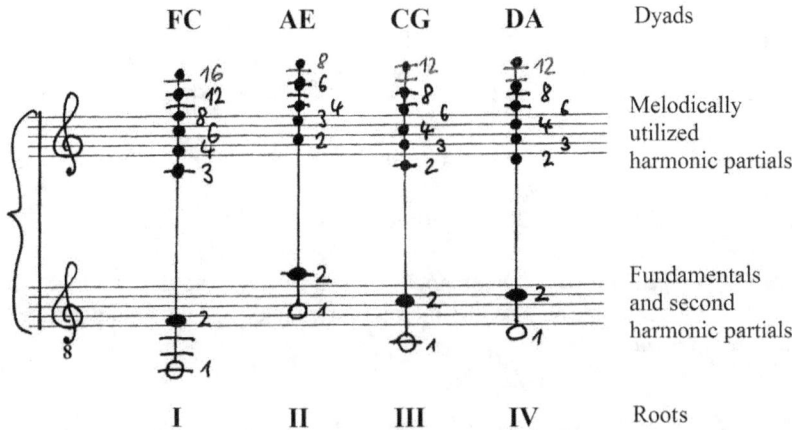

Figure 2.23 *Chipendani*: Selection of mouth-filtered harmonic partials, arranged in columns. Note the cross-stabilizing commonalities between the columns of roots I and III, and between those of roots IV and II! Illustration: Klaus-Peter Brenner.

> → Audio 2. *Chipendani*: selection of mouth-filtered harmonic partials, arranged in columns. The played sequence is: $I_{4-6-8-12-16-12-8-6-4}$ $II_{2-3-4-6-8-6-4-3-2}$ $III_{3-4-6-8-12-8-6-4}$ $IV_{2-3-4-6-8-12-8-6-4-3-2}$. – Demonstration played by Klaus-Peter Brenner. Duration: 0'42".

The descending scalewise representation of that selection of mouth-filtered harmonic partials shows the hexatonic structure C D E F G A (Figure 2.24, Audio 3).

> → Audio 3. *Chipendani*: selection of mouth-filtered harmonic partials, arranged as descending scale. The played sequence is:
> $\quad\quad\quad\quad I_{16}\ II_6\ IV_8$
> $I_{12}\ II_4\ III_6\ I_8\ II_3\ IV_4$
> $I_6\ II_2\ III_{(3)}\ I_4\ II_{(-)}\ IV_2.$
> Focus attention on the <u>partials</u>! – Demonstration played by Klaus-Peter Brenner. Duration: 0'27".

And, as we can see, its production depends technically on a specific sequential occurrence of the four roots on which they are based. This cyclical sequence is, in its basic manifestation, either: [I → II → III → I → II → IV →], or: [I → II → IV → I → II → III →], depending on the chosen starting point. Other temporal cyclical permutations as, for example, [II → IV → I → II → III → I →] (fifth temporal cyclical permutation), do also occur, though.

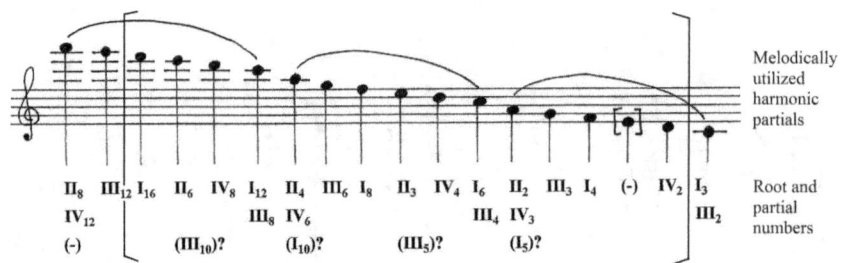

Figure 2.24 *Chipendani*: Selection of mouth-filtered harmonic partials, arranged as descending scale. Brackets refer to the ambitus represented in Audio 3. Illustration: Klaus-Peter Brenner.

This corresponds very well with two further observations (Figure 2.25, Audio 3):

(1) A systematic examination of the technical availability of immediate progressions from one root to another yields a significant result: among the six theoretically existent 1-step progressions five are indeed executable, and equally so in both directions. But the sixth one, connecting roots III and IV, turns out to be technically inexecutable, also in both directions. The reason for this technical restriction is that in order to execute this progression the player would have to switch with his right hand from stopping the short segment to plucking the long one or the other way round. This simply does not work without disturbing the motional and sonic flow, and is therefore consequently avoided.

(2) In the previously described 6-step progression, the five technically available 1-step progressions are represented in one direction each, while roots III and IV, though inexecutable as an immediate progression, are most prominently structuring the harmonic cycle by establishing the difference between its two corresponding halves.

> → Audio 3 (second listening). Description as above. – This time focus attention on the <u>fundamentals</u> forming the 6-step 'standard' root progression!

How then does this distinctively structured tone material show through when it comes to actual *chipendani* music? How does it shape it in space and time? With respect to the dimension of tonal space and register, the *chipendani* polyphony typically combines a tetratonic lower voice on the scale, F A C D, provided by fundamentals and/or second harmonic partials, with a hexatonic upper voice on the partial tone scale, C D E F G A, with multiple octave extension. With respect to its

Chipendani: *Origin of the Shona* Mbira *System* 57

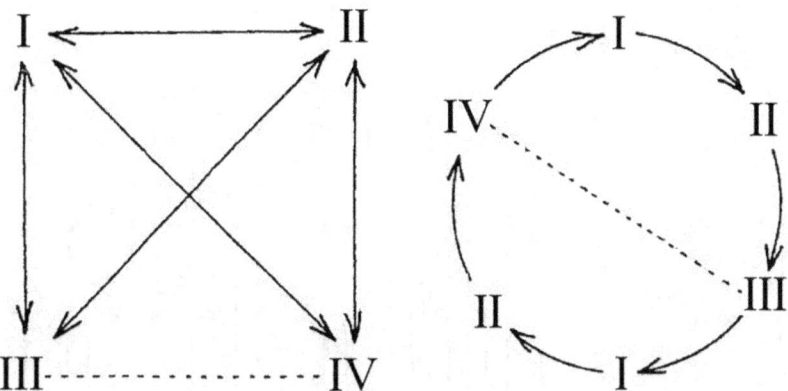

Figure 2.25 *Chipendani*: (a) technically possible (straight lines) versus impossible (dotted line) root progressions, (b) the 6-step 'standard' root progression. Illustration: Klaus-Peter Brenner.

temporal dimension, this two-voice polyphony emerges from a stock of distinctively structured and closely interrelated root progressions, the most elementary and typical variety of which is the 6-step 'standard' progression [FC → AE → DA → FC → AE → CG →] (first described by A. Tracey 1961 for Shona *kalimba* music).

The afore-described bundle of traits manifests in an ideal-typical way in the following music example, the *chipendani* piece, 'Kwa ambuya asina keriya' ('You must bring your mother-in-law a present on your bicycle carrier when you go to see her, or she will be angry'), as played by Mr. Muchabaiwa in the Marondera District of Zimbabwe (then Marandellas, South Rhodesia) and recorded by Hugh Tracey in 1951 (H. Tracey 1955–70 and 1973: TR-174 (A-6), H. Tracey et al. 2000: Track 19, *cf* Kyker 2018). My condensed transcription (Figure 2.26) provides a synopsis of the sonic and the motional aspects of this piece. It shows, in correlation to the grid of twenty-four elementary pulses and eight reference beats,

(1) two varieties of the hexatonic upper voice,
(2) the tetratonic lower voice,
(3) the root progression *in abstracto*, and
(4) the underlying motional pattern.

The corresponding two audio examples provide a looped and slightly slowed down excerpt from Hugh Tracey's recording, comprising two cycles of the root progression (Audio 4), and subsequently the complete recording in its original tempo (Audio 5).

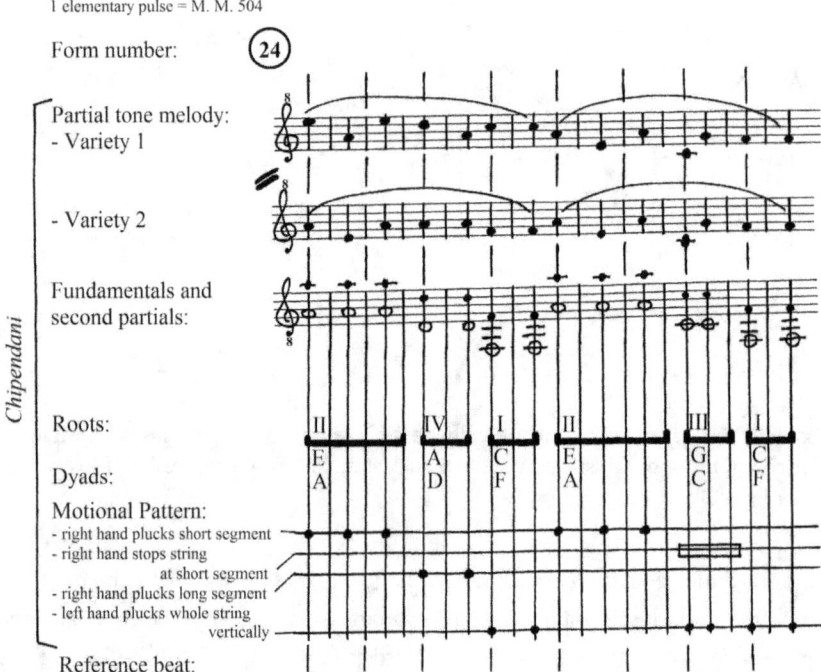

Figure 2.26 A *chipendani* piece based in the most elementary way on the 6-step 'standard' root progression: 'Kwa ambuya asina keriya', played by Mr. Muchabaiwa, supported by two unidentified singers, Marondera District, Zimbabwe (then Marandellas District, South Rhodesia), 1951. Recording by Hugh Tracey (H. Tracey 1955–70 and 1973: TR-174 (A-6)). Condensed transcription, restricted to sound and motional pattern of *chipendani* part. (For an extended transcription which also includes some typical lines of the two polyphonic vocal parts, see Brenner 1997: 57). Transcription: Klaus-Peter Brenner.

→ Audio 4. *Chipendani* piece 'Kwa ambuya asina keriya', played by Mr. Muchabaiwa, supported by two unidentified singers, Marondera District, Zimbabwe (then Marandellas District, South Rhodesia), 1951. Recording by Hugh Tracey (H. Tracey 1955–70 and 1973: TR-174 (A-6)). Excerpt: Two cycles of *chipendani* solo, looped and slightly slowed down. Duration: 0'52". – Copyright: International Library of African Music. Courtesy Prof. Diane Thram, director/ILAM.

→ Audio 5. *Chipendani* piece 'Kwa ambuya asina keriya', played by Mr. Muchabaiwa, supported by two unidentified singers, Marondera District, Zimbabwe (then Marandellas District, South Rhodesia), 1951. Recording by Hugh Tracey (H. Tracey 1955–70 and 1973: TR-174 (A-6)). Complete recording in original tempo. Duration: 1'19". – Copyright: International Library of African Music. Courtesy Prof. Diane Thram, director/ILAM.

In the following short video clip (Video 1), the author demonstrates the playing technique of the *chipendani* in motion.

> → Video 1. Author demonstrates playing technique of *chipendani* by playing 'Kwa ambuya asina keriya'. Excerpt from footage for exhibition trailer video 'Schätze des Wissens' ('Treasures of Knowledge'). Duration: 0'43". Production and Copyright: Georg-August-Universität Göttingen, Germany, 2011.

In the next three video examples (Videos 2–4), recorded in an informal workshop situation during the 1st Bow Music Conference in Durban, 2016, Sekuru Compound Muradzikwa demonstrates some of the more complex pieces from his *chipendani* repertoire, 'Ndezvemeso Muromo Chinyarara' and 'Mabhiza', along with one that he considers a beginners' piece, 'Tsoko', and which he combines in a medley with another one that I was not able to identify. These examples show how the 6-step 'standard' progression relates to and is structurally contained in individual root progressions which are derived from it by means of

(1) cyclical permutation in the temporal dimension,
(2) insertion of elements,
(3) iteration of groups of elements,
(4) as well as combinations of these three operations.

In addition to the underlying sequence of roots *in abstracto*, it is its metro-rhythmic phenotype ('harmonic rhythm', *cf* Berliner 1993: 77) *in concreto* that – often together with a kind of melodic 'catch phrase' – shapes the musically distinctive character and identity of an individual *chipendani* piece.

The piece 'Ndezvemeso Muromo Chinyarara' ('It is for the eyes; mouth, keep quiet') (Video 2, *cf* Kyker 2007) is based on a metro-rhythmic cycle of 8 x 2 = 16 elementary pulses (occasionally ternarized towards a cycle of 12 elementary pulses) and, harmonically, on the root progression

16 (= 12 EP)

IV		I			II	III		I			II	

which is the sixth temporal cyclical permutation of the 6-step 'standard' progression.

> → Video 2. Sekuru Compound Muradzikwa plays the *chipendani* piece 'Ndezvemeso Muromo Chinyarara'. Recorded at the 1st Bow Music Conference in Durban, 2016. – Duration: 1'23". Video: Klaus-Peter Brenner. Copyright: Compound Muradzikwa and Klaus-Peter Brenner.

The piece 'Mabhiza' ('Horses') (Video 3, *cf* Kyker 2007) is based on a metro-rhythmical cycle of 8 x 3 = 24 elementary pulses and, harmonically, on the root progression

24 EP

IV		I		IV		I		IV		I		II		III			I			II		I	II
IV										I	II			III								I	II

which is the sixth temporal cyclical permutation of the 6-step 'standard' progression, extended by insertions and internal iterations. The inherent 'standard' form is shown in grey in the second line.

> → Video 3. Sekuru Compound Muradzikwa plays the *chipendani* piece 'Mabhiza'. Recorded at the 1st Bow Music Conference in Durban, 2016. – Duration: 0'43". Video: Klaus-Peter Brenner. Copyright: Compound Muradzikwa and Klaus-Peter Brenner.

The piece 'Tsoko' ('Monkey') (Video 4, *cf* Kyker 2007) is based on a metro-rhythmical cycle of 8 x 3 = 24 elementary pulses (inferred from the vocal part, because in this case the *chipendani* pattern is rhythmically restricted to a manifestation of the beat) and, harmonically, on the root progression

24 EP

II			I			IV			I			II			III			II			I		
II									IV			I			II			III					I		

which is the fifth temporal cyclical permutation of the 6-step 'standard' progression, extended by insertions. Along with it, the author can be heard picking up and humming the catch phrase 'Tsoko, tsoko, tsoko, tsoko' on the (relative) notes, a f d f, a g e f, in the background.

24 EP

a			f			d			f			a			g			e			f		

Occasionally, Muradzikwa switches to a simplified variation that replaces root III for root I, thereby omitting root III (and partial g) altogether:

24 EP

II			I			IV			I			II			I			II			I		
II									IV			I			II			–			II			I		

The unidentified second piece of the medley (Video 4, beginning at 1'16") is based on a metro-rhythmical cycle of 8 x 3 = 24 elementary pulses and, harmonically, on the root progression

24 EP

II		IV	I	IV		I		II		III	II	III		I	
II		IV				I		II		III				I	

which is again the fifth temporal cyclical permutation of the 6-step 'standard' progression, extended by insertions.

> → Video 4. Sekuru Compound Muradzikwa plays a medley of two *chipendani* pieces, 'Tsoko'/[second piece unidentified]. Recorded at the 1st Bow Music Conference in Durban, 2016. – Duration: 2'20". Video: Klaus-Peter Brenner. Copyright: Compound Muradzikwa and Klaus-Peter Brenner.

As we have seen, the organization of the tone material is distinctively characterized by the combination of three features which together form the unique *chipendani* system:

(1) the register-dependent distribution of the tone material which is tetratonic at the bottom, as opposed to being hexatonic at the top,
(2) the inventory of four roots in a specific intervallic relationship, and the fifth dyads erected upon them, and
(3) the typical temporal manifestation of that inventory, that is, the 6-step 'standard' root progression.

The transference of this system to a small lamellophone in the remote past yielded the 8-key 'basic *kalimba* core', identified by Andrew Tracey (A. Tracey 1972, 1974, 2013), and it triggered and coherently channelled the evolution and gradual branching-out of the 'family' of Zimbabwean and circum-Zimbabwean lamellophone tuning plans (A. Tracey 1972, 1974, 2013), and, interdependently with it, it also triggered and coherently channelled the evolution and gradual branching-out of the Shona *mbira* system of harmonic patterning (Berliner [1978] 1993, 2019, Berliner and Magaya 2019, Brenner 1997, 2004a, 2013, 2015, 2019a, Grupe 1998, 2004, Kubik 1987, 1988b, A. Tracey 1961, 1970, 1989, 2015).

The following condensed four-quadrant graphic representation (Figure 2.27) visualizes the evidence for the first point: Andrew Tracey's 'basic *kalimba* core' (top left) (A. Tracey 1972, 1974, 2013), that is, the tuning plan of the hypothetic common ancestor of the Zimbabwean and circum-Zimbabwean family of *mbira* lamellophones bears a close and encompassing structural affinity to the tonal-harmonic system of the *chipendani* in terms of the distribution of its pitches in physical space (bottom left): each of the four dyads can be played with two thumbs, the distribution of its pitches in tonal space (top right): the tetratonic lower versus hexatonic upper representation of the tone material is preserved, and in terms of its most typical manifestation in temporal respect, the 6-step 'standard' root progression (bottom right) on which all present-day Shona *karimba* music is based. The corresponding audio example (Audio 6) demonstrates this threefold affinity *in abstracto*.

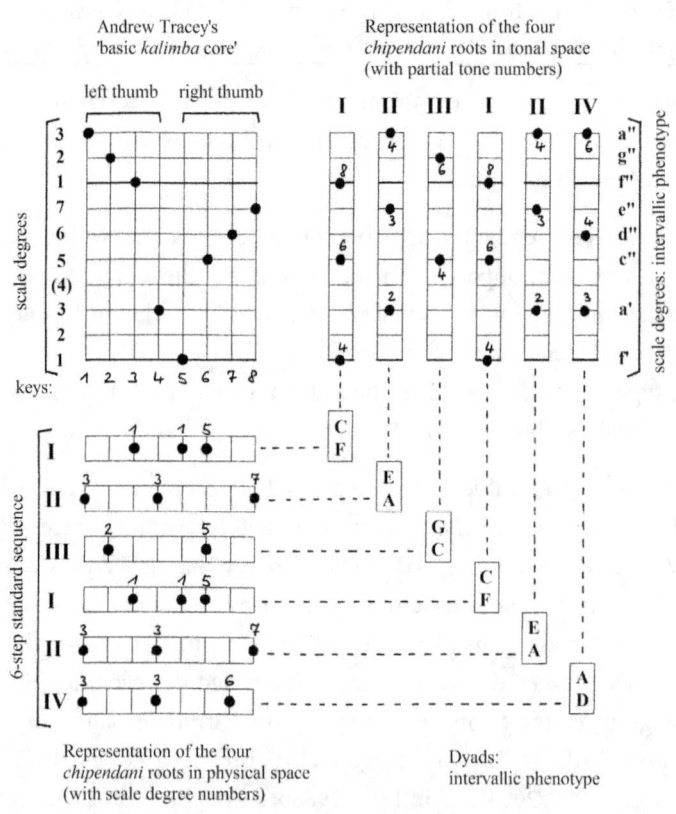

Figure 2.27 Andrew Tracey's 'basic *kalimba* core' (top left) and its structural affinity to the *chipendani* system in terms of pitch distribution in physical space (bottom left) and tonal space (top right), and its most typical manifestation in temporal respect, the 6-step 'standard' root progression (bottom right). Illustration: Klaus-Peter Brenner, incorporating an illustration by Andrew Tracey.

→ Audio 6. Demonstration of Andrew Tracey's 'basic *kalimba* core', keys from left to right, notes from lowest to highest, and available two-thumb combinations of keys producing the 6-step 'standard' root progression. Duration: 1'18".

The lower manual of the present-day Shona *karimba* (Figure 2.28) is structurally identical to Andrew Tracey's 'basic *kalimba* core', as marked on the depicted specimen. Its music is exclusively based on a stock of distinctively structured and closely interrelated root progressions, the most elementary and typical variety of which is the 6-step 'standard' progression [FC → AE → DA → FC → AE → CG →] (*cf* A. Tracey 1961, Kauffman 1970, Kaemmer 1973, Berliner [1978] 1993)!

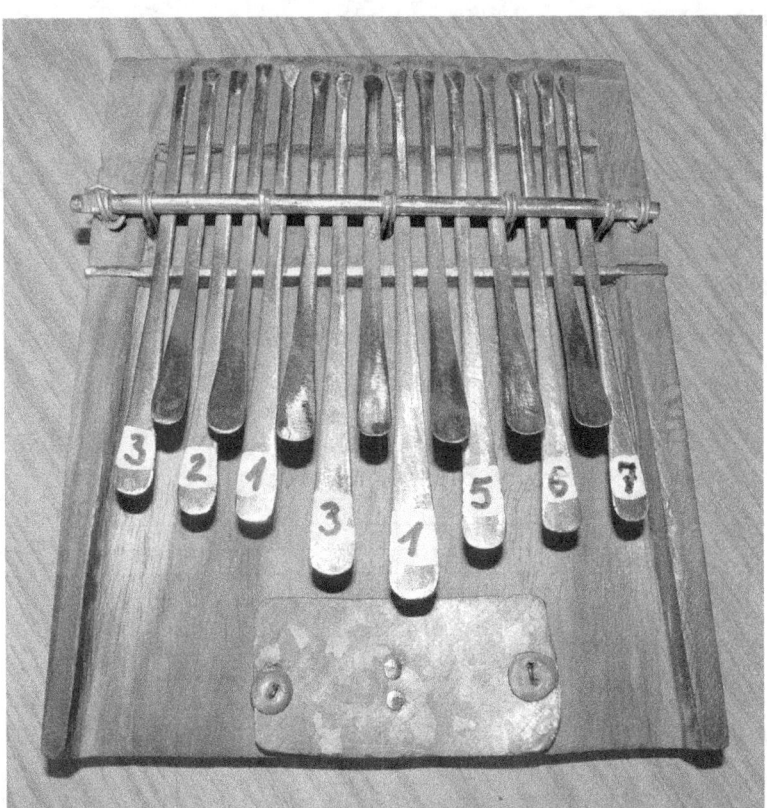

Figure 2.28 Present-day Shona *karimba* whose lower manual is identical with the 'basic *kalimba* core'. Depicted specimen made by Chris Mhlanga, New Canaan, Harare, Zimbabwe, before 1993; now: Georg-August-Universität Göttingen, Collection of Musical Instruments, inventory number 1311; 'basic *kalimba* core' assigned to the lower manual by author. Photo: Klaus-Peter Brenner.

In the following excerpt from a YouTube tutorial video (Video 5), Eric Orem gives a typical example of this: he demonstrates an elementary version of the Shona *karimba* piece 'Chemutengure' ('That which carries', 'Wagon') (*cf* A. Tracey 1961, Kauffman 1970, Berliner [1978] 1993, Matiure 2008), based on the 6-step 'standard' root progression and restricted to the lower manual, which conforms to and preserves the 'basic *kalimba* core'. My corresponding transcription (Figure 2.29) shows how the pattern relates to the root progression.

> → Video 5. Shona *karimba* piece 'Chemutengure', based on the 6-step 'standard' root progression, elementary version restricted to the lower rank of keys which is identical with the 'basic *kalimba* core'. Excerpt from: Orem 2013. – Duration: 0'39". Copyright: Eric Orem. Courtesy Eric Orem.

Figure 2.30 shows, on the highest level of abstraction, my reconstruction of how the 12-step and 9-step harmonic progressions of Shona *mbira* music are likely to have evolved from the 6-step *chipendani/karimba* 'standard' progression (Brenner 1997) as their origin and embryonic prototype. In the synopsis, fundamentals of dyads/triads are shown in terms of heptatonic scale degree numbers. From the synopsis, their structural and hypothetic evolutionary relationship becomes evident.

Let us finally focus on the 12-step 'standard' *mbira* progression (first described by A. Tracey 1970 for Shona *matepe* music) (Figure 2.30, Audio 7).

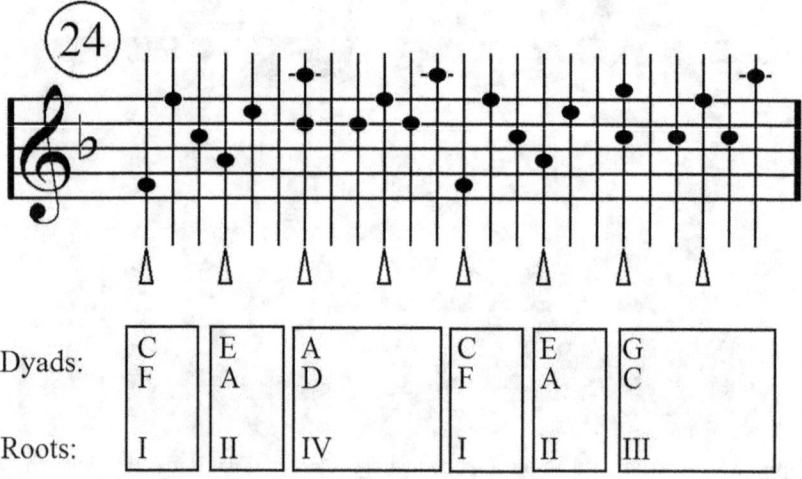

Figure 2.29 Shona *karimba* piece 'Chemutengure', based on the 6-step 'standard' root progression, elementary version restricted to the lower manual which is identical with the 'basic *kalimba* core', transcribed from Video 5 (Excerpt from Orem 2013). Transcription: Klaus-Peter Brenner.

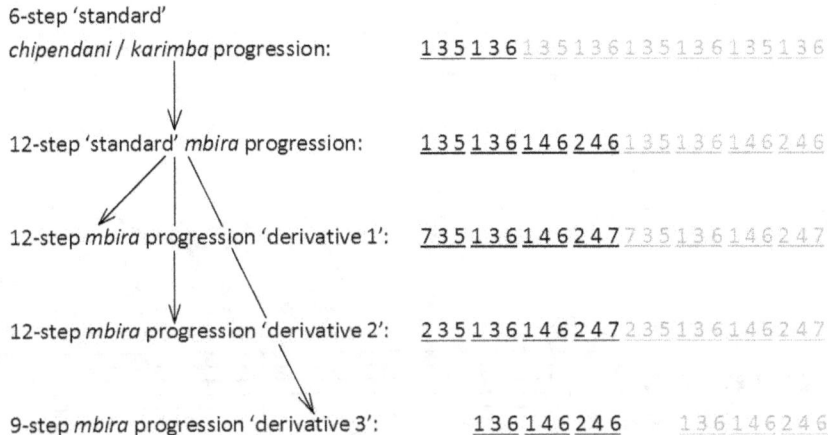

Figure 2.30 Evolution of harmonic progressions of Shona *mbira* music from *chipendani*/*karimba* progression (Brenner 1997) (figures = fundamentals of dyads/triads in terms of scale degree numbers).

> → Audio 7. Shona *mbira dzavadzimu* piece 'Kariga mombe', based on the 12-step 'standard' root progression, elementary version of *kushaura* part (*cf* transcription: Brenner 1997: 219, Brenner et al. 2013) restricted to the central upper region of the tuning plan which is a heptatonisized derivative of the 'basic *kalimba* core' (*cf* A. Tracey 1972, 1974, Brenner 1997). – Version according to Ephat Mujuru Mbire. Demonstration played by Klaus-Peter Brenner. Duration: 1'16".

How did this ingenious musical invention possibly come about? Where and how did the cognitive transgression and breakthrough occur that led from the well-established 6-step *chipendani*/*karimba* progression to what was to become the 12-step 'standard' *mbira* progression of Shona music? The following hypothetic model (Figures 2.31 and 2.32) offers a plausible explanation: the 12-step 'standard' progression resulted from the fusion of the 6-step 'standard' progression with a fourth-transposed temporal cyclical permutation of itself. This is theoretically realizable by a duet of two alternating *zvipendani* (pl. of *chipendani*) tuned a fourth apart. In this model, the first *chipendani* provides the roots F A C D, while the second one provides the roots B♭ D F G. As the roots F and D occur in both *zvipendani*, though in different positions on the instrument, their combination yields the common inventory of the six roots F G A B♭ C D.[4]

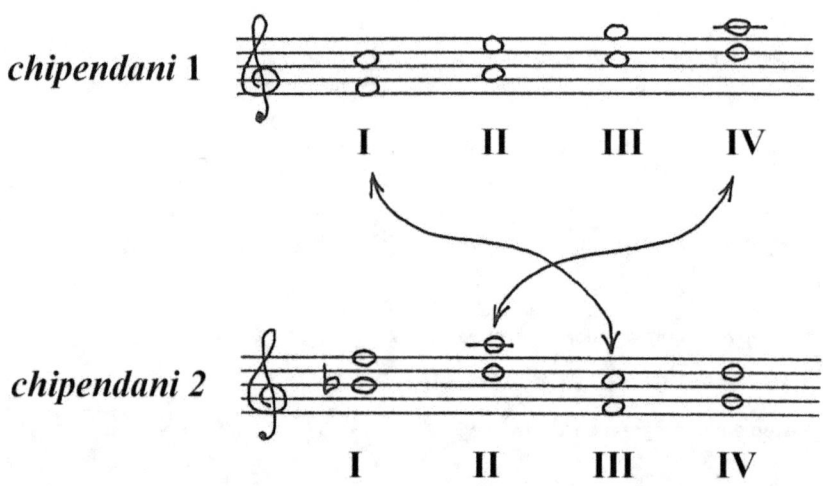

Figure 2.31 Inventory of dyads of two *zvipendani* with root I tuned in F vs. B♭.

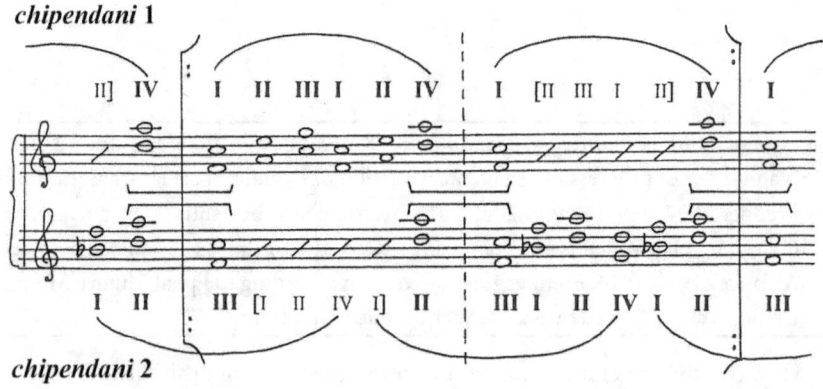

Figure 2.32 12-step 'standard' *mbira* progression as potentially realizable by a duet of two alternating *zvipendani*.

The following audio example (Audio 8) demonstrates *in abstracto* their playing in overlapping alternation.

→ Audio 8. Demonstration *in abstracto* of the 12-step 'standard' progression resulting from the fusion of the 6-step 'standard' progression with a fourth-transposed temporal cyclical permutation of itself – as played by an alternating duet of two *zvipendani* (pl. of *chipendani*) tuned a fourth apart. The sequence starts at root IV of *chipendani* 1 (= root II of *chipendani* 2). – Demonstration played by Klaus-Peter Brenner. Duration: 1'34".

Whether or not this self-referential reduplication and transposed recombination of the *chipendani* progression really emerged from a praxis of *chipendani* duet playing in the remote past, or whether it emerged rather from some creative transposition experiments, carried out by an inventive and explorative *kalimba* player, remains beyond our knowledge. But whatever was the case historically, this much is certain: the style-molding impact of the *chipendani* on the harmonic and polyphonic foundations of Shona *mbira* music is perfectly obvious. This is cogently demonstrated by the last audio example (Audio 9, Figure 2.33). In the Shona *mbira dzavadzimu* piece 'Ndodzungaira' ('I wander around') the 12-step harmonic 'standard' progression is materialized in the most exemplary way, with the roots being pointedly articulated in the bass register throughout the cycle.

> → Audio 9. Shona *mbira dzavadzimu* piece 'Ndodzungaira'. Rendition by Cosmas Muza and John Gandidze, in Karanda village near Gora Primary School, Mashayamombe chiefdom, Mhondoro Communal Land, Chegutu District, Mashonaland West Province, Zimbabwe, 1993. – Analytical two-channel recording: Klaus-Peter Brenner. Duration: 2'35".

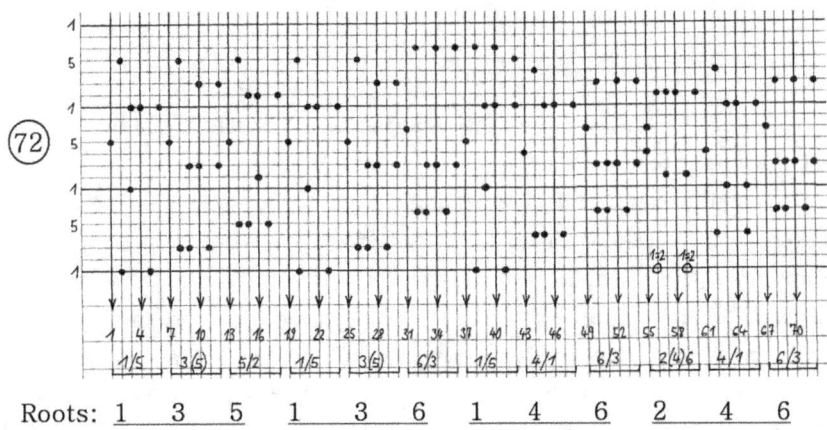

Figure 2.33 'Ndodzungaira', a perfect example of a Shona *mbira dzavadzimu* piece based on the 12-step harmonic 'standard' progression. Rendition by Cosmas Muza and John Gandidze, recorded by author in Mhondoro, Zimbabwe, 1993. Transcription shows one harmonic cycle of superimposed complementary *kushaura* and *kutsinhira* parts. (For an extended transcription which also shows the two parts separately, see Brenner 1997: 238–43.) Transcription: Klaus-Peter Brenner.

I always wondered what, in the remote past, the precise sociocultural circumstances, position and function of the *chipendani* might have been that enabled it to wield – as a kind of 'gravitational' force – such a formative, pervasive and lasting influence on the grammatical foundations of Shona *kalimba/mbira* lamellophone music. There was every indication that these must have significantly differed from the comparably marginal present-day position of the *chipendani*. In her insightful and corrective reassessment of the latter, Jennifer Kyker (2017, 2018) presented in this respect a most thrilling and crucial finding, namely, the evidence for a local use of the *chipendani* – instead of the *mbira* (!) – in religious possession ceremonies of the ancestral cult (called *bira*, pl. *mapira*, in chiShona, *cf* Gelfand 1959, 1962, Kaemmer 1975, 1989, Berliner 1975/1976, [1978] 1993, Brenner 1997, Rutsate 2010) in recent times. This, when considered in correlation with the above-presented evidence of the musical continuity, reveals the possibility that the *kalimba/mbira* did inherit not only the nucleus of its harmonic system from the *chipendani*, but also its religious function. At least, such an assumption would offer a plausible explanation of where and why the *chipendani-kalimba/mbira* system transfer is likely to have occurred and to have become so firmly established that it was able to configure the harmonic deep structures of much of Shona (and Sena) music for centuries to come.

Appendix

The Venda *tshihwana*: a different tonal-harmonic system based on the same set of acoustic principles

Among the historically related southern neighbours of the Shona, the Venda, the organological equivalent of the Shona *chipendani*, is known as *tshihwana* (*cf* Kirby [1934] 1968, University of Washington n. d. b). The material published so far as well as my own research with *tshihwana* player Mrs. Avhapfani Constence Dima from Sibasa, Limpopo province, South Africa, during the 'South African Music Village' festival at the Berlin 'Haus der Kulturen' in July 1996 reveal the alternative use of (at least) two fundamentally different tunings:

(1) The first tuning is essentially identical with the above-described Shona one in using the interval of a 'fifth' (*c.* 702 cents) for the basic string division, though the tonal-harmonic system erected upon it is reduced to the three roots I, II and IV in this case, as the instrument is plucked with a plectrum

instead of the pinching grip which prevents the player from stopping the string for root III (*cf* Kruger 1986, 2006: 55–6 with transcription Figure 3.10,[5] University of Washington n. d. a: Track 9).

(2) The second tuning is based on a somewhat elastic interval whose size ranges between a 'minor third' (*c.* 300 cents) and a 'major third' (*c.* 400 cents) (*cf* Brenner 1997: 48–52, Dargie 1990, 2001, 2003, Kruger 1986, 2006: 53–5 with transcription Figure. 3.9a–b, *ILAM Digital Sound Archive* 2016, University of Washington n. d. a: Track 7) and that allows for a reductive approximation to the tonal-harmonic system and polyphonic structure of the prestigious *tshikona* reed-pipes dance (*cf* Blacking 1965, 1973, Brenner 2015, Kirby [1934] 1968, Kruger 1999, 2006, 2007, A. Tracey and Gumboreshumba 2013).

The following example shows the 'minor-third' phenotype of the second tuning. It demonstrates how a completely different tonal-harmonic system (different from the Shona one as well as from the first of the two Venda ones) is generated on the basis of the same set of acoustic principles, when firstly the cultural choice of the interval of the basic string division and secondly the cultural choice of the melodically utilized partials are a different one. As opposed to the *chipendani* system, no use is made of the stopping-technique, as the player's right hand holds a plectrum and is therefore not available for the pinching grip required to stop the string in order to shorten its vibrating length. But the left-hand index finger action is identical to that of the *chipendani* system in that it plucks the bent whole string from above.[6]

So how is the one-dimensional string-divider utilized in this tuning? When the string is divided in such a way that the interval between the two segments is roughly a 'minor third', this implies that the whole string is divided approximately by 11, and the string length ratio of 5:6 (or something close to it) is established (Figure 2.34).

The three musically utilized string lengths are then:

11:5:6

From this set of string length ratios, we calculate the corresponding frequency ratios and hence the intervals between the three fundamentals (Figure 2.35). Expressed in relative pitch, these are:[7]

F^+:g:e

Henceforth we also address them as:

Root I:II:III

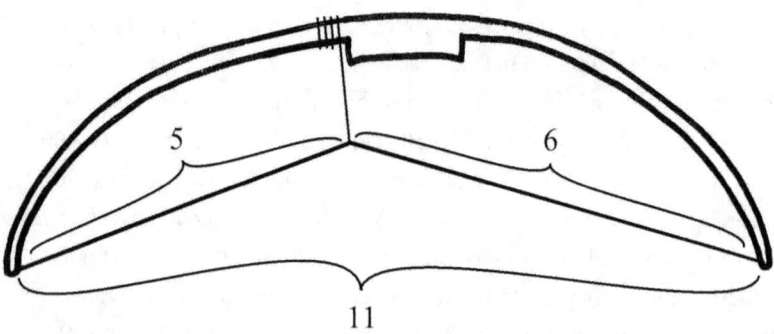

Figure 2.34 *Tshihwana*, 'minor-third' tuning: ratios of vibrating string lengths. Division of whole string by 11. Illustration: Klaus-Peter Brenner.

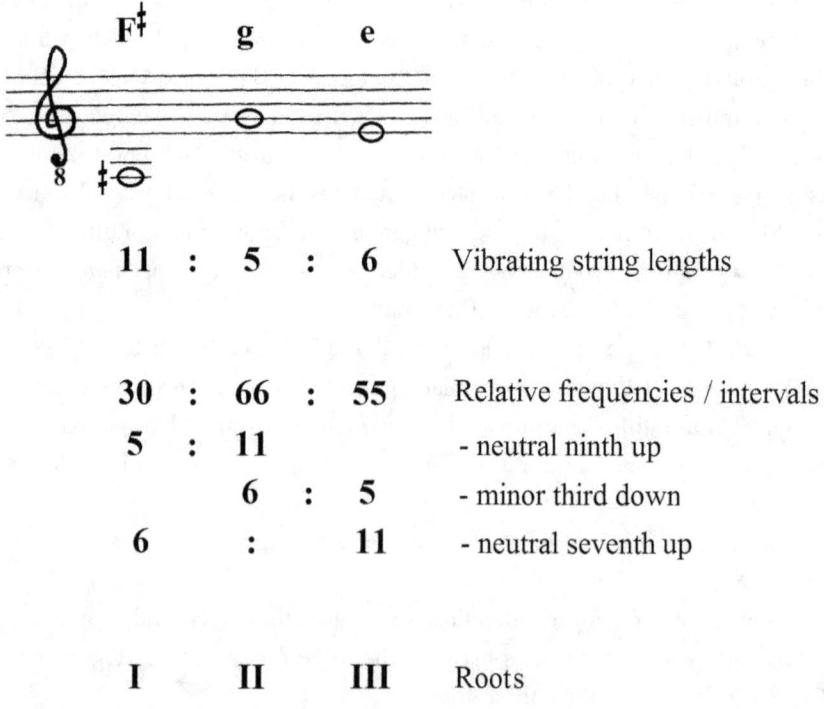

Figure 2.35 *Tshihwana*, 'minor-third' tuning: intervals between fundamentals. Illustration: Klaus-Peter Brenner.

> → Audio 10. Venda *tshihwana*, 'minor-third' tuning: fundamentals F⁺, g, e. – Duration: 0'17". Demonstration played by Klaus-Peter Brenner (on a retuned *chipendani* with attached secondary rattle *chijaka*).

The tonal-harmonic system of this variety of Venda *tshihwana* music, as it can be inferred from the bow part of Mr. P. Munyayi's *tshihwana*-based song 'Nga vha mu rende Yesu' (Audio 13), is based on the three fundamentals F⁺, G and E, and the triad/dyads F⁺A⁺C⁺, GD and EB, which are obtained by selectively mouth-filtering them from their respective columns of partials. The columnar representation of this tone material (Figure 2.36) shows that mainly those harmonic partials are selected which are octave equivalents of the first to third partials, i.e. of the fundamentals and their respective fifths, however with one systemically significant exception: the fifth partial of root I and its octave equivalent, the tenth partial, complete the so far hexatonic tone material towards a heptatonic scale. As opposed to the *chipendani* system, there exist no cross-stabilizing commonalities between the columns in this variety of the *tshihwana* system which is likely to account for its greater intervallic elasticity.[8]

> → Audio 11. Venda *tshihwana*, 'minor-third' tuning: selection of mouth-filtered harmonic partials, arranged in columns. The played sequence is: I₄₋₅₋₆₋₈₋₁₀₋₈₋₆₋₅₋₄ II₂₋₃₋₄₋₃₋₂ III₂₋₃₋₄₋₆₋₄₋₃₋₂. – Duration: 0'44". Demonstration played by Klaus-Peter Brenner (on a retuned *chipendani* with attached secondary rattle *chijaka*).

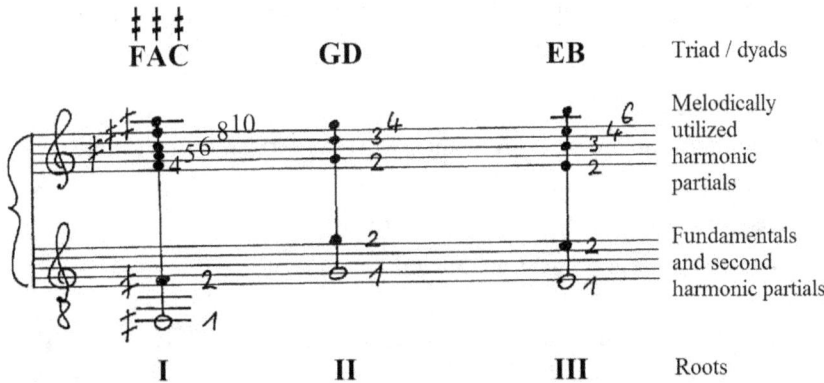

Figure 2.36 *Tshihwana*, 'minor-third' tuning: selection of mouth-filtered harmonic partials, arranged in columns. (Note the absence of any cross-stabilizing commonalities between the columns in this tonal-harmonic system!) Illustration: Klaus-Peter Brenner.

Figure 2.37 *Tshihwana*, 'minor-third' tuning: selection of mouth-filtered harmonic partials, arranged as descending scale. Illustration: Klaus-Peter Brenner.

> → Audio 12. Venda *tshihwana*, 'minor-third' tuning: selection of mouth-filtered harmonic partials, arranged as descending scale (Figure 2.37). The played sequence is:
>
> $$III_6 \quad I_{10} \quad II_4 \quad I_8 \quad III_4$$
> $$II_3 \quad I_6 \quad III_3 \quad I_5 \quad II_2 \quad I_4 \quad III_2$$
>
> Duration: 0'31". Demonstration played by Klaus-Peter Brenner (on a retuned *chipendani* with attached secondary rattle *chijaka*).

A photograph taken by Dave Dargie in 1988, when 'Nga vha mu rende Yesu' was recorded, shows Mr. P. Munyayi playing his *tshihwana* with an opened safety pin as a plectrum (Figure 2.38). The one-dimensional string-divider is clearly recognizable: it is made of a strand of cotton, one end of which is permanently fixed at the string which is then tightened by pulling the other end towards the bow stave and winding/lashing it several times around it, with the free end loosely hanging down. My condensed transcription of the *tshihwana* part of P. Munyayi's 'Nga vha mu rende Yesu' (Figure 2.39, Audio 13) comprises

(1) two ph(r)ase-shifting varieties of the partial tone melody,
(2) the pattern formed by the fundamentals and for the most part more prominently audible second partials,
(3) their abstract representation as root progression, and
(4) an analytical representation of the motional pattern of the two hands.

> → Audio 13. 'Nga vha mu rende Yesu', *tshihwana*-based Christian worship song composed in traditional Venda style, played and sung by Mr. P. Munyayi and accompanied by female response singers, recorded by Dave Dargie during a workshop at Lumko Music Department, Delmenville, Gauteng, South Africa, in 1988 (Dargie 1990: Track A-11; 2003: Track 13; mislabelled 'Yehova nga a rendwe', title given here according to Dargie's corrected metadata at *ILAM Digital Sound Archive* 2016). Complete recording. Duration: 5'01". Courtesy Prof. Dave Dargie.

Figure 2.38 Mr. P. Munyayi with his *tshihwana*. Photo: Dave Dargie (*cf* Dargie 2001: Handbook: xi). Courtesy Prof. Dave Dargie.

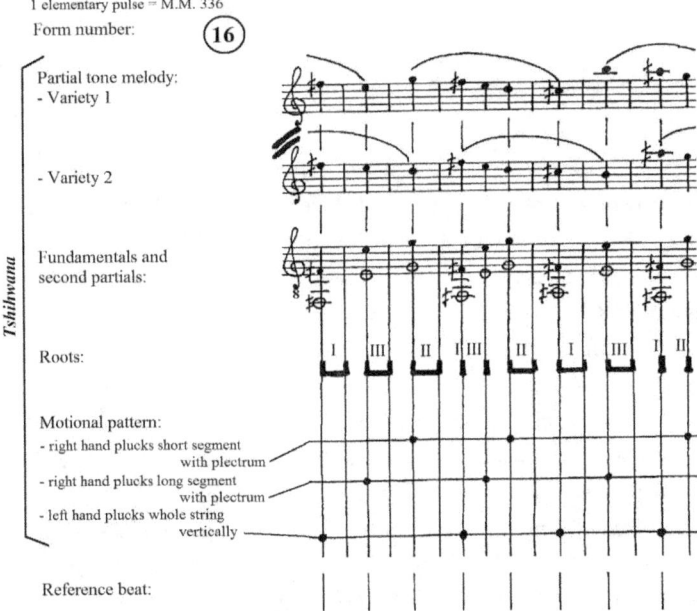

Figure 2.39 *Tshihwana*-based song 'Nga vha mu rende Yesu' in 'minor third' tuning (Audio 13): Condensed transcription of sound and motional pattern of *tshihwana* part. Transcription: Klaus-Peter Brenner.

While the two phrases within each of the two varieties of the partial tone melody display an alternating shift downward and upward by one heptatonic scale degree, there exists a shift-relationship of yet another kind between the two varieties themselves. In these a structural linkage between the spatial and the temporal dimension causes a tricky *gestalt* effect: once the initial notes of the two phrases of variety 1 are replaced by their respective lower octave equivalents in order to achieve variety 2, a different grouping is foregrounded that preserves their descending melodic contours, however, in a position shifted downward by one step spatially and delayed by one beat in temporal respect. In effect, the entry points of the two phrases of variety 1 interlock with those of the phrases of variety 2, and both pairs of phrases show an overlapping relationship on the common background of the *ostinato* of the root progression. This feature reveals, on the one hand, structural affinities with southcentral and southern African forms of polyphonic multi-part singing with interlocking entry points of phrases as can be found from the Shona and Sena in the north to the Xhosa in the south (*cf* Brenner 2020) and, on the other hand, with musical strategies to 'Shepardize'[9] the tone material – an aspect that I have comparatively discussed with regard to certain central African chordophone and idiophone musics (*cf* Brenner 2004b).

Notes

1. The Shona *chipendani* specimens in the Collection of Musical Instruments, University of Göttingen, vary in length: inventory number L-88 = 50 cm, 1344 = 68 cm, L-171 = 89 cm, L-89 = 80 cm, 1345 = 96.5 cm. Opposed to these, the Shangana-Tsonga *xipendani* [*xipendana*] specimen, inventory number L-172, measures 114.5 cm. Further information on these six specimens is given in the general catalogue of the collection (Brenner 2019b: 383–5).
2. Tomas F. Johnston reports for the organologically equivalent, though differently tuned, *xipendana* of the Shangana-Tsonga, that the string used to be made of 'a length of tendon from a hind leg of cattle' before the tendency emerged to replace this older material by copper wire (Johnston 1980: 263).
3. As predicted by himself, the tentative three-bow merger model suggested by Gerhard Kubik in his San substratum theory (Kubik 1987, 1988b, *cf* A. Tracey 1989, Brenner 1997) proved to be an expedient heuristic means on the way to this finding. Thus, having fulfilled its purpose, it must now be considered obsolete.
4. The playing of equally tuned pairs of mouth bows with one-dimensional string-divider has been reported for the Venda *tshihwana* (Blacking 1973: Fig. 'A duet on

two mouth bows'), the Shangana-Tsonga *xipendana* (Johnston 1971: 68–71; 1972: Plate 42; 1980; A. Tracey 2005), the Pedi *lekope* (Kirby [1934] 1968: 233–4), as well as for the Mbuti *andôbu* (*cf.* Schebesta 1957: Fig. 15).

5   However, Kruger's transcription (Figure 3.10) is not completely consistent with his description of the playing technique insofar as it shows roots II (fundamental tone D), IV (A), and III (C), the latter of which cannot be produced by vertically plucking the bent whole string with the left-hand index finger unless it is stopped by the right-hand pinching grip which in turn is technically impossible as long as the player uses a plectrum. Doubtlessly, instead of root III (fundamental C) as erroneously transcribed by Kruger, it must have been root I (fundamental F) that was actually played; but possibly the real fundamental was barely audible so that its partial tone No. 3, which is indeed a C, could easily be mistaken for the fundamental. This would also offer a consistent explanation for Kruger's so-called ghost notes: the melodic note f at the end of his transcription is not, as he suggests, obtained as an acoustically enigmatic partial of root III (fundamental C), but rather as partial No. 8 of root I (fundamental F). The melodic passing note g, which occurs immediately before that f, is hence obtained as partial No. 9 of root I.

6   This peculiar action of the *tshihwana* player's left-hand index finger has already been described by Kirby ([1934] 1968: 229–31) and Kruger (2006: 56), both of whom however missed the point regarding the acoustic principle exploited by it.

7   The symbol '+' signifies a micro-intervallic upward alteration by roughly a quarter tone and is used here as a substitute for the proper half sharp used in Figures 2.35–2.37 and 2.39.

8   In Dave Dargie's recordings, the size of Mr. P. Munyayi's tuning interval can be heard to vary between roughly a 'minor third' (Dargie 1990: Track 4 'Nga vha mu rende Yesu') and a 'major third' (Dargie 2001: Track 10 'Setimela').

9   The notion of 'Shepardization' refers to musical strategies that strive, by juggling with octave equivalents, to foreground the circularity of tone chroma while attempting to mask out the linearity of tone height. As an aspect of the respective musical grammar, these strategies manifest in the way the tone material is structured in the process of composing or improvising a piece of music according to its rules. But it can even manifest itself organologically, as for instance in the octave-doubling and re-entrant tuning plans of certain central African xylophones such as the Nzakara *nzangu^{n}la*, or it may be codified in the musical organization of an instrumental ensemble such as the *nanga* reed-pipes of the Venda dance, *tshikona*, whose sound structure bears a striking resemblance with the psychoacoustic paradox known as the 'falling Shepard scale', or more exactly: with two simultaneously sounding 'Shepard scales' descending in parallel fifths (*cf* Blacking 1965, 1973, Brenner 2015, Kirby [1934] 1968, Kruger 1999, 2006, 2007, A. Tracey and Gumboreshumba 2013).

References

Berliner, Paul F[ranklin] (1975/1976), 'Music and Spirit Possession at a Shona Bira', *African Music* 5 (4): 130–9.

Berliner, Paul F[ranklin] ([1978] 1993), *The Soul of Mbira: Music and Traditions of the Shona People of Zimbabwe. With an Appendix: Building and Playing a Shona Karimba*, Chicago and London: University of Chicago Press.

Berliner, Paul F[ranklin] (2019), *The Art of Mbira: Musical Inheritance and Legacy. Featuring the Repertory and Practices of Cosmas Magaya and Associates*, Chicago: The University of Chicago Press.

Berliner, Paul F[ranklin], and Cosmas Magaya (2019), *Mbira's Restless Dance: An Archive for Improvisation*, Chicago: The University of Chicago Press.

Blacking, John (1965), 'The Role of Music in the Culture of the Venda of the Northern Transvaal', in *Studies in Ethnomusicology* 2 (ed.), Mieczyslaw Kolinski, 20–53, New York: Oak Publications.

Blacking, John (1973), *How Musical Is Man?* Seattle et al.: University of Washington Press.

Brenner, Klaus-Peter (1997), *Chipendani und Mbira. Musikinstrumente, nichtbegriffliche Mathematik und die Evolution der harmonischen Progressionen in Musik der Shona in Zimbabwe*, Abhandlungen der Akademie der Wissenschaften in Göttingen, Philologisch-Historische Klasse, 3rd Series, 221, with 2 companion audio CDs, Göttingen: Vandenhoeck and Ruprecht.

Brenner, Klaus-Peter (2004a), 'Das akustische Prinzip des 1-dimensionalen Saitenteilers und seine musikalische Nutzung beim *chipendani* (Mundbogen) der Shona', in Erich Stockmann, Eszter Fontana, and Andreas Michel (eds.), *Studia instrumentorum musicae popularis* 12, 27–44, Leipzig: Verlag Janos Stekovics.

Brenner, Klaus-Peter (2004b), *Die kombinatorisch strukturierten Harfen- und Xylophonpattern der Nzakara (Zentralafrikanische Republik) als klingende Geometrie – eine Alternative zu Marc Chemilliers Kanonhypothese* (EthnomusiCologne, 4, ed. Rüdiger Schumacher), with English summary and 1 companion audio CD, Bonn: Holos-Verlag.

Brenner, Klaus-Peter (2013), 'The *Mbira/Chimurenga* Transformation of "Dangurangu" – A Music-Analytical Case Study from Zimbabwe at the Intersection of Ethnomusicology and Popular Music Research', with an appendix by Laina Gumboreshumba, in Gerd Grupe (ed.), *Ethnomusicology and Popular Music Studies* (Grazer Beiträge zur Ethnomusikologie/Graz Studies in Ethnomusicology 25), 53–146, with 23 audio examples, Aachen: Shaker.

Brenner, Klaus-Peter (2015), 'Squaring the Circle: Venda/Shona Grammatical Ambiguity and the Amalgamation of Mutually Exclusive Systems of Harmonic Patterning in Barangarani Mudzanani's *Mbila dzaMadeza* Piece "Bidera"', in Anja Brunner, Cornelia Gruber and August Schmidhofer (eds.), *Transgressions of a*

Musical Kind. Festschrift for Regine Allgayer-Kaufmann on the Occasion of Her 65th Birthday, 25–50, with 1 audio example, Aachen: Shaker.

Brenner, Klaus-Peter (2019a), 'A Cognitive Firework of Model-bound Two-handed Improvisation: *Mbira dzaVadzimu* Master Ephat Mujuru's "Deep" *Kutsinhira* Rendition of "Bukatiende Diki"', in Klaus-Peter Brenner (ed.), *Mbira Music | Musics. Structures and Processes. Papers Presented at the Symposium III.4 of the 15th International Conference of the Gesellschaft für Musikforschung at the University of Göttingen, 4–8 September 2012* (Göttingen Studies in Musicology, ed. Andreas Waczkat and Birgit Abels, 9), 293–344, with 1 audio and 1 video example and 276 pp. of graphic figures available on the companion website, Hildesheim: Olms.

Brenner, Klaus-Peter (2019b), *Musikinstrumentensammlung des Musikwissenschaftlichen Seminars der Georg-August-Universität Göttingen. Bestandskatalog: Klassifikation, Objektbeschreibungen und -abbildungen, Bibliographie, Verzeichnisse* (version as of 10 October 2019, 931 pages), PDF. Available online: https://www.uni-goettingen.de/en/71170.html (accessed 7 November 2019).

Brenner, Klaus-Peter (Brenner 2020), 'A Grammatical Merger of Heterogeneous Musical Structures: The Vocal Polyphony *Ntano* of the Sena of Southern Malaŵi', in Malik Sharif and Kendra Stepputat (eds.), *Understanding Musics: Festschrift on the Occasion of Gerd Grupe's 65th Birthday*, 27 pages, with 56-pages extended version and 3 audio examples available online, Düren: Shaker Verlag.

Brenner, Klaus-Peter, Laurent Bartholdi and Radhika Gupta (2013), *The '12-step Harmonic Standard Sequence' of the Shona mbira Music of Zimbabwe: Animated Visualization of Its Rotational Symmetric Structure on Plane and Torus, with Synchronized Music Example*, sounding computer animation according to → Brenner (1997: 119–20), with explanatory notes, Göttingen: Georg-August-Universität Göttingen, Mathematical Institute, http://www.uni-math.gwdg.de/laurent/torus and http://www.youtube.com/watch?v=ds_I2q7C5Po (accessed 9 February 2016).

Dargie, Dave (recordings, notes, ed.) [1990], *Missa Africa: African Sunday IV*, Lumko Music Dept. Tape No. 153, tape cassette, Delmenville, Gauteng, South Africa: Lumko Music Department.

Dargie, Dave (recordings, notes, ed.) (2001), *Magical Musical Bows: A CD with Accompanying Article/Handbook, to Introduce the Sounds of the Wonderful Musical Bows of Southern Africa*, audio CD and 28-pages handbook, Alice, South Africa: Prof. Dave Dargie, University of Fort Hare.

Dargie, Dave (recordings, notes, ed.) (2003), *New World, Ancient Harmonies*, Audio CD and 12-pages booklet, Alice, South Africa: Prof. Dave Dargie, University of Fort Hare.

Dias, Margot (1986), *Instrumentos Musicais de Moçambique*, with companion audio tape cassette, Lisboa: Instituto de Investigação Científica Tropical/Centro de Antropologia Cultural e Social.

Gelfand, Michael (1959), *Shona Ritual. With Special Reference to the Chaminuka Cult*, Cape Town et al.: Juta & Co., Ltd.

Gelfand, Michael (1962), *Shona Religion. With Special Reference to the Makorekore*, Cape Town etc.: Juta & Co., Ltd.

Grupe, Gerd (1998), 'Traditional *mbira* Music of the Shona (Zimbabwe): Harmonic Progressions and Their Cognitive Dimension', in Till Förster/Iwalewa-Haus/Afrika-Zentrum der Universität Bayreuth (eds.), *Iwalewa Forum – Working Papers in African Art and Culture* 98 (2): 5–23.

Grupe, Gerd (2004), *Die Kunst des mbira-Spiels. The Art of Mbira Playing. Harmonische Struktur und Patternbildung in der Lamellophonmusik der Shona in Zimbabwe* (Musikethnologische Sammelbände, ed. Wolfgang Suppan, Institut für Musikethnologie an der Universität für Musik und darstellende Kunst in Graz, 19), with 1 companion audio CD, Tutzing: Hans Schneider.

ILAM Digital Sound Archive (2016), http://greenstone.ilam.ru.ac.za/cgi-bin/library?site=localhost&a=p&p=about&c=ilam&l=en&w=utf-8 (accessed 8 April 2016, however, on 11 September 2019 no longer available), search result for → "Nga vha mu rende Yesu".

Johnston, Thomas F[rederick] (1971), 'Shangana-Tsonga Drum and Bow Rhythms', *African Music* 5 (1): 59–72.

Johnston, Thomas F[rederick] (1972), *The Music of the Shangana-Tsonga* (PhD diss., University of Witwatersrand, South Africa), Ann Arbor: University Microfilms International, No. 74-3773.

Johnston, Thomas F[rederick] (1980), 'The Mqangala and Xipendana Musical Bows of the Shangana-Tsonga', *Afrika und Übersee: Sprachen, Kulturen* 63 (2): 257–68.

Jones, Claire (2019), 'Shona *Mbira* Tunings and the Production of New Sounds: Modal Tunings and the Emergence of the *Mbira* Orchestras', in Klaus-Peter Brenner (ed.), *Mbira Music | Musics. Structures and Processes. Papers Presented at the Symposium III.4 of the 15th International Conference of the Gesellschaft für Musikforschung at the University of Göttingen, 4–8 September 2012* (Göttingen Studies in Musicology, ed. Andreas Waczkat and Birgit Abels, 9), 201–34, with 7 audio examples available on the companion website, Hildesheim: Olms.

Kaemmer, John Edmund (1973), Review of Two 12" 33 1/3 rpm Discs: (a) *The African Mbira; Music of the Shona People of Rhodesia. Performed by Dumisani Abraham Maraire*, Nonesuch H-72043 (Explorer Series), notes by Dunisani Abraham Maraire, 1971, and (b) *Mbira Music of Rhodesia. Performed by Dumisani Abraham Maraire*, University of Washington Press, UWP-1001 (University of Washington Ethnic Music series), notes by Dumisani Abraham Maraire and Robert Kauffman, 1971, *Ethnomusicology* 17 (2): 366–8.

Kaemmer, John Edmund (1975), *The Dynamics of a Changing Music System in Rural Rhodesia* (PhD diss., Indiana University), Ann Arbor: University Microfilms International, No. 76-11,423.

Kaemmer, John Edmund (1989), 'Social Power and Music Change among the Shona', *Ethnomusicology* 33 (1): 31–45.

Kauffman, Robert [Allen] (1970), *Multi-Part Relationships in the Shona Music of Rhodesia* (PhD diss., University of California, Los Angeles), Ann Arbor: University Microfilms International, No. 71-650.

Kirby, Percival ([1934] ²1968), *The Musical Instruments of the Native Races of South Africa, Second Edition*, Johannesburg: Witwatersrand University Press.

Kruger, Jaco (1986), 'Venda Instrumental Music. With Reference to Certain Chordophones and Idiophones', M.Mus. diss., University of Cape Town.

Kruger, Jaco (1999), 'Singing Psalms with Owls: A Venda Twentieth Century Musical History', *African Music* 7 (4): 122-46.

Kruger, Jaco (2006), 'Tracks of the Mouse: Tonal Reinterpretation in Venda Guitar Songs', in Suzel Ana Reily (eds.), *The Musical Human: Rethinking John Blacking's Ethnomusicology in the Twenty-First Century* (SOAS Musicological Series), 37-70, Aldershot, England, and Burlington, United States: Ashgate Publishing Company.

Kruger, Jaco (2007), 'Singing Psalms with Owls: A Venda 20th Century Musical History Part Two: *Tshikona*, Beer Songs and Personal Songs', *African Music* 8 (1): 36-59.

Kubik, Gerhard (1987), 'Das Khoisan-Erbe im Süden von Angola. Bewegungsformen, Bogenharmonik und tonale Ordnung in der Musik der !Kung' und benachbarter Bantu-Populationen', in Erich Stockmann (ed.), *Musikkulturen in Afrika*, 82-196, Berlin: Verlag Neue Musik.

Kubik, Gerhard (1988a), 'Ikonologie der afrikanischen Musik', in Gerhard Kubik (ed.), *Zum Verstehen afrikanischer Musik. Aufsätze* (Reclams Universalbibliothek, 1251), 114-40, Leipzig: Verlag Philipp Reclam jun.

Kubik, Gerhard (1988b), 'Nsenga/Shona Harmonic Patterns and the San Heritage in Southern Africa', *Ethnomusicology* 32 (2): 39-76.

Kubik, Gerhard (1998), *Kalimba, Nsansi, Mbira: Lamellophone in Afrika* (Veröffentlichungen des Museums für Völkerkunde Berlin, Neue Folge 68, Musikethnologie X), Berlin: Staatliche Museen zu Berlin - Preußischer Kulturbesitz, Museum für Völkerkunde.

Kubik, Gerhard (2002), *Lamelofones do Museu Nacional de Etnologia*, Lisboa: Museu Nacional de Etnologia/Instituto Português de Museus/Ministério da Cultura.

Kubik, Gerhard, Moya Aliya Malamusi and András Varsányi (2014), *Afrikanische Musikinstrumente. Katalog und Nachdokumentation der Musikinstrumente aus Afrika südlich der Sahara in der Sammlung Musik des Münchner Stadtmuseums*, Berlin: Nicolai Verlag.

Kyker, Jennifer, recordist and ed. (2007), *Sekuru Compound Muradzikwa: Chipendani Music from Zimbabwe*, audio CD with 8-pages booklet, [Hungwe Records].

Kyker, Jennifer, recordist and ed. (2015), 'Sekuru Compound Muradzikwa Performs a Medley of Several Chipendani Songs', video clip on *YouTube*, https://www.youtube.com/watch?v=P0GbuYjgB7k (accessed 5 February 2016).

Kyker, Jennifer (2017), 'Mabimbi Ehurukuro Dzangu Navaridzi Vechipendani Vanonzi Sekuru Tute Wincil Chigamba Nasekuru Compound Muradzikwa/Excerpts from

Interviews with Chipendani Players, Sekuru Tute Wincil Chigamba and Sekuru Compound Muradzikwa', in Sazi Dlamini (ed.), *First International Bow Music Conference Proceedings, University of KwaZulu-Natal, Durban, South Africa, 24–27 February 2016*, 95–110, Grahamstown, South Africa: International Library of African Music, Rhodes University.

Kyker, Jennifer (2018), 'Reassessing the Zimbabwean *Chipendani*', *African Music* 10 (4): 40–66.

Matiure, Perminus (2008), 'Learning How to Play *Karimba/Nyunganyunga* the Easy Way for Beginners', *The Talking Drum* 30, 15–20, Durban, South Africa: School of Music, UKZN. Available online: http://www.disa.ukzn.ac.za/samap/sites/default/files/resources/Talking%20Drum/TDno30dec2008.pdf (accessed 11 April 2016).

Orem, Eric (2013), 'Tutorial – Chemutengure for mbira nyunga nyunga', video clip on *YouTube*, https://www.youtube.com/watch?v=FAGd4Bdncnw (accessed 5 February 2016).

Rutsate, Jerry (2007), *Performance of Mhande Song-Dance. A Contextualized and Comparative Analysis*, Master's Thesis in Ethnomusicology, Grahamstown, South Africa: Rhodes University. Available online: http://eprints.ru.ac.za/2783/1/RUTSATE-MA-TR08-130.pdf (accessed 24 June 2014).

Rutsate, Jerry (2010), '*Mhande* Dance in the *Kurova Guva* Ceremony: An Enactment of Karanga Spirituality', *Yearbook for Traditional Music* 42: 81–99.

Schebesta, Paul (1957), *Baba waBambuti. Vater der Zwerge. Vier Fahrten zu den Bambuti-Pygmäen* (Fahrt-Reihe, 1), Mödling bei Wien: St. Gabriel-Missionsverlag.

Tracey, Andrew (1961), 'Mbira Music of Jege A. Tapera', *African Music* 2 (4): 44–63.

Tracey, Andrew (1970), 'The Matepe Mbira Music of Rhodesia', *African Music Society Journal* 4 (4): 37–61.

Tracey, Andrew (1972), 'The Original African Mbira?', *African Music* 5 (2): 85–104.

Tracey, Andrew (1974), 'The Family of the Mbira: The Evidence of the Tuning Plans', *Zambezia* 3 (1): 1–10.

Tracey, Andrew (1989), 'The System of the Mbira', in Andrew Tracey (ed.), *Papers Presented at the Seventh Symposium on Ethnomusicology*, 43–55. Grahamstown: International Library of Music, Rhodes University.

Tracey, Andrew (2005), 'Indigenous Instruments', in Christine Lucia (ed.), *The World of South African Music: A Reader*, 237–43, Newcastle, UK: Cambridge Scholars Press.

Tracey, Andrew (2013), 'Predicted Mbira Found', *African Music* 9 (3): 21–4.

Tracey, Andrew (2015), 'The System of the Mbira', *African Music* 10 (1): 127–49.

Tracey, Andrew, and Laina Gumboreshumba (2013), 'Transcribing the Venda Tshikona Reedpipe Dance', *African Music* 9 (3): 25–39, with 1 audio and 1 video example on companion DVD.

Tracey, Hugh (1955–1970), *The Sound of Africa Series. 210 Long Playing Records of Music and Songs from Central, Eastern and Southern Africa*, Roodepoort, South Africa: International Library of African Music.

Tracey, Hugh (1973), *Catalogue. The Sound of Africa Series. 210 Long Playing Records of Music and Songs from Central, Eastern and Southern Africa*, 2 vols., Roodepoort, South Africa: International Library of African Music.

Tracey, Hugh (1991), Pastel of MuKaranga Babu Runesu Chipika playing *chipendani*, painted in 1931, reproduced as cover illustration with a comment by Andrew Tracey, *African Music* 7 (1), front cover and backside of front cover (unpaginated).

Tracey, Hugh (recordings and comments), Andrew Tracey (comments), and Michael Baird (ed.) (2000), *Other Musics from Zimbabwe. Southern Rhodesia: Ndau, Sena, Tonga, Shona. 1948 '49 '51 '57 '58 '63* (Historical Recordings by Hugh Tracey series), audio CD and 24-pages booklet, SWP 012, Utrecht, The Netherlands: SWP Records, Stichting Sharp Wood Productions; Grahamstown, South Africa: International Library of African Music, Rhodes University.

Tracey, Hugh (recordings and comments), Andrew Tracey (comments), and Michael Baird (ed.) (2003), *Southern Mozambique, Portuguese East Africa: Chopi, Gitonga, Ronga, Tswa, Tsonga, Sena Nyungwe, Ndau. 1943 '49 '54 '55 '57 '63* (Historical Recordings by Hugh Tracey series), audio CD and 20-pages booklet, SWP 021, Utrecht, The Netherlands: SWP Records, Stichting Sharp Wood Productions; Grahamstown, South Africa: International Library of African Music, Rhodes University.

University of Washington, School of Music, Seattle (n.d. a), *John Blacking: Venda Music*, audio field recordings. Available online: https://music.washington.edu/john-blacking-venda-music (accessed 11 September 2019), here especially John Blacking's 1956 and 1958 Venda *tshihwana* recordings Track 7d and 9c.

University of Washington, School of Music, Seattle (n.d. b), *Musical Instrument Collection*, digital representations. Available online: https://music.washington.edu/musical-instrument-collection (accessed 11 September 2019), here especially the search result for 'tshihwana': 4 specimens.

van Dijk, Marcel (2019), 'A Multipurpose Tuning-Plan: The "Basic *Kalimba* Core" in a Musical Perspective', in Klaus-Peter Brenner (ed.), *Mbira Music | Musics. Structures and Processes. Papers Presented at the Symposium III.4 of the 15th International Conference of the Gesellschaft für Musikforschung at the University of Göttingen, 4–8 September 2012* (Göttingen Studies in Musicology, ed. Andreas Waczkat and Birgit Abels, 9), 51–80, with 3 audio examples available on the companion website, Hildesheim: Olms.

For audio and visual examples, see https://www.bloomsbury.com/us/musical-bows-of-southern-africa-9781501346743/.

3

Musical bows of Namibia

Dave Dargie

Abstract

Namibia is a sparsely populated, large country, but the population includes peoples of a number of languages and with cultural differences. There is a broad spectrum of musical bow types, to which the monochord zither types are added in the chapter because, despite their different method of construction, they are closely related to the bows by their method of playing and sound production. It is beyond the scope of a short chapter to provide detailed examinations of all the bow types and their music; therefore, the chapter is designed as an introduction to the instrument types and their music. The author has based this introduction on recordings he himself has made in Namibia, to which are added recordings made by other, more noted musicologists. The chapter is illustrated with photographs, drawings and music scores.

Introduction

Namibia is a huge country (826,615 square kilometres) with a sparse population (2,606,917 in 2017), with twelve recognized national and regional languages, about thirty actual spoken languages and more than ten ethnic groups. To offer a comprehensive study of the musical bows of Namibia and their music is not possible in this short chapter. Therefore, I am presenting a small insight into the music of those bows, based on fifteen recorded songs.

I recorded nine of those songs: being recordings of four Kavango songs, two Ovambo songs and three Damara songs. A team of dedicated researchers, Dr Minette Mans, Dr Emmanuelle Olivier and Dr Hervé Rivière, collected six

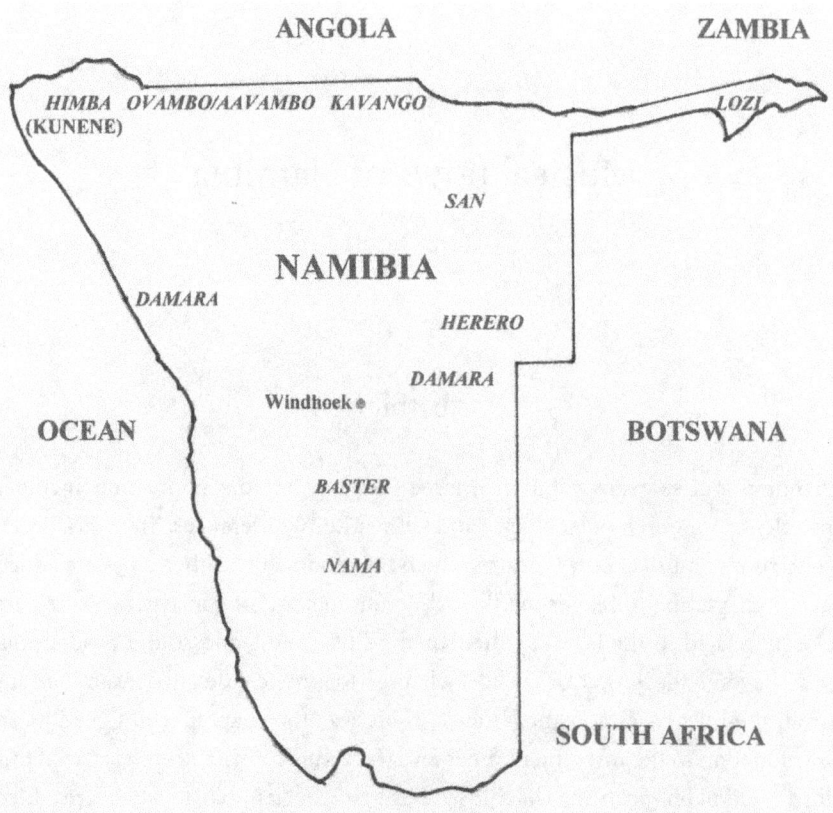

Figure 3.1 People map of Namibia. The map includes the names of the main population groups of Namibia and shows their most important areas of habitation. Source: D. Dargie.

of the songs. These are songs of the ovaHimba and OvaZimba people of the Kunene (Figure 3.1). These fifteen songs, because they represent a number of musical bow types and several branches of bow music theory, serve to give some insight into the styles of bow music in that vast region. As an example of the inter-relationship of musical styles, we learn from the work of Gerhard Kubik (Kubik 2010, vol. 1: 217–24) that the San bow players in Angola use the same three tetratonic scales as those used by Kavango musicians, as shown in the transcriptions below of the Kavango songs. This is a strong suggestion that such scales are also used by San musicians in Namibia, and that perhaps this scale usage has passed from the San to the Kavango people.

I have taken one small liberty by including in my presentation two songs with the Damara *gorito*. *Gorito* is made, not with a bowed stick, but with a straight piece of wood, so that in fact it is a monochord zither, according to the revised Hornbostel-Sachs classification of instruments (MIMO 2011: 3111.2). However, this instrument is also made using a bowed stick – see the photograph and drawing of *ikatari*, in the chapter on Xhosa musical bows in this collection and see also plates 59, 60 and 61 in Kirby 1934/68. The musical product of both forms of the instrument is the same. The Damara songs recorded with *gorito* show that traditional singing techniques of the Damara can be accompanied by *gorito*, so it is meaningful to include these songs.

Musical bows are among the simplest of all musical instruments; yet, their music is among the most touching. It is the music of people living in the most human way, very close to the earth, which has its own unique types of beauty. It is a testimony to the intelligence and spirit of those people, who have not only made their own lives and culture meaningful and valuable to themselves, but have shown that humanity can shine in beauty without technology apart from the simple techniques of bow making and playing, even out of dire poverty – because even blind people, poorest of the poor, can give beauty through their bow music.

It is with deep sincerity that I thank Dr Minette Mans for being allowed by her, despite the illness which is afflicting her, to use photographs and recordings from her excellent book on the music of the Kunene (Mans 2004), and I also offer sincere thanks to Dr Emmanuelle Olivier, currently based at the Georg Simmel Centre of the École des H Études en Sciences Sociales (EHESS) in Paris, France, and gratefully acknowledge the work of the late Dr Hérvè Rivière who contributed to the research on which Mans 2004 is based. Dr Mans is known for her fine work on music and culture in Namibia, as evidenced by her publications – Mans 2004, Mans 2005 and Mans 2017 – in the table of references below. Dr Olivier kindly gave me permission to use recordings and photographs made by her. If, as I hope, this chapter will give an insight into some techniques of Namibia bow music, it can be complemented by the work of other scholars. Dr Olivier, for example, over a research period of eight years and more, collected many photographs and recordings of bow music in Namibia. Her collection of photographs of San and Damara musical bows can be described as kaleidoscopic. It is very much to be hoped that contributions on her work will appear in succeeding publications edited by Dr Sazi Dlamini.

All score transcriptions in this chapter are by the author, as are also all photographs and illustrations, except when otherwise stated. The transcriptions are intended primarily for analysis, and not for performance, of the music. All the Namibian bow songs recorded by Dave Dargie may be heard on the CD 'Musical Bows of Namibia', in *Dargie 2000 to Present* (the *Dave Dargie Collection*), available from the International Library of African Music, Rhodes University (ILAM). All the recordings transcribed for this chapter from the book Mans 2004 may be heard on the CD accompanying that book.

Kavango musical bows and bow theory

The bow music of the Kavango people provides a useful starting point for this study.

When a string vibrates it produces sound. The vibration of the full length of the string produces the fundamental tone of the string. The string also vibrates in fractions of its length, and these partial vibrations give rise to higher tones called partials, or overtones. Figure 3.2 shows what tones the different lengths of the string produce if the fundamental tone is G on the lowest line of the bass clef (written as a black note). The hollow notes indicate the overtones. Vibrations of the fractions of the string, 1/1, 1/2, 1/3, 1/4, 1/5 and 1/6, produce respectively the octave, the perfect fifth above the octave, the double octave, and above that the major third and the perfect fifth as shown. These are the tones of the G major chord.

It is seldom that a musical bow is used to produce higher overtones than these, and in many cases bows are played using only the octaves and the fifth of the chord. This is the case with the bow recordings which I made among Kwangali people in Kavango. With only those overtones Kavango musical bows create three different four-note (tetratonic) scales.

Figure 3.3 shows three different overtone systems used in Kavango bow playing, namely, with the fundamentals a whole tone (A), or a minor third (B), or a major third (C) apart. The Kavango system is to use only the octaves and fifths above

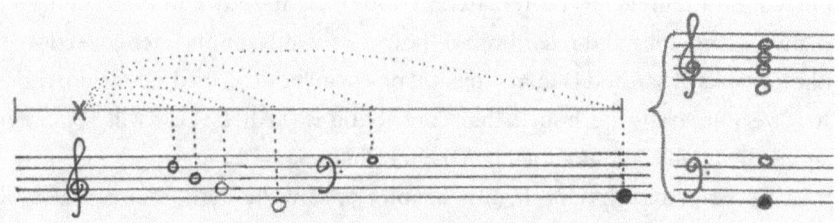

Figure 3.2 The overtones of a vibrating string.

Figure 3.3 Kavango musical bow theory.

each fundamental tone, even though the audible overtones of the fundamental, up to the sixth harmonic, in fact produce all the tones of a major triad.

There is no doubt that the use of this bow theory came to the Kavango, and other peoples of Namibia, from the San people. Gerhard Kubik found exactly the same system, the use of three sets of fundamental tones a whole tone apart, or a minor third apart, or a major third apart, resulting in the use of three different tetratonic scales (Figure 3.3), among the !Kung people of south-eastern Angola. The different intervals between fundamentals came from the use of those three different intervals in tuning the two segments of string in braced mouth bows (Figure 3.22). Kubik found that tones above the fourth partial (the double octave, e.g. 'G' above 'middle C' in Figure 3.2) were not used, resulting in the use of only four-note scales.[1]

The Rugoma *mouth bow*

Rugoma (plural *marugoma*) is a bow of bamboo, about 50 cm in length, strung (when I encountered it) with nylon fishing line, and played by plucking with the finger as seen in the photo. The player holds the bow against the side of the mouth using the mouth as resonator and selects the required overtone by shaping the mouth. Fingers of the hand holding the bow are used to depress the string to change the fundamental tone. It is the same bow as the Xhosa *inkinge* discussed by Kirby together with similar instruments used by a number of Southern African peoples.[2] The photograph shows two women in Rundu in 1981, playing a duet with *marugoma*. Transcriptions of two of these duet performances are given below. They used only tetratonic scales as shown in the bow theory example above, unlike Ms D. Rukunde, whom I recorded playing *rugoma* at Nyangana in 1988.[3] The overtone patterns and scales used by Ms Rukunde are shown in Figure 3.5 (at approximate pitch). She used one tetratonic scale (G-B flat-D-F) based on the minor third interval between fundamental tones (G and B flat), and one pentatonic (G flat-A flat-B flat-D flat-E flat), based on overtone patterns with fundamentals a whole tone apart (G flat and A flat).

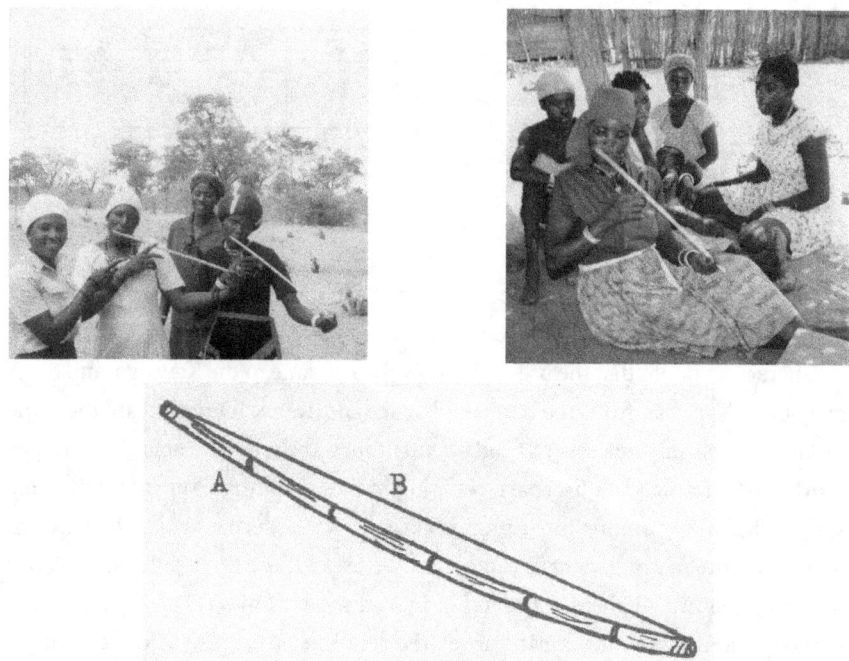

Figure 3.4 The Kavango mouth bow *Rugoma*. Left: *Rugoma* duet players. Kapande & M. Mpinga, Rundu, 1981 – transcriptions below. Middle: *Rugoma*: A: the stick, of bamboo, and B: the string, of nylon fishing line; playing method: plucking. Right: Ms D. Rukunde plays *rugoma*, Nyangana (Gciriku/Ju/hoansi), 1988. Photographs & Drawing: D. Dargie.

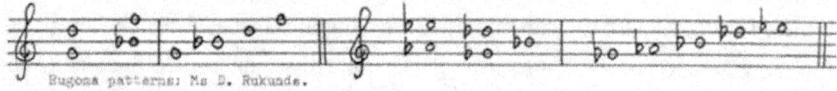

Figure 3.5 *Rugoma* overtone patterns used by Ms D. Rukunde, Nyangana, 1988.

Figure 3.6 Traditional song, with two *marugoma* plucked mouth bows played in duet by Ms J. Kapande and Ms M. Mpingana, and women singers, recorded at Rundu, 1981.

Descriptions of the scores

With each transcription a description will be given, with some description of the performance and focusing on style elements in the score. The transcriptions and the descriptions are intended to promote a stylistic understanding of the music. Attention is paid to scales, for instance, to make the point that musical bows influence the way people sing. The bow songs themselves fit into the patterns of traditional songs. By analysing the bow songs one may focus on the role of the bows, but the bows songs are also typical of the traditional songs themselves. Allowance must be made for the differences found in solo performances – the greater use of improvisation, for example.

Description of the above transcription

As shown in Figure 3.6, both bows followed the same melody. The singers sang two independent polyphonic parts, but using harmonic parallelism. As they sang they clapped, not using a cross-rhythm but with the claps falling between the *rugoma* beats. The scale (written as A-B-E-F sharp) is tetratonic, based on two fundamentals (A and B) a whole tone apart. The cycle is six main beats. The clap falls on a weak beat after the bow main beat.

In this performance the two bows had their own individual parts, overlapping each other polyphonically. The lower bow part follows the voice part 1. Voice part 2 reflects part of the upper bow part. The tetratonic scale (written B-D-F sharp-A) is based on two fundamentals a minor third apart (B and D). The

Figure 3.7 Traditional song with *marugoma* duet, same performers as the previous example.

clapping imitates the bow rhythm a beat later, hinting at the use of two main beats, one for bow and singers, one (a beat later) for the body rhythm. The cycle is 4x3=12 beats. The songs in Figures 3.6 and 3.7 illustrate scales A and B in Figure 3.3.

The Kaworongongo *mouth bow*

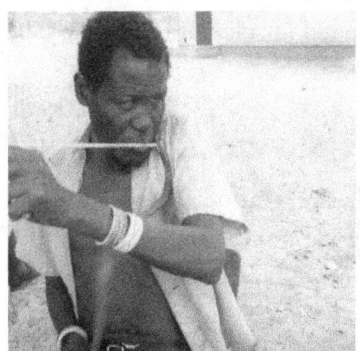

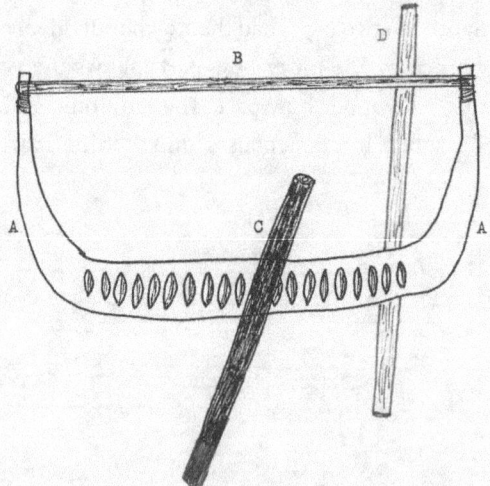

Figure 3.8 Photographs and drawing: Kavango mouth bow *Kaworongongo*. Left: Blind Mr Eugen. Hango plays *Kaworongongo*, Rundu, 1981. Middle: *Kaworongongo*: A. The notched stick; B. The string – a strip of palm leaf; C: the scraper; D. Stick applied to the string to raise the fundamental; played by friction. Right: the same bow, called *Kaholo* in Caprivi. Photo: Minette Mans.

Mr Eugen Hango, shown in the photograph in Figure 3.8, was a blind man who kept body and soul together by soliciting small donations, wandering around Rundu playing his *kaworongongo* bow. He was one of several blind musicians recorded by the author in Namibia. Such musicians were among the last people keeping treasures of musical heritage alive. *Kaworongongo* is a bow with a notched stick, strung with a strip of palm leaf, played by rubbing the notches with a small stick (held in his right hand) and changing the fundamental tone by touching a stick held in his left hand to the palm leaf string. The two songs transcribed in Figures 3.9 and 3.10 show that he used the same two four-note scales as did the *rugoma* players.

The semiquaver pattern (indicated by the lines crossing the stems of the notes in the bass clef) shows the scraping rhythm used by Mr Hango. In the treble clef, the notes with tails pointing down are played using bow overtones and the notes with tails pointing up are tones sung by him. The transcription shows two cycles of the song (each six main beats), played in the same way by the bow, but with Mr Hango varying the sung melody. The sung melody uses the characteristic falling pattern which follows the speech tones. The short phrases of the bow melody are leader parts to which the voice melodies respond. The tetratonic scale (written F-G-C-D) is based on an interval of a whole tone between the fundamentals (F and G).

Mr Hango's song shown in Figure 3.9 was relatively simple. The song in Figure 3.10 is more complex, with a longer cycle (6x4 = 24 beats). In between the cycles in which the bow alone performed the melody, he sang a voice part during one full cycle (voice notes with tails pointing up, bow melody overtones

Figure 3.9 Traditional song with *kaworongongo* mouth bow: Mr E. Hango, Rundu, 1981.

Figure 3.10 Traditional song with *kaworongongo* mouth bow, by Mr E. Hango, Rundu, 1981.

with tails pointing down). The three voice entries have irregular numbers of beats, the voice part growing longer each time. The 'key signatures' at the start of each clef mean that, in the treble clef, the tones written A and E are always A flat and E flat, and in the bass A is always A flat. The tetratonic scale used is F-A flat-C-E flat, based on the fundamentals F and A flat.

A most unusual musical bow – Lipuruboro

Lipuruboro, constructed with a large hunting bow, is purely a rhythm instrument, a combined 'drum' and rattle. There is no use of overtones or melody. His was the only such musical bow encountered by the author.

> The photo: Mr P.M. Karufere and Mr P. Haididira play *lipuruboro*; one holds the bow onto a mat on top of a three-legged pot with his left hand, and in his right hand has a mug with seeds (mealies) to apply to the vibrating string as a rattle. The other beats the leather bow string with two sticks, as if playing a drum. The drawing: A: the bow stick; B. the string, a strip of leather; C: sticks for beating the string; D: mug containing seeds; E: grass mat which rests on; F: three legged iron pot as resonator. Photograph & Drawing: D. Dargie.

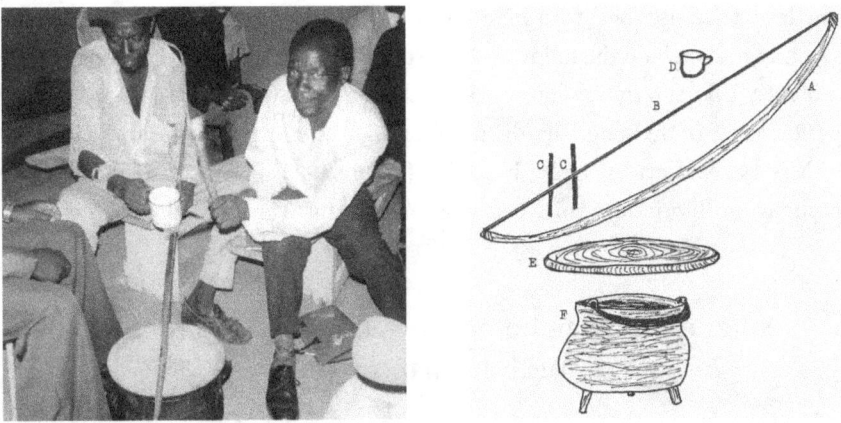

Figure 3.11 *Lipuruboro*, Shambyo (Sambiu), Kavango, 1982.

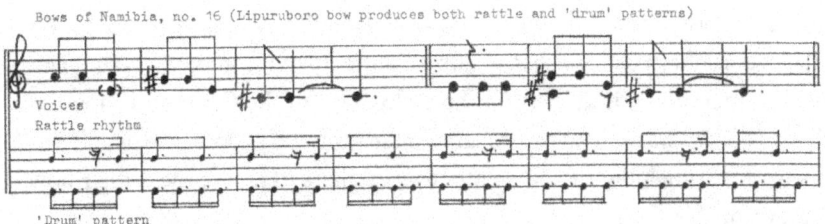

Figure 3.12 Traditional song accompanied by the *lipuruboro* musical bow: recorded Sambyu, 1981 (Sambyu).

I had the good fortune to 'discover' *lipuruboro* at Sambyu (Sambiu) in 1981, thanks to missionary Father van Roosmalen. The players came to take part in a church music composition workshop which I was conducting. *Lipuruboro* is a large hunting bow strung with leather, which is converted into a combination 'drum' and rattle.

This song uses the rarest tetratonic bow scale, based on an interval of a major third between the bow fundamentals. The scale is transcribed as A-C sharp-E-G sharp, the bow overtone (perfect fifth) intervals being A-E and C sharp-G sharp, with fundamental tones A and C sharp. Although the scale is bow-derived, it cannot come from *lipuruboro* which is not an overtone instrument, but rather perhaps from *rugoma* or *kaworongongo*. The upper line of the score shows the sung melodies. The leader sang the first sentence of the melody (before the double bar) several times, each time the sentence being repeated by the followers.

The leader (transcribed with note tails down) then sang the first phrase of the second sentence, and the followers (transcribed with note tails up) completed the sentence. This pattern was followed a number of times, to the end of that particular performance of the song. The 'drum' and rattle patterns performed on *lipuruboro* by Messrs P.M. Karufere and P. Haididira (Figure 3.11) are shown in the lower line of the score. 'Drum' and voice beats form a 4-versus-3 cross-rhythm.[4]

Among the Ovambo people – *Okamburumbumbwa* – the bow that travelled

Okamburumbumbwa almost certainly came from Angola across the Kunene with the Ovambo/Aavambo people, into Namibia. From Angola it crossed the Atlantic with the slaves taken by the Portuguese colonists to Brazil, where today it is a celebrity, called *berimbao*.[5] It is apparently the only musical bow with attached calabash (or calabash ersatz – Figure 3.24) resonator in Namibia. Like the Kavango bows, it influenced the scale usage of the Ovambo people. It was the only bow I was able to record among the Ovambo people. The people I asked knew of no other, but of course other researchers have recorded other bows in that region.

The traditional scale used in unaccompanied Ovambo singing is a seven-note equal spaced scale, similar to that used in Chopi (Mozambique) xylophones. The Western well-tempered scale has 1,200 cents to the octave, with each semitone exactly 100 cents.

The Ovambo singing scale has seven equal steps, each about 171 cents. This may be heard in the song *Vashitwa va Kalunga*, track 5 on the CD 'Missa Namibia', in the collection *Dargie 2000 to Present*. The system with *okamburumbumbwa*, however, is to use two fundamental tones (e.g. the tones F and G) a whole tone apart, similar to that used for the isiXhosa *uhadi* bow. The resultant Xhosa scale, as also the *okamburumbumbwa* scale, combines the tones of two major triads a whole tone apart. This scale is shown in Figure 3.14.

Mr Emanuel Namulo was another blind bow player, keeping *okamburumbumbwa* alive in his area. In 1982 I held a church music composition workshop at Oshikuku Mission in Ovamboland. People coming to the workshop from the West reported seeing a bow player singing for coppers in the market when passing through Ombalantu. I was unable to leave Oshikuku, but most fortunately Andrew Tracey, director of ILAM, was with me. He immediately went back to Ombalantu with

Musical Bows of Namibia

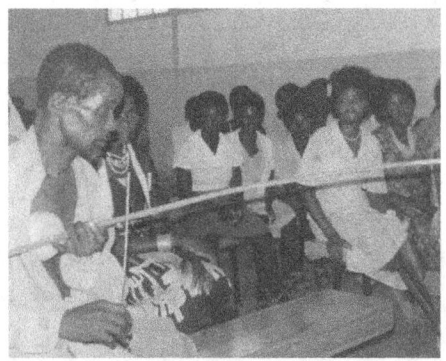
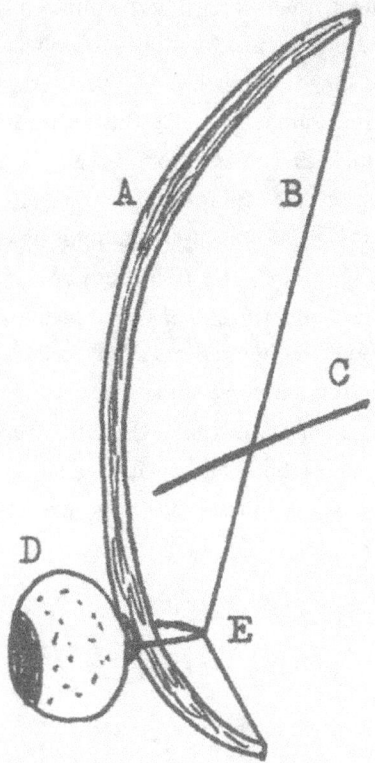

Figure 3.13 *Okamburumbumbwa* – Photographs and drawing. Blind Mr Emanuel Namuro (both photos) with his *okamburumbumbwa* at a composition workshop at Oshikuku Mission, Ovamboland, 1982. Middle: *Okamburumbumbwa*: A. The bow stick; B. the string, braced near the end; C. the beating stick; D. the calabash resonator; E. the loop attaching the resonator to the bow stick by passing around the string. Photograph and Drawing: D. Dargie.

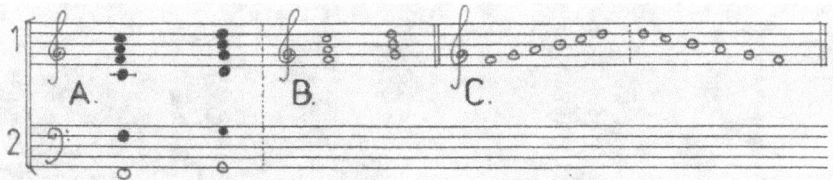

Figure 3.14 Hexatonic Bow Scale used by Xhosa Bows and by *Okamburumbumbwa*. A: The two fundamental tones (hollow) with the overtones derived from them (black notes). B: The two overtone triads. C: The six-note (hexatonic) scale which combines the two overtone chords.

the driver of the vehicle and returned with Mr Namulo and his bow. Mr Namulo was clearly living in poverty, clad in rags. In the photos he may be seen wearing a new shirt which Andrew bought for him in Ombalantu (Figure 3.13). He recorded five traditional songs and worked with the workshop group to compose two church songs in OtshiKwambi language. The two transcriptions which follow show uses of this scale, including a variant of the scale.

This is a simple song set in verse form. The stave (1) shows the bow cycle, the bow using the tones G-A-B-C sharp-D. The sixth tone of the scale (E) is not used in this song. Line (2) is the voice part. Both bow and voice use the same melody. Mr Namulo plays and sings, first only playing the bow, then singing several verses with the bow. He then repeats the procedure with further verses of the song, and further passages for bow solo.

Line 1 shows the fundamental tones (hollow) and the overtones used in the songs (black notes). Line 2 (the stave) shows the bow fundamentals (bass clef) and the part sung by Mr Namulo (treble clef). Lines 3 and 4 continue the song, combining voice

Figure 3.15 A song about a Kudu and a girl: Emanuel Namulo, with *Okamburumbumbwa*, Oshikuku, 1982.[6]

Figure 3.16 A song about migrant workers going to the mines, and their poverty. Emanuel Namulo with *Okamburumbumbwa*, Oshikuku, 1982.[7]

and bow fundamentals on one line. The song bursts into life with a stirring use of the seventh of the chord, sung by Mr Namulo. He repeats the note, to the beating of the bow, sixteen times, with the exclamation 'Ye, ye …'. This is clearly a lamentation for the sufferings of the migrant miners, far from their Ovambo home, working like slaves for a pittance and subject to indignities and hard conditions. In addition to the unusual use of the 7th of the chord (F), the song uses the full hexatonic scale (G-A-B-C sharp-D-E) as Mr Namulo apparently improvises his setting of the words.

A Damara single string zither and a musical bow

Gorito

My first work tour to Namibia was in 1979. One of the places I had church music composition workshops was a large mission at Gobabis, east of Windhoek. Cecilia Gildenhuys, living in Windhoek, asked to accompany me. She took a great interest in Namibian musical instruments.[8] She had a collection of instruments, including some she had made herself.

She brought to Gobabis a monochord zither closely related to similar instruments called *segankuru* in Setswana. For the workshop the missionary had brought together a number of elderly Damara church members, who made a number of compositions during the workshop. When Mr P. !Gawiseb, one of the group, saw the *segankuru* he enthusiastically took it up, told us that his father, who had called it *gorito*, used to play it at home every day, and himself began to play. After a short practice he recorded four traditional songs, and then composed a church song, working with the group members. There is very little doubt that the instrument came to the eastern Damara people from their Tswana neighbours – many Tswana people live in the eastern part of Namibia. What is extremely interesting is how different Mr !Gawiseb's music is from the Tswana music produced with *segankuru*: see the DVD 'Tswana Music – Traditional and neo-Church', in the collection Dargie 2000 to Present.

> A man playing the *gorito/segankuru* type instrument, and (underneath) the instrument itself, showing the boat-like body, the string running from tuning peg to the back of the body, the oil-tin resonator and the small bow for bowing the string. Photo and Drawings: D. Dargie.

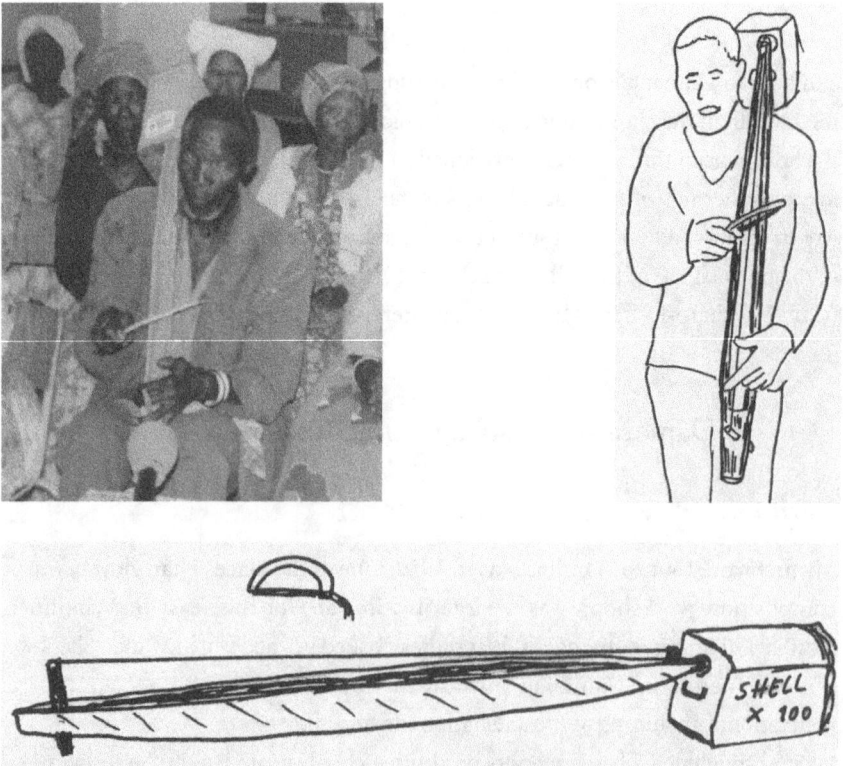

Figure 3.17 *Gorito* – In the photo Mr P. !Gawiseb plays the *gorito*. The drawings:

In the photo Mr P. !Gawiseb plays *gorito*. Around and behind him sat people attending the workshop, and in front of him is one of the author's microphones. The drawing beneath the photo illustrates the instrument. At the right is a drawing of a Northern Sotho musician playing *tsorwani*, which is the same instrument. The player bows the string with a small bow strung with fibre or animal hair.

The score shows the *gorito* part in line 1, and lines sung by Mr !Gawiseb in lines 2, 3 and 4.

Mr !Gawiseb's voice covered a large range, the highest notes sung with countertenor. He used a mixture of yodelling and normal voice, the latter for the lower tones. In line 1 the solid notes show the fundamentals (lower with open string, upper with string touched by his left thumb, the hollow diamonds show the overtones). The bowing method is the only control the player has to bring out the overtones. Bowing across the string makes it vibrate; bowing along the string brings out the overtones, hence the circular bowing pattern.

Line 1 of Figure 3.19 shows (above) the *gorito* part (Figure 3.18) and the beginning of the leader part sung by the player. Lines 2 and 3 show the interplay between the song leader and a woman singing the follower part. Both parts are highly improvisatory, with both using yodelling at times. This type of improvisation was used very much in the group singing, which in fact was live composition of the song, of church songs at a workshop with Damara people at Okombahe in 1982. At Okombahe the singers used two four-note scales, one which could be written as C-E-G-B flat and one as A-C-E-G.[10] In Figure 3.18 Mr !Gawiseb used the notes written (at approximate pitch) as D-E-A-B, all four notes related to the bow fundamentals D and E. In Figure 3.19 the singers used the notes

Figure 3.18 Traditional song with *Gorito* by Mr P. !Gawiseb, Gobabis, 1979.[9]

Figure 3.19 Traditional song with *Gorito* by Mr P. !Gawiseb, Gobabis, 1979.

written as B-D-E-F sharp, again related to the bow fundamentals D and E, plus the striking high tone C sharp. Its high pitch, especially in the counter-tenor of Mr !Gawiseb, lets one hear it as an interval of a major 7th rather than a semitone with the bow fundamental D, so that it is an acceptable dissonance to the ear.

A Damara mouth bow

In 1982 I had a church music composition workshop with Damara people at the oasis town of Okombahe, north of Karibib. Andrew Tracey of the ILAM was with me. There we met Mr Moses Heibeb, who played the mouth bow called/ *noukhas*. I was able to record one song by Mr Heibeb. His brother sang with him for the recording. It was a simple song, nevertheless very attractive. We bought the bow, which is now in the ILAM.

Lines 3 and 4 show the beginning of the song. The bow begins, playing patterns. The solid notes in the bass clef are the fundamentals, a minor third apart. The hollow diamonds show audible overtones. The voice begins as shown. Line 1 shows the voice beginning and continues the song, continuing further with line 2. The singer treats the tones of the four-note scale as consonant with either fundamental.

Figure 3.20 /*noukhas*: A Damara mouth bow. /*noukhas* is a braced mouth bow, played by percussion (tapping the string). The constituent parts, shown in the drawing, are the stick, the string and the brace loop. The method of playing is similar to that shown in the photograph by Minette Mans, of a Damara man playing a bow called *gomakhas*. With/*noukhas* the sections of the string are of different length, providing two fundamental tones a minor third apart. Drawing: D. Dargie. Photo: Minette Mans.

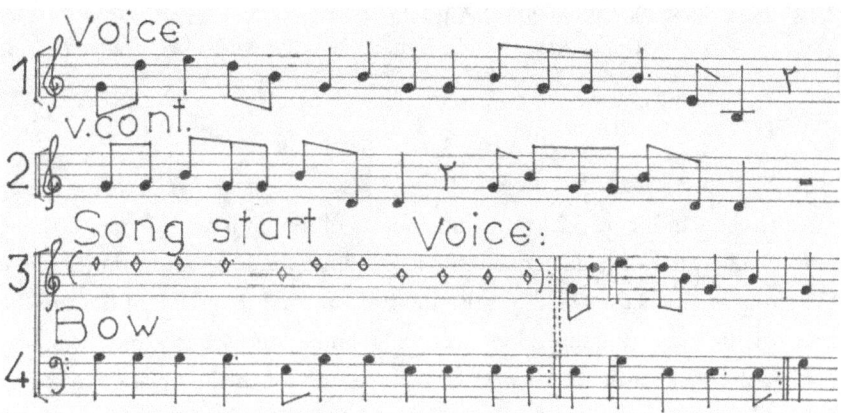

Figure 3.21 Song with the mouth bow/*Noukhas*.

Musical bows of the people of the Kunene

This section looks at the musical bows discussed in the book Mans (2004). Sincere thanks to her for her permission to use photos by her and photos and recordings from the book, and also to Dr Emmanuelle Olivier for permission to use her photo of the man playing the pluriarc (Figure 3.26).

The mouth bow Outa

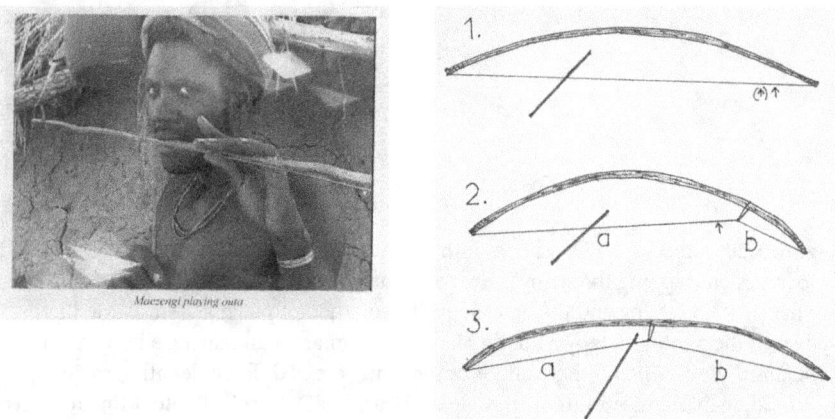

Figure 3.22 *Outa*. Photo (M. Mans): *Outa* is played by Maezengi, an omuHimba (Man of the Himba people of the Kunene). Drawings (by the author, based on drawings in Mans 2004, 33): *Outa* Constructions: 1. Unbraced; 2: End braced; 3. Middle braced. The *Ondendele* shown in Figure 3.31 is the same as a braced *outa*.

Playing a mouth bow

The drawings in Figure 3.22 show three forms of mouth bows: 1. Unbraced: the bow is held by the stick and tapped with a light stick; the small arrow shows where the string is touched or held to raise the fundamental tone. 2. End-braced: the brace divides the string into a long section (a) and a short section (b). The bow is held by the stick, or by the stick and the brace, and touched (at place marked by the small arrow) to raise the fundamental tone. Only the long section of the string (a) is played. 3. Middle-braced: the bow is held by the stick. The two sections of the string [(a) and (b)] are of different lengths, tuned to a desired interval, usually a whole tone or a minor third, sometimes a major third. The player strikes either section of the string according to the fundamental tone required.

Dr Mans described the playing method for *outa* in Mans (2004: 33–4). The description includes amplifying the overtones by use of the mouth cavity, as with other mouth bows.

The player in this recording however uses a type of whistling which is more hiss than melody. The pitch starts around a high octave of the fundamental and descends each time by a hissing glissando. The main purpose in the playing seems to be to demonstrate different rhythm patterns in a series of passages, embellished by the whistling. The score in Figure 3.23 shows examples from five of these passages. However, in passage 5 the whistling rests on two beats out of three, and on these two beats one may hear the overtones. What one apparently hears may be what is called an 'otic illusion' in the score, shown in Illusion (i). The ear may interpret the short melody as the tones written 'A-G-F'. But the tone G is not an overtone of the fundamental D. What is happening is shown in the score, where the symbol ↓ indicates a microtonal lowering of the fundamental F, and therefore also of the overtone A. The ear may therefore interpret the interval between the fundamentals as a minor third, but the interval between 'A' and 'G' as a whole tone – an 'otic illusion'. Perceptions of rhythmic emphasis in this passage may also be deceptive, as shown in 'Illusions' (ii) and (iii).

In the transcription (Figure 3.23) the notes are placed at approximate pitch. The small arrows in the score indicate microtone changes of pitch. The 'whistling' is described in the paragraph above the transcription. The transcribed passages

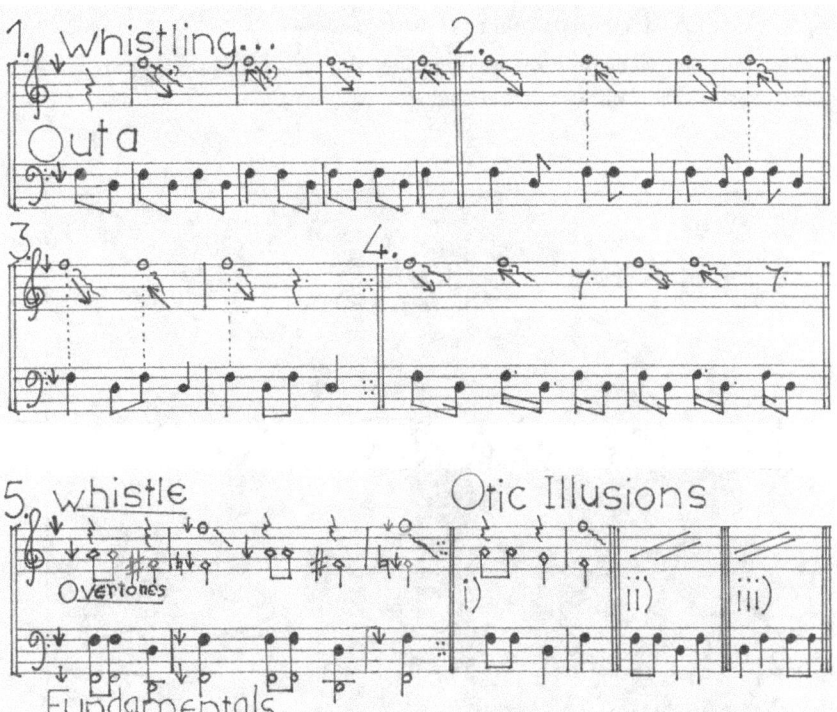

Figure 3.23 *Outa* mouth bow performance, Track 3 of the *Kunene* CD.

are as follows – 1: at 0m00s of the recording, 2: at 0m35s, 3: at 1m20s, 4: at 1m40, 5: at 2m03s (continued at 2m29, after a short break). (One passage at 1m03s is omitted, as are the passages after no. 5.)

Ombulumbumba – *the same bow as* Okamburumbumbwa

This bow was recorded among the OvaZimba people of the Kunene, the area lying west of Ovamboland and along the Kunene River (Figure 3.1). The player was Mr Petrus Tjisuta.[11, 12]

In the photo one may clearly see the manner of holding the bow, with the little finger of the player's left hand hooked onto the brace which joins the resonator (possibly a plastic flower pot) to the bow. The player's left forefinger can hold the string onto the thumbnail in order to obtain the higher fundamental tone. In the player's right hand is the small stick used for tapping the string. The resonator is opened and closed against the breast to release or damp the overtones in following the melody.

> The score shows one bow cycle of the song. The player constantly repeats this cycle, at times singing short phrases in snatches.
>
> The score shows one bow cycle of the song. As with the previous example, the player sings short phrases in snatches.

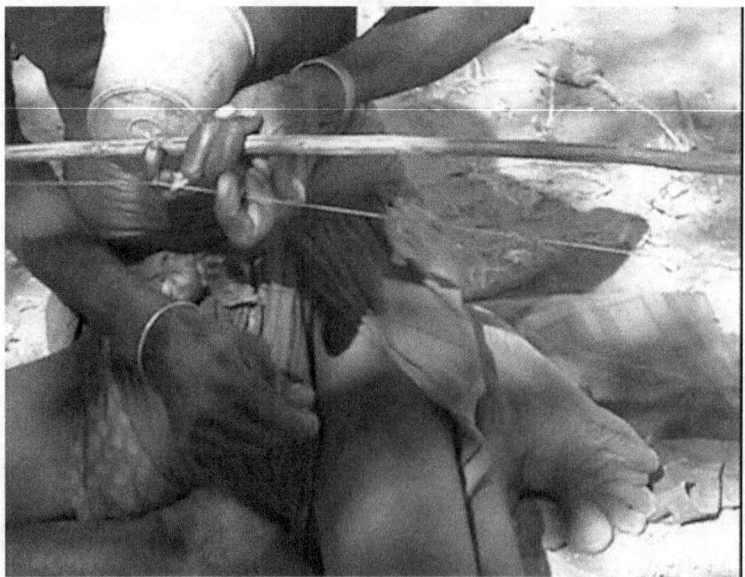

Figure 3.24 Mr Petrus Tjisura playing *Ombulumbumba*. Photo: Minette Mans.

Figure 3.25 Song with *Ombulumbumba* – by Twahuma Elenene. (Rec. E. Olivier & H. Rivière.)

Figure 3.26 Song with *Ombulumbumbwa* – by Tjingwe Tjiponyo. (Rec. E. Olivier & H. Rivière.)

The two *ombulumbumba* songs transcribed in Figures 3.25 and 3.26 use the same playing method as the songs of Mr Namulo (Figures 3.15 and 3.16). The complete scale is not used, but the harmonic system is clear – two major chords a whole tone apart.

Pluriarc – The bow lute, a multi-bow

On my trips to Namibia (1979–88) sometimes I saw one or more pluriarcs for sale in tourist shops in the north. I was told that San people made them. I never heard one played, and of course was unable to record the instrument. The San people had been driven out of their northern homes, made to serve the South African army as trackers and guides. I am extremely grateful to Minette Mans that I could use her photos of the instrument, and also transcribe the two songs which are on the CD accompanying the book Mans 2004. I am also very grateful to Dr Olivier for providing me with the fine copy of her photo in Figure 3.28.

Figure 3.27 Pluriarc. *Okuimba otjihumba*, a pluriarc of the OvaZimba people of the Kunene. (Photo: Dr. M. Mans; touched up by the author.)

Figure 3.28 The player of the pluriarc, and the finger technique. Left: Mr Metatu Munekamba playing the pluriarc. (Photo: Dr E. Olivier.) Right: A player demonstrates the fingering for playing the pluriarc. (Photo: Dr M. Mans.)

Figure 3.29 The first song with pluriarc, Track 21 on the CD. (Rec. E. Olivier & H. Rivière.)

Scores of the two pluriarc songs by Mr Munekamba, on the CD accompanying the Kunene book (Mans 2004), are given in Figures 3.29 and 3.30. The most remarkable thing impacting on one is undoubtedly what fine music can be made with just four tones. The song in Figure 3.29 can move the hearer beyond any expectation from just looking at the score. The deep voice of the singer sets a powerful atmosphere, supported by the pattern playing of the instrument. The instrument is tuned to (approximately) the scale G sharp-A sharp-B-C sharp in the bass, with the fifth string tuned to the C sharp an octave higher. The four lower strings set up an accompanying pattern. The loud playing of the high(er) C sharp, reinforcing that note at times when it is used an octave lower, emphasizes the rhythm and prepares for the entry of the voice. The player sings two phrases, falling patterns of three and four tones.

Figure 3.30 The second song with pluriarc, Track 29 on the CD. (Rec. by E. Olivier & H. Riviere.)

For the performance transcribed in Figure 3.30 the instrument is tuned to tones which could be written as E sharp-G sharp-A sharp-C sharp, reflecting the same tuning of three strings as in Figure 3.29. For convenience I have written these tones as F-A flat-B flat-D flat, with the D flat repeated an octave higher by the fifth string (again used for emphasizing the use of the lower D flat – see line 6 of the score. It is not clear if the string tuned to B for the song in Figure 3.29 was re-tuned to F for the song in Figure 3.30, or if more than one string was re-tuned. The other tones are at exactly the same pitches in both songs. The voice part includes the tone C flat (= B), a tone used in the pluriarc tuning and the voice in the first song. What is sung may look monotonous in the score, but in performance it seems forceful and highly atmospheric, as in the first song.

In conclusion

In this chapter the study of Namibian musical bows has been based on nine different instruments: *rugoma* (Kavango), *kaworongongo* (Kavango), *lipuruboro* (Kavango), *okamburumbumbwa* (Ovambo)/*ombulumbumba* (otjiZimba), *gorito*

Figure 3.31 Mouth bows of the OvaZimba people. Photos by M. Mans, from Mans (2004). Left: *Elumba* – the same instrument as *Kaworongongo* (Figure 3.8); Right: *Ondendele*, described in the book (p. 105) as a braced mouth bow looking exactly like *Outa* (Figure 3.22).

(Damara),/*noukhas* (Damara), *outa* (otjiHimba) and the pluriarc (otjiZimba). Although the number of instruments studied is small compared to the full treasury of Namibian musical bows, it is clear that at least to a reasonable extent the study does stretch widely, because the same instruments occur among different peoples of Namibia. For example, the photos in Figure 3.31 show otjiZimba versions of instruments of other peoples included in the study. The bow *elumba* is the same as used by two other peoples, shown in Figure 3.8. Tuning and scale usage clearly passed from one people to another, and so did instrumental usage. The findings in this chapter should help in understanding bow music not directly studied here.

Notes

1. Kubik (2010, vol. 1: 217–24).
2. *Kirby 1968*, 220 and 225, with photographs of nine such instruments of different peoples on his plates 62 and 63. The revised Hornbostel-Sachs classification describes such a bow as a 'mono-heterochord musical bow without resonator and without tuning noose', with classification number 311,121,11: *MIMO 2011*, 13. See Dargie 2019 – the author's other chapter in this volume.
3. *Dargie 2003C*, tracks 33 and 34.

4   There seem to be excellent grounds for thinking that the name *lipuruboro*, like the name *kaworongongo*, is derived onomatopoeically from the sound of the bow - _*purupuru* for the rattle sound and - *boro boro* from the drumming of the string.
5   The renowned scholar Gerhard Kubik studied this bow as *ombulumbumba* in Angola and as *berimbao* in Brazil. See Kubik 1973, 1975/1976, 1979 and 1987.
6   Track 24 on the CD 'Musical Bows of Namibia', *Dargie 2000 to Present*.
7   Ibidem, Track 26.
8   See Gildenhuys (1981).
9   Mr !Gawiseb's songs are recorded as no's 20 to 23 and no. 37 on the CD 'Musical Bows of Namibia', in the collection Dargie 2000 to Present. Figure 3.18 shows the song on track 21 and Figure 3.19 shows track 23.
10 Examples of this are no's 8 (Credo) and 22 (Gloria) on the CD 'Missa Namibia' in Dargie (2000 to Present).
11 *Ombulumbumba* is the same bow as *okamburumbumbwa* ("see a section on 'Among the Ovambo people'.").
12 Photographs by Dr Mans and by Dr Emmanuelle Olivier are used with permission.

References

Dargie, D. (1995), 'Developing Local Church Music for the Catholic Church in Namibia', in *Papers presented at the Ninth Symposium on Ethnomusicology [at the] University of Namibia*, 8–15, Grahamstown: Rhodes University: International Library of African Music.

Dargie, D. (2000 to Present), The 'Dave Dargie Collection', series of CDs, DVDs and handbooks, Grahamstown, Rhodes University: International Library of African Music.

Dargie, D. (2013), 'Kavango Music', *African Music* 9 (3): 122–50.

Dargie, D. (forthcoming), 'Musical Bows of the AmaXhosa', in S. Dlamini (ed.), *Musical Bows of Southern Africa*, New York: Bloomsbury.

Gildenhuys, C. (1981), 'Musical Instruments of South West Africa/Namibia', *Papers presented at the Second Symposium on Ethnomusicology, Rhodes University*, 28–33, Grahamstown: ILAM.

Kirby, P. R. (1934), *The Musical Instruments of the Native Races of South Africa* [First Edition], Johannesburg: Witwatersrand University Press.

Kirby, P. R. ([1934, 2013],1968), *The Musical Instruments of the Native Races of South Africa*, Johannesburg: Witwatersrand University Press.

Kubik, G. (1973), *Muziek van de Humbi en de Handa uit Angola*, Tervuren: Belgische Radio en Televisie.

Kubik, G. (1975/1976), 'Musical Bows in South-Western Angola, 1965', *African Music* 5 (4): 98–104.

Kubik, G. (1979), 'Angolan Traits in Black Music, Games and Dances of Brazil: A Study of African Cultural Extensions Overseas', *Estudos de antropologia cultural* (10): 7–55.

Kubik, G. (1979), *Angolan Traits in Black Music, Games and Dances of Brazil: A Study of African Cultural Extensions Overseas* (Estudos de antropologia cultural, no. 10), Lisboa: Junta de Investigações Científicas do Ultramar.

Kubik, G. (1987), 'Das Khoisan-Erbe im Süden von Angola', in E. Stockmann (ed.), *Musikkulturen in Afrika*, 82–196, Berlin: Verlag Neue Musik.

Kubik, G. (2010), *Theory of African Music*, Chicago: University of Chicago Press.

Mans, M. (2004), *Discover Musical Cultures in the Kunene – A Guide to the Living Music and Dance of Namibia*, Windhoek: Namibia Scientific Society.

Mans, M. (2005), *Research Report – Musical Instruments of Namibia* 1. Available online: www.academia.edu

Mans, M. (2017), *The Changing Faces of Aavambo Musical Arts*, Basel, Switzerland: Basler Afrika Bibliographien.

MIMO Consortium (2011), 'Revision of the Hornbostel-Sachs Classification of Musical Instruments', in *Musical Instrument Museums Online* (MIMO). Available online: www.mimo-international.com

Links to San musical bows videos available online:

https://www.youtube.com/watch?v=sSHuzzUCGJIPluriarc. Alan Kuehner. On sale in Bushman shop. (Shown by white lady only.) Four strings, wooden body. Wood – very similar to Mans photos.

https://www.youtube.com/watch?v=e12MUnOU5YI
Braced mouth bow played by tapping. Joe Leeming, 1972. !Xo (!Ko). ('San Bushmen'.) Interval between fundamentals: minor third. Long bow – c. 1½ metres. Kalahari (Botswana). Two bows, two players (men) in duet.

https://www.sciencephoto.com/media/320963/view/bushman-playing-traditional-instrument
Bow 'like hunting bow' (Bogen " das wie Pfeil und Bogen ähnelt"). Chris Sattlberger. Man playing, photo only. Near Tsumkwe, Kalahari, Namibia.

https://blogs.bl.uk/music/2013/02/kalahari-san-bushmen-music-online-1.html
Blog: Joe Brearley, many recordings of Kalahari San music (Botswana). Blog posted by Janet Topp. Brearley recorded between 1982 & 2007, available on the British Library Sounds website. Photos in the Blog show woman playing pluriarc (& singing), four strings, oil tin body; also large unbraced mouth bow played by tapping by two women, one end rests on small upturned bowl as resonator, one woman can touch the string near an end with forefinger.

http://www.bushmanmusicinitiative.org/

Website constructed by Aris Aurellano, for possibility of downloading recordings of Kalahari San music in Botswana. CD entitled 'When We Were Free'.
https://www.youtube.com/watch?v=yktziU75QI0
Postings by Dr Nicole Apelian. A recording of San group (Nharo Bushmen, western Kalahari in Botswana)) with bow. Large bow, one end resting on upturned bowl, played by tapping by two people, a woman who touches a stick to the bow string, and another woman and a man who take turns during the song.
https://www.youtube.com/watch?v=srNeyqcQ2cw
A recording of same bow and people as previous: large bow resting on bowl, played by two people while others sing.

For audio and visual examples, see https://www.bloomsbury.com/us/musical-bows-of-southern-africa-9781501346743/.

4

Umakhweyana and *ugubhu* Zulu musical bows as *inkokha, imvingo, inkohlisa, uqwabe* and *isiqwemqwemana*

Sazi Dlamini

Abstract

Southern African musical bows are referred to by a profusion of indigenous terms whose meanings and theoretical significance remain unexplored. A case in point are definitions of Zulu musical bows named as *umakhweyana, ugubhu, nkokha (inkokha/unkokha), imvingo, inkohlisa, uqwabe, isiqwemqwemana*. In descriptions of Zulu musical bows of supposedly different constitutive structural layout of parts and visual appearance, the references of these terms are invariably generic. The lack of correctly labelled historical artefacts or analysable illustrations of 'distinguishing' traits of each 'named' bow conveys impression of unverified diversity. This nomenclature however embeds indigenous cultural understandings of – among other characteristics – structure and technical processes of sound production, including Zulu sociocultural contexts for playing musical bows. My chapter essay explores *inkokha, imvingo, inkohlisa, uqwabe* and *isiqwemqwemana* as terms articulating rooted understandings of *ugubhu* and *umakhweyana* calabash-resonated musical bows in their Zulu traditional indigenous practice.

Introduction

Southern Africa is home to several cultural ethnicities whose indigenous musical traditions include the use of mono-heterochord musical bows. The braced[1] *umakhweyana*[2] and to a lesser extent the unbraced *ugubhu*[3] calabash-resonated musical bows have persisted in relatively marginal practices among isiZulu and siSwati speaking Bantu (Figure 4.1).

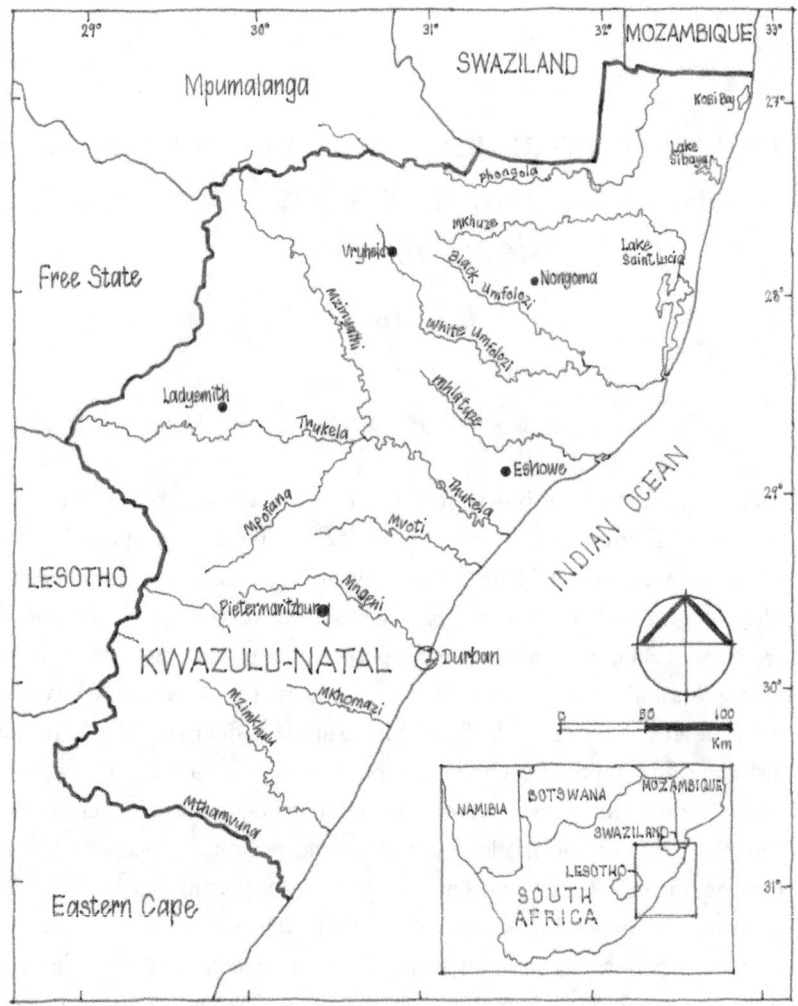

Figure 4.1 Map of KwaZulu-Natal. Drawing: Maria Cristina Giampietri.

Widely accessible encyclopaedic references regard *imvingo*, *inkohlisa*, *isiqwemqwemane*, *uqwabe* and *inkokha/unkokha* as alternate names (among others) for a musical bow commonly known as *umakhweyana* by both the Zulu and the Swati (Kirby [1934, 1968] 2013, Rycroft 1984b: 698). In addition, geographical proximity between several Bantu dialects in Southern Africa gives rise to different names for what are practically similar musical bows in all aspects of design, construction materials and methods of playing. For example, the common usage of the term *inkokha/unkoka/unkokha* among the Zulu, Swati, Chopi and Thonga/Tsonga people illustrates a widespread occurrence of a braced musical bow known variously as *dende* (Venda), *sekgapa* (Pedi), *umakhweyana/ umakhweyane* (Zulu) and by the Swati as *umakhweyana/umakhoyana* (Kirby [1934, 1968] 2013, Rycroft 1984b).

Zulu terminological references to *ugubhu* and *umakhweyana*

Understanding *[i]nkokha, imvingo, inkohlisa, isiqwemqwemane* and *uqwabe* as synonyms for Zulu *umakhweyana* and/or *ugubhu* does not reveal the historical, theoretical, technical and cultural significance of these terms. With particular regard to Zulu calabash-resonated bows such as *umakhweyana* and *ugubhu*, the vagueness in meaning of such Zulu terms provokes their theoretical consideration as rooted in indigenous conceptualizations and knowledge of musical bows. The underpinning of indigenous knowledge of musical bows in observation, experimentation and technical innovation was conceded by Kirby as follows:

> [A]lthough the musical instruments of the native peoples of South Africa may, at first sight, appear simple and their players unsophisticated, in reality they display not only constructive ingenuity on the part of their makers but a real understanding of certain of the basic phenomena of sound.
>
> ([1934, 1968], 2013: xvi)

Structural features of *umakhweyana* and *ugubhu*

The widespread occurrence of musical bows among diverse Southern African cultural ethnicities continues to challenge organological classification, understanding of their comparable features of distinction and nuanced contexts of their traditional practices. Historical descriptions by European ethnological observers of musical bows indigenous to Southern Africa have been in contestation since Gardiner (1836), Angas (1849), Von Hornbostel (1933), Von Hornbostel and Sachs (1961) and others.

The Zulu *ugubhu* and *umakhweyana* are differentiated by – among other aspects – visual appearance due to structure, their distinctive harmonic sensibilities in traditional tuning and techniques of playing. *Ugubhu* and

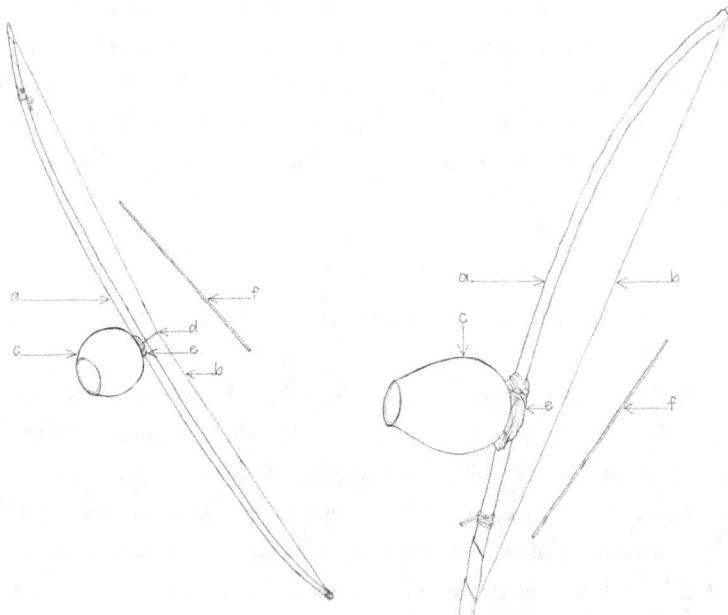

Figure 4.2 *Umakhweyana* [left] and **Figure 4.3** *Ugubhu* [right]. Figure labels: a. *U[lu]thi* or *induku* (bow stick or stave), b. *Intambo* or *uthaka* (string), c. *Igobongo* or *iselwa* (calabash resonator), d. *Ingona* (loop brace), e. *Inkatha* (support cushion), f. *Ubhaqa* or *u[lu]thi lokushaya* (grass stalk playing stick). Drawings: Maria Cristina Giampietri.

umakhweyana are commonly characterized by three structural parts, namely, (*a*) *uluthi/induku* (stave), (*b*) *intambo/uthaka* (string) and (*c*) *igobongo/isigubhu* (resonator) made out of *iselwa* (calabash). A primary structural and thus visual distinction between *umakhweyana* and *ugubhu* is the division (or non-division) or presence (or absence) of *ingona* (*d*) loop brace on the string. On *umakhweyana* the string division coincides with the position of the calabash resonator near the middle of the stave, whereas on *ugubhu* the resonator is located near the bottom end of the bow stave (Figures 4.2 and 4.3). The stick or stave (referred to as *induku* or *u[lu]thi*) is a tree branch sapling measuring, on average, 1,500–1,800 mm in length and 15–20 mm in diameter. Preferred tree species are light of weight when dry, such as *uthathawe* (*acacia ataxacantha*), *iphahla* (*brachylaena discolor*) which in South Africa is commonly known as 'coastal silver-oak' and *umbangandlala* (*heteromorpha arborescens*).

The structural significance of *imvingo*[4]: The spring potential energy of the bow stave

A simple definition of *imvingo* as a calabash-resonated musical bow (Doke-Vilakazi 1990: 835) – without specifying division [or non-division] of the string – is only useful as a general reference. Because of a common usage of similar wood materials in the structure of several Zulu musical bows, the accuracy of *imvingo* as a reference is only to the tree-branch saplings used in fashioning bow staves. The traditional Zulu understanding of *imvingo*[5] as a bundle of wood pertains to its primary function as *izintingo*[6] (Figure 4.4) the branch sapling structural framework used in the construction of the dome-shaped, indigenous 'beehive'[7] hut.

For *umakhweyana* the ideal length of the bow stave (*induku* or *u[lu]thi*) is estimated from shin or knee level to the top of the standing player's head, approximately 1,200–1,500 mm. For *ugubhu*, which was traditionally played in a seated position, the lowest point of the stave is around hip level, with the rest (slightly more than half) of the bow projecting well above the players head. To make a bow stave, an *imvingo* sapling of appropriate thickness is seared over flames and its bark peeled off. If selected from stockpile material, *imvingo*

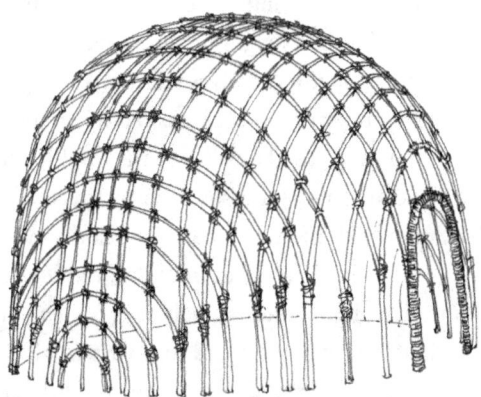

Figure 4.4 Structural use of *imvingo* as *izintingo*. Drawing: Maria Cristina Giampietri.

saplings are initially soaked in water to regain flexibility prior to debarking (Nyembezi-Nxumalo 1982: 41). Furthermore, as Angela Impey observed, an *imvingo* of appropriate diameter thickness (40–50 mm) is required to fashion a bow stave employing the traditional method 'by shaving the inner side of the arched stick into a flat surface so that the branch, which was originally circular in diameter, is reduced to a semi circle' (Impey 1983: 7). Using rope or wire to join the two ends of the stick into a shallow bow curve, the stick is left to dry in the sun for several days.[8] The use of traditional raw material resource avails the term *imvingo* to Zulu calabash-resonated musical bows in general, and in particular, as a reference to *ugubhu* and *umakhweyana*. The flexible property of *imvingo* for use as *induku* bow stave provides the physical mechanical forces required to exert tension on the string of a musical bow. The spring potential energy of *imvingo* material is utilized in the maintenance of structural form in indigenous Zulu architecture and also to provide forces required for tuneable string tension in musical bow making.

Imvingo elastic potential energy and *nkokha/inkokha* equilibrium restoring forces

The term *inkokha*[9] encapsulates the understanding – in an indigenous conceptual sense – of a functional manipulation of the energy potential of musical bow structural materials. In resistance to forceful stretching by bending into to a curved bow shape, the equilibrium restoring force[10] due to elastic physical properties of *imvingo* establishes tension in a length of string tied between its two ends. The knowledge of building musical bows involves selection of appropriate materials and harnessing their physical properties to elicit desired musical sounds when a string under tension is mechanically caused to vibrate. The resulting sounds are amplified by various methods and materials of resonation for musical use as fundamental pitches and for derivation of harmonic partials for melodic manipulation.

Bowstrings – referred to by the Zulu as *intambo* or *uthaka* – were traditionally obtained from domestic animal material including *ishoba* (oxtail hair), *umsipha* (sinew from the back of the leg), or a cured thin strip of hide or lining of animal gut. Strings were also made from *ilala* (*hyphaene crinita*) palm leaves and from *igceba (scirpus)* species of rush. Fibrous material harvested from *utakataka* and *ikhamanga* (*strelitzia angusta*) [wild-banana] plant stems was also twisted to function as strings for musical bows. Nowadays recycled thin-gauge industrial

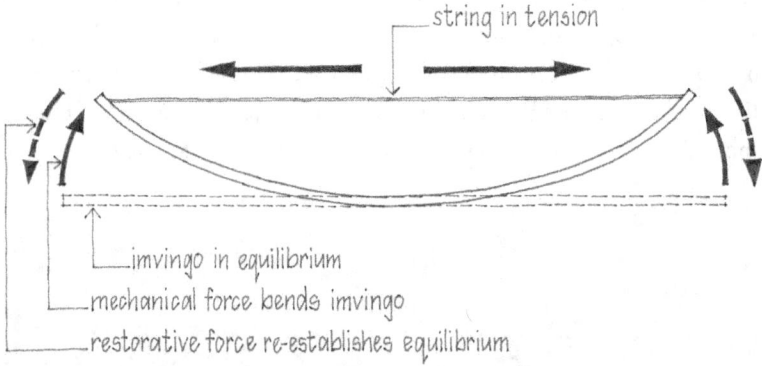

Figure 4.5 Tension exerted on an undivided string (cf. *ugubhu*). Drawing: Maria Cristina Giampietri.

wire is normal to use, including straightened-out bangle wire, crane-sling, curtain-rail coil and any thin wire possessing reasonable qualities of resonance.

In an undivided string such as on *ugubhu*, the significant potential energy is stored in the critical flexibility of *imvingo* (bow stave) and *intambo/uthaka* (string) when bent by force into the shape of an arc. The natural tendency of *imvingo* material to retain its original form in resistance to bending provides the force that is transmitted as tension to a string tied to the two ends of *u[lu]thi/induku* bow stave (Figure 4.5).

String division – redistribution of *inkokha* functional forces with *ingona*[11]

The asymmetrical division of *umakhweyana* string using *ingona* loop as a brace and tensioning the string between the two ends of the bow stave provide the structural basis for tuning *umakhweyana* string by pitch adjustment. The smallest of the two resonator apertures of *umakhweyana* is used to affix *ingona* on the inside of the calabash to secure it behind the stave.

On the outside of the calabash *ingona* is looped around the string to function as a brace in dividing it into two slightly unequal lengths. For stability, an *inkatha* made of cloth, soft hide or woven grass is inserted as a cushion between the stave and calabash. In a braced bow such as *umakhweyana*, dividing the string using *ingona* loop brace doubles the number of string segments and also increases the magnitude of tension exerted on each segment. As a result of the inverse proportional relationship between frequency of vibration and length in a stretched string, each of the two segments will be higher in pitch than the undivided string.[12] In *umakhweyana*, the unequal division of the string into shorter segments using *ingona* loop brace redistributes *inkokha* primary

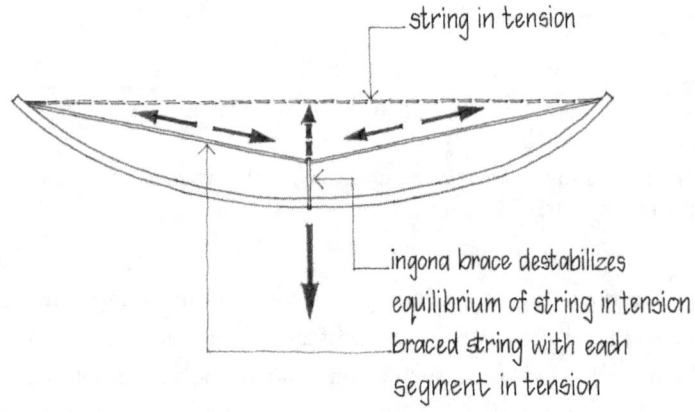

Figure 4.6 Tension exerted on the divided *umakhweyana* string. Drawing: Maria Cristina Giampietri.

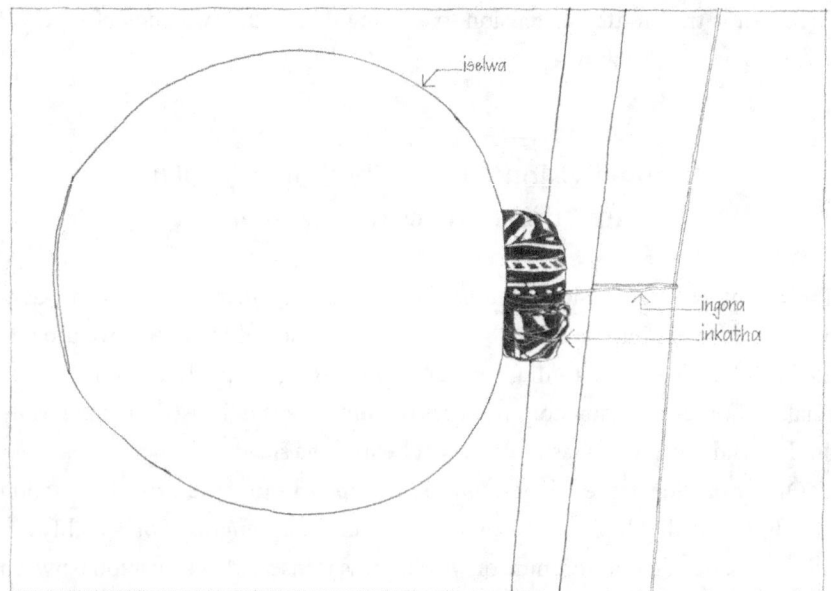

Figure 4.7 Detail of *iselwa*, *ingona* and *inkatha*. Drawing: Maria Cristina Giampietri.

tension forces (Figure 4.6). Thus among the Swati the brace in *umakhweyana* is referred to as *inkokha* which, in dividing the string, technically provides a tensioning function (Stacey 2017: 93).

The single division of *umakhweyana* string enables further manipulation of tension – an aspect of tuning reliant on the material tensility of the stave and the string as well as the latter's bracing with a moveable *ingona* loop (Figure 4.7). The addition of another open fundamental pitch as a result of the unequal division of *umakhweyana* string has a bearing on tuning and playing technique. Depending on the ratio of the difference in length, different intervallic relationships between fundamental pitches of the two segments are utilized. In an unsymmetrical division of its string, *umakhweyana* behaves like a composite bow whose two unequal string segments share a tension node provided by *ingona*.

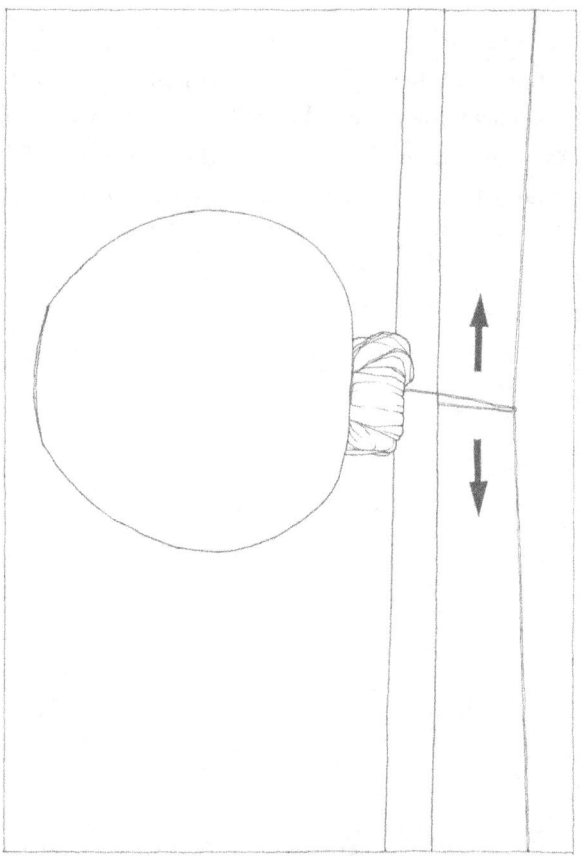

Figure 4.8 Positional method of tuning using *ingona*. Drawing: Maria Cristina Giampietri.

Positional *ingona* method of fine-tuning *umakhweyana*

The positional adjustability of *ingona* brace along the length of the string enables the use of its unequal divisions as a mechanism for tuning. The domestication of such ratios is encountered in the open fundamental pitches used as common tuning in the Zulu *umakhweyana* tradition. The positional adjustments of *ingona* (Figure 4.8) determine specific pitches of the two string segments and – depending on the contrapuntal characteristics of a song to be accompanied – the intervallic relationships between the pitches may range from a major second to a perfect fifth (Kirby [1965] 2013: 274).

Rotatory *ingona* method of fine-tuning *umakhweyana*

In addition to its structural division of *umakhweyana* string, *ingona* has another important function in the heteromonochordal assemblage of string-bearer and resonator. The bracing tension exerted with *ingona* loop on the string also serves to attach the calabash around the middle of the concave arch of the bow stave. A delicate fine-tuning method of slightly adjusting the tension in the loop, and

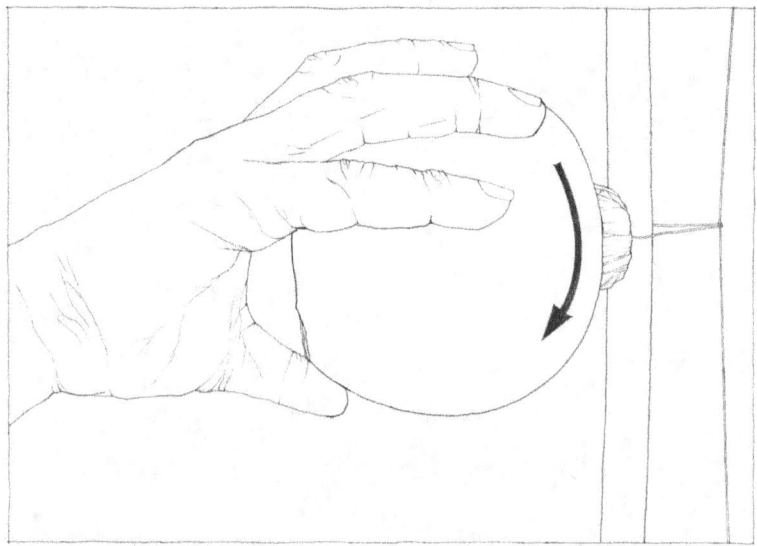

Figure 4.9 Rotatory method of fine-tuning using *ingona*. Drawing: Maria Cristina Giampietri.

thereby raising or lowering the open fundamental pitches of the string makes use of the *iselwa* calabash resonator. This involves holding the bow with one hand in the normal playing position just under the calabash and, using the free hand, to rotate the resonator carefully in the clockwise or anticlockwise direction as required. The functionality of this tuning manoeuvre is however critical due to the limited tolerance of wire material of *ingona* loop, which cannot withstand repeated manipulation by twisting (Figure 4.9).

Iselwa (calabash) as resonator

Upon witnessing a !Kung musical performance in the 1920s, social anthropologist Dorothy Bleek had concluded that the musical bow used was 'not a special instrument, but the singer's own hunting bow with the string with the string [braced] at about a third of its length', and that the calabash resonator was 'an ordinary household utensil not kept for playing' (Kirby 1968: 205). This instrument was considered by Kirby to be a prototype of braced musical bows that included the Zulu *umak[h]weyana*, among others that have calabashes attached as resonators *(ibid.)*.

The resonator *(igobongo)* for *umakhweyana* is traditionally a well-formed dried calabash *(iselwa)* of between 100 mm and 150 mm in circumference. Industrially produced tin or plastic containers are also recycled for use as resonators. Although also preferred by some *umakhweyana* players, calabashes of a larger size are normally associated with the slightly longer *ugubhu*. To make a resonator, a circular hole of average 70–80mm diameter is opened on the 'flower' aspect of a dried *iselwa*. Seed is scooped out and the calabash filled with water to soak until the inside material is mushy soft, and then scraped off. Once dried, an aperture of approximately 3 mm diameter is made on the scar of the calabash stalk for use in attaching the resonator to the bow stave.

Sounding of fundamental notes on *ugubhu* and *umakhweyana*

The characteristic sound of calabash-resonated musical bows is partly the result of mechanically induced vibrations of a single string. On both *ugubhu* and *umakhweyana* the lowest pitched fundamental note is sounded on an open string. Additional fundamental notes of a higher pitch are obtained by various methods of stopping the string at some considered position along its length. This obstructing action has a dual function of silencing an already-vibrating string and of shortening the length of a segment of string. Depending on the size of the interval desired, when played, the resulting fundamental note of the shortened string segment is of a higher order of pitch. The selected intervals of choice are determined by their melodic and harmonic compatibility with diverse musical approaches to Zulu bow song repertoires.

Ugubhu and *umakhweyana* are played by tapping on the string using a dried stalk of *isiqunga* or *uqunga* ['tambootie'] or *uhlonga [Cymbopogon hirtus]* grass species. Traditionally the Zulu used such grass types as thatching and musical bow beaters are also named *ubhaqa* ('torch') because of their household usage as indoor firelighters. To play a bow *ubhaqa* is held lightly between thumb and forefinger (or forefinger and middle finger) like a 'chopstick' or a pen and is supported by the rest of the fingers (Figure 4.10). In this way the player is able to tap on the string with 'whip-like' hand-wrist movements to elicit a characteristic 'staccato' sound.

To facilitate for their differing techniques of stopping the vibrating string, *ugubhu* and *umakhweyana* differ in the method of holding the bow stave (Figures 4.11 and 4.12).

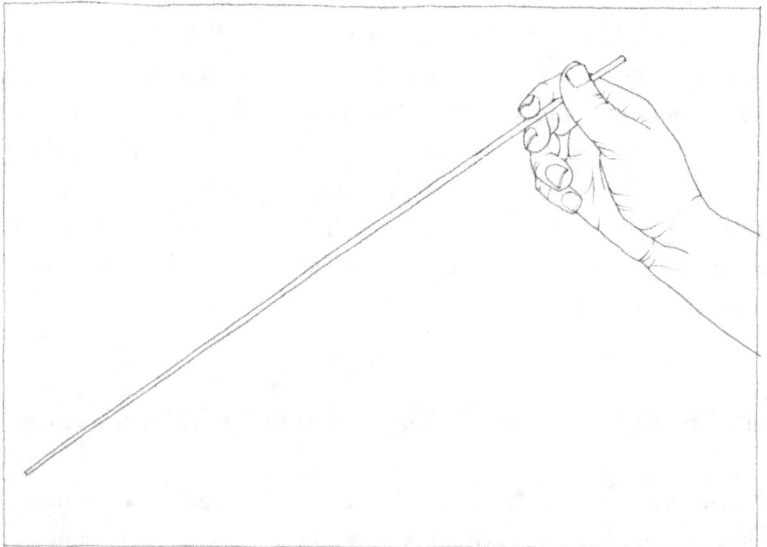

Figure 4.10 *Ugubhu* and *makhweyana* playing technique – holding *ubhaqa* playing stick. Drawing: Maria Cristina Giampietri.

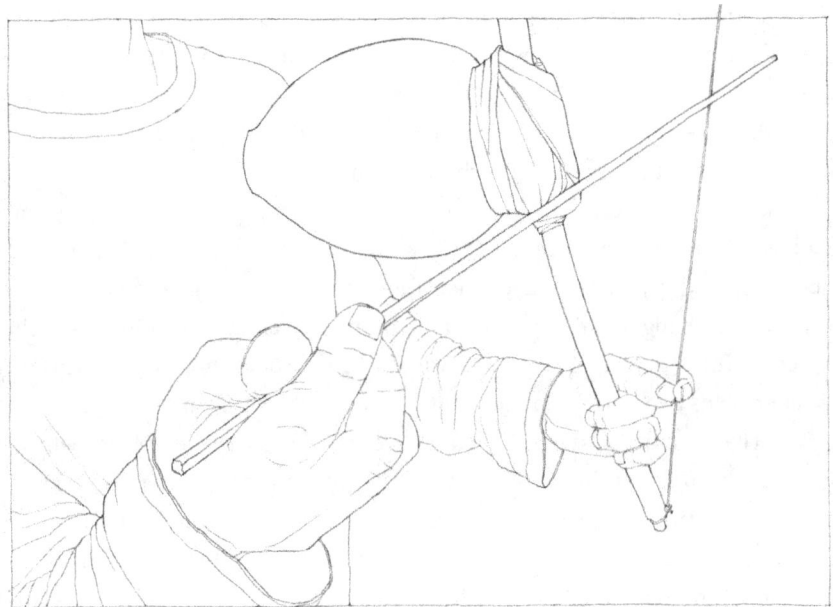

Figure 4.11 *Ugubhu* three-finger grip and string stopping-by-pinching. Drawing: Maria Cristina Giampietri.

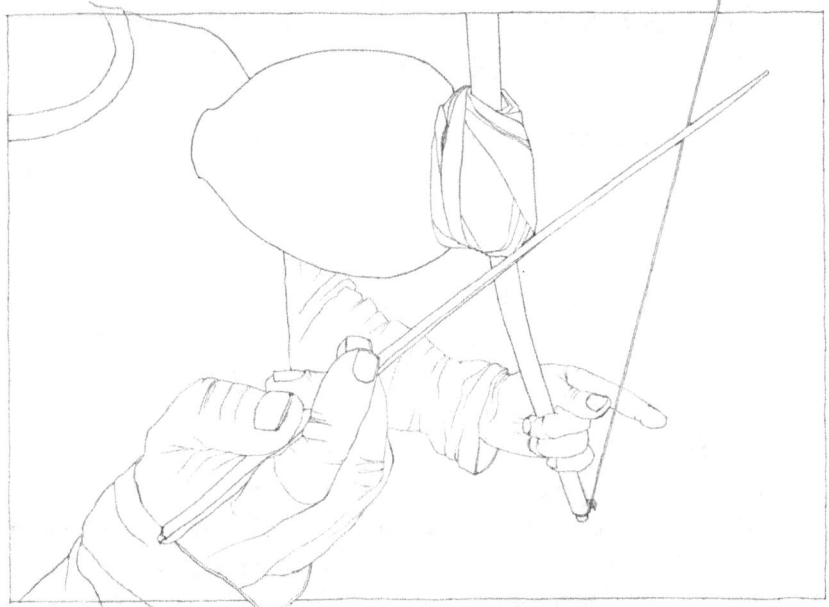

Figure 4.12 *Ugubhu* technique of playing the open fundamental note. Drawing: Maria Cristina Giampietri.

In the upright playing position, one hand is used to hold *ugubhu* just below the calabash, with the opening of the resonator close to the player's breast on the same side as the hand holding the bow. The second, third and fourth fingers grasp the lower end of the bow, leaving both the index finger and the thumb free to stop the vibrating string by pinching (Figure 4.12).

Held like a pen or chopsticks on the other hand, *ubhaqa* thatching-grass stalk is used to tap the lower end of the string in a staccato action. When played upon, the string yields a low-pitched fundamental note together with several harmonics, giving a listener an overall sound of a chord. Pinching the string raises the fundamental pitch an interval of semitone or a whole tone. In this way *ugubhu* yields two harmonic chords of a semitone or a tone interval apart.

For right-handed playing, *induku* (stave) of *umakhweyana* is held with the left hand just below the calabash, with the opening close to the player's left breast. Only the thumb and three fingers are used – leaving the index finger free to stop the string using the flesh of the outside (knuckle) aspect. This string stopping movement yields a third fundamental note of a variable pitch – from a minor second to a fourth or fifth interval – higher than the open note of the shorter segment. For self-accompaniment of a sung melody the player selectively amplifies desired overtones by carefully moving the calabash resonator closer or further away from the breast.

Indigenous references to fundamental pitch sounding technique

With respect to *umakhweyana*, Zulu women bow players referred to the technique of sounding fundamental notes on the upper and lower string segments as *ukushaya ngaphezulu* and *ukushaya ngaphansi* respectively (Impey 1983: 10). Technical references to the open and stopped fundamental note positions as *vuliwe* (open) and *banjiwe* (held or stopped) respectively were documented with regards to Xhosa *uhadi* and *umrhubhe* bows (Dargie 1988: 50).

Some adjustment to the applicability of *vuliwe* and *banjiwe* as technical concepts for fundamental pitch elicitation is necessitated by the linguistic subtleties of isiXhosa and isiZulu dialects. For example the selective amplification of overtones in calabash-resonated bows also involves manipulating the resonator in an opening and closing movement against the player's body. The relative proximity of the mouth of *iselwa* (calabash) to the player's body as technical process of dampening and amplifying overtone harmonics may appropriately be referred to as *vuliwe* (open) and *valiwe* (closed). However, to eliminate possible confusion requires distinguishing between the technical references of *vuliwe* – as the 'open' position – to either resonator or string. In *umakhweyana* particularly, it is preferable to refer to the open string position as *dedelwe* (lit. 'released') rather than *vuliwe* (lit. 'open') and similarly to the stopped string position as *thiyiwe* (lit. 'obstructed') instead of *banjiwe*. For open string positions, these considerations recognize a structural and technical distinction between *uhadi* and *umrhubhe* on the one hand, and *umakhweyana* on the other. Furthermore, *umakhweyana* has not one but two open fundamental notes in *vuliwe* or *dedelwe* position[s] due to the division of its string. Thus, the open fundamental notes on *umakhweyana* upper and bottom string segments require technical specification as *dedelwe ngaphezulu* ('upper [segment] released') and as *dedelwe ngenzansi*[13] ('bottom [segment] released') respectively. In the stopped string position, understanding the *banjiwe* ('held') stopping technique as *thiyiwe* ('obstructed') particularizes difference between techniques of stopping the vibrating string. On both *uhadi* and *umrhubhe* the vibrating string is commonly stopped by pinching between thumb and index finger. The Xhosa term *banjiwe* ('held') documented by Dargie (1988) is a causative grammatical derivative of the Nguni verb *[uku]bamba* (Eng. 'to hold'). However, a common *umakhweyana* string-stopping technique uses the outside aspect of the index finger or knuckle. This action, which in isiZulu is *ukuthiya* (Eng. 'to obstruct' or 'to trap'), is appropriately expressed in the verb's causative form, *thiyiwe* ('obstructed').

Figures 4.13–4.15 illustrate the location and sounding of fundamental notes on *umakhweyana* as a dynamic techno-structural process involving string-division, string-playing and string-stopping. In the normal vertical playing position, the unstopped note on the upper string segment is the lowest in pitch of all fundamental notes (Figure 4.13). As a method of playing, *ukushaya ngaphezulu* (Eng. 'to play on the upper segment') elicits the first and lowest pitched fundamental note in a *dedelwe ngaphezulu* (open upper string segment) position. The technique of *ukushaya ngenzansi* (Eng. 'to play on the bottom segment') elicits the second open fundamental note in the *dedelwe ngenzansi* (open bottom string segment) position (Figure 4.14). The third fundamental is a stopped note played in the *thiyiwe siqalo* (first obstruction) position on the bottom string segment using the technique of *ukushaya ngenzansi* (Figure 4.15).

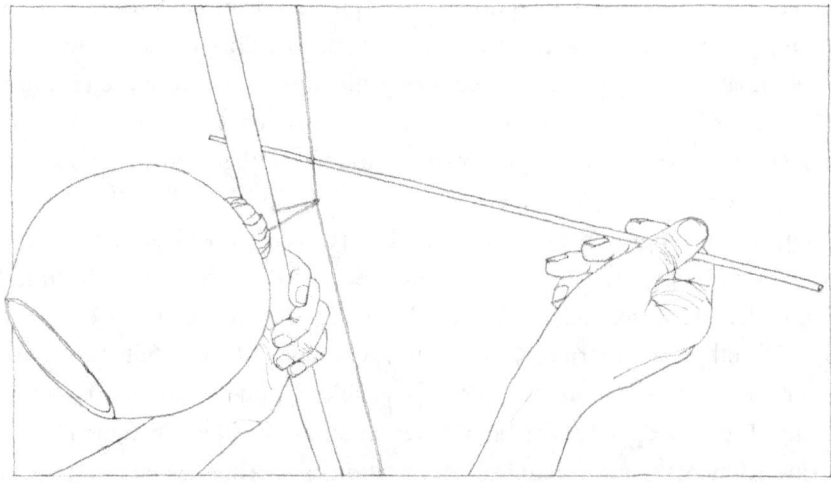

Figure 4.13 *Ukushaya ngaphezulu* to elicit the upper open (*dedelwe ngaphezulu*) fundamental note. Drawing: Maria Cristina Giampietri.

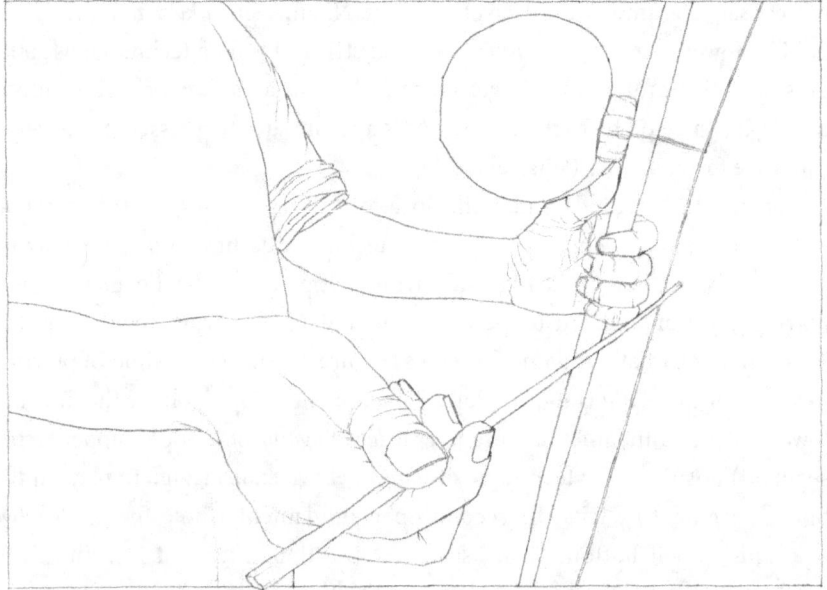

Figure 4.14 *Ukushaya ngenzansi* (*umakhweyana* bottom open/*dedelwe ngenzansi* fundamental). Drawing: Maria Cristina Giampietri.

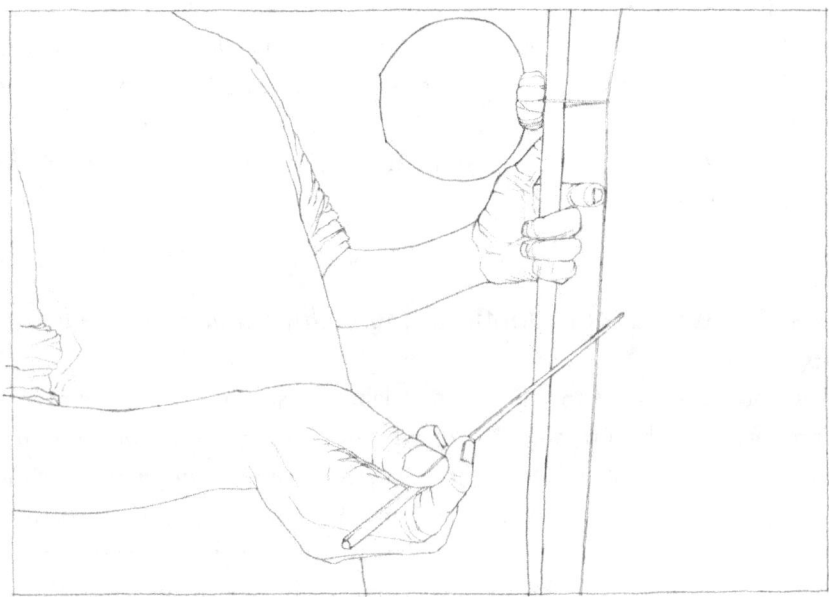

Figure 4.15 *Ukushaya ngenzansi* to elicit the first obstruction (*thiyiwe siqalo*) fundamental note. Drawing: Maria Cristina Giampietri.

In a common *umakhweyana* open fundamental note tuning interval of a whole tone, two notes are obtained on each *dedelwe* segment of the divided string. Following above and playing the bottom segment of *umakhweyana* string in the stopped *thiyiwe siqalo* position would elicit a third fundamental note – a technique similar to that referred to by other practitioners as *ukuvala uthaka*.[14] For *umakhweyana*, the most commonly used interval of stopping the bottom string segment in the *thiyiwe siqalo* (first obstruction) position varies between a minor second and a whole tone.

Uqwabe/isiqwemqwemana as synonyms for *umakhweyana*

The terms *uqwabe* and *isiqwemqwemana*[15] are among several Zulu synonyms for the braced, calabash-resonated musical bow commonly known as *umakhweyana* or *umakhweyana* by the Zulu and the Swati (Kirby [1934, 1968], 2013: 274, Rycroft 1985: 698 and Impey 1983: 1). Zulu linguistic references in general describe *isiqwemqwemana* as a 'species of musical bow' that is 'comparable to *umakhweyana*', while *uqwabe (uluqwabe)* is compared to *inkokha* and explained as a 'large musical bow with a calabash attached and string tied down to the stave in the middle' (Doke-Vilakazi 1990: 718). As mere synonyms, these definitions do not adequately convey the musical, structural and technical characteristics specific to *umakhweyana*.

The hypothesis of adoption of *umakhweyana* as *u[Q]wabe*

A historical reference to the braced, calabash-resonated bow as *uqwabe* is implicated in a hypothesis[16] that regards the occurrence of *umakhweyana* among the Zulu and the Swati as a 'relatively recent' adoption from the Thonga (Kirby [1968] 2013: 274], Rycroft 1985: 698). Another explanation of the Zulu reference to the braced calabash bow as *uqwabe* draws from an imaginary of inter-clan 'borrowing' of *umakhweyana* as *u[Q]wabe*.[17] The assumption of a borrowing presupposes an unlikely, staggered process of cultural socialization between the families of siblings sons of Malandela, namely Qwabe and Zulu (Khumalo 1995: 14). In the plausibility of a common, contemporaneous usage of the musical bow by subjects of both Qwabe and Zulu, the hypotheses are inadequate in their implicit assumption of asynchronous occurrence of *umakhweyana* in the implicated pre-Zulu and Bantu trans-ethnic diaspora.

A significant cultural context for *umakhweyana* is the musical socialization of girls in gendered age stratifications of successive Zulu female rites of passage.[18] The prohibition among the Zulu, of *umakhweyana* playing by married women, was reason enough for its disparagement by the Princess Magogo kaDinizulu (Rycroft 1975: 58). A royal matriarch in her mid-1970s when she was interviewed, Princess Magogo was not likely to break with Zulu *ukuhlonipha* traditions,[19] of which observance she was expected to be exemplary.[20] Furthermore, the narrative of *umakhweyana*'s adoption from the Thonga of Mozambique does not adequately account for the occurrence and similar naming of the musical bow among the Swati and the Zulu. Such considerations as above invite alternate hypotheses to those articulating *uqwabe* to the Zulu people's genealogic siblinghood to Qwabe and *umakhweyana* to transcultural musical borrowings from the Thonga.

Uqwabe, onomatopoeia and equal-pulse rhythm *umakhweyana* playing technique

Among Xhosa women in the Eastern Cape, Dave Dargie encountered *umrhubhe* and *umqangi* as the two names for one simple mouth bow. The relevance of each term is its direct onomatopoeic imitation of sound elicited from the mouth bow when using a different method of playing. The term *umrhubhe* is an onomatopoeic

Figure 4.16 A transcription in equal pulse notation illustrating the repetitive perpetual sound-motion of *[uku]qhwabaqhwaba* from which derives the noun *uqwabe*. Refer to Audio #1.

imitation of the scraping sound – *rhu! rhu! rhu!* – that is elicited when the string is played like a friction bow using a thin, roughened playing stick. Alternatively, tapping repeatedly on the string using the same playing stick elicits a resonant twangy sound resembling *qang! qang! qang!*[21] (Dargie 2001a: 7).

Similar references of *uqwabe* and *isiqwemqwemana* may be onomatopoeically elicited from the Zulu linguistic characterization of both terms by a radical click consonant 'q'. When pronounced as force-beat syllables, the rhythmic sonicity of successive radical click consonant 'q,' mimics *umakhweyana* characteristic sonic patterns of equal-pulse durations. Such small, equal units of durations are considered pivotal and a defining trait of the African concept of musical time.[22]

The onomatopoeic mimicking of a vowel-conjugated *q*, which in isiZulu is pronounced as a palato-alveolar, 'radical' click consonant (Doke-Vilakazi 1990: xvi), bears a similar grammatical relationship to the naming of *uqwabe*. Sonically perceived as units in a sequential rhythmic tapping, the sounds *'q[w]á!* or *q[w]é!* closely resemble the repetitive verb form *q[h]wábá-q[h]wábá*, from whose root *qhwábá*[23] is derived the noun *uqwabe* (Doke-Vilakazi 1990: 705). In its linguistic function of under-emphasizing the action of its reference, the verb form thereby justifies the necessity for repetitive, thus quantitive increment of the action. Figure 4.16 is a transcription, using equal pulse notation, of the repetitive pattern illustrating the repetitive perpetual sound-motion of *[uku]qhwabaqhwaba*, the verb root of the noun *uqwabe*. An audio example is also provided.

Isiqwemqwemana: Onomatopoeia and calabash resonation technique

Isiqwemqwemana pronunciation onomatopoeically mimics the sound – *qwem!* – as a rhythmic pattern – *qwem! qwem! qwem!* – that is heard when *umakhweyana* string is played upon using a 'staccato' technique employing 'whip-like' movement of the player's wrist. As one of the Zulu names for *umakhweyana* (Doke-Vilakazi 1990: 719, Kirby [1934, 1968] 2013: 274) the term *isiqwemqwemana* conjugates Zulu grammatical process with string resonation techniques using the *iselwa* calabash. This is easily demonstrated by sounding *umakhweyana* string segment once in the *dedelwe* (open) position with the calabash away from the body, and immediately closing the calabash mouth against the body to attenuate the sustaining note. The twangy tones of a vibrating single string elicited by repeating this technique several times imitates the sound *qwem! qwem! qwem! qwem! qwem!* etc. as heard in Audio #2.

Resonation: *Amakhweyana* or 'little whistles' as overtone-derived harmonics

Southern African musical bows are characterized with amplification techniques by resonation to isolate pitches of the harmonic overtone series, usually from two or more fundamental notes. Overtone harmonics function to outline song melodies, providing secondary melodic and contrapuntal framework to bow songs. The significance of overtone harmonics articulates to an understanding of their reference to rooted meanings and usage in the Zulu *umakhweyana* tradition. The term *umakhweyana* is a diminution of the plural form of the Nguni noun *ikhwelo/i(li)khwelo* (Eng. 'shrill whistle') to *amakhwelana* (English: 'little shrill whistles'). A synonym of *ikhwelo* is *umlozi* or 'soft whistling', a term also given to 'a whistling spirit', a 'spiritual being who manifests ... in whistling within the hut' or 'ventriloquist' (Doke-Vilakazi 1990: 464). The technique of vocally eliciting audible overtone harmonics while playing the Xhosa *umrhubhe* mouth bow is also referred to as whistling (Dargie 1988: 53).

Overtone harmonics in bows with undivided string – biradical tonal organization

In common with other musical bows with undivided single strings such as *uhadi* (Xhosa) and *ligubhu* (Swati), *ugubhu* yields two fundamental notes when its string is sounded in the open and stopped positions. From each of the bows' two fundamental notes and their selected overtone harmonics is derived a six-note (hexatonic) scale for melodic and polyphonic use. The harmonic theoretical process of deriving musical bow scales from two fundamental notes and their selective corresponding harmonic partials was first referred to by David Rycroft as 'biradical tonal organisation' (1967: 96). In a biradical tonal organization, hexatonic scales are linear derivatives of two harmonic triads each comprised of the third, the fourth and fifth partials of overtones isolated from two fundamental pitches (Figure 4.17). The interval between the two fundamental notes depends on the string-stopping interval that is commonly used for each musical

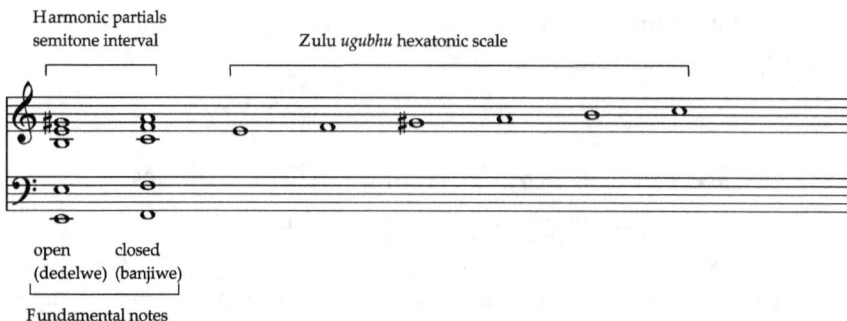

Figure 4.17 *Ugubhu* hexatonic scale – a biradical tonal organization (See Rycroft 1967: 96).

bow. Unlike *uhadi* (Xhosa) and *ligubhu* (Swati) whose fundamental notes are invariably a whole tone apart, *ugubhu* string is traditionally stopped at an interval of a semitone. This distinguishes *ugubhu* derivative hexatonic scale and imbues its Zulu repertoires with their characteristic melodic and polyphonic modalities.

Triradical tonal organization[24] – overtone harmonics on a divided string

The concept of triradical tonal organization was also introduced by David Rycroft to scalar and polyphonic material derivatives of three fundamental notes elicited from musical bows with a divided string such as *umak[h]weyana*[25] and *xitende* (Rycroft 1967: 97). The third fundamental note elicited by stopping *umakhweyana* bottom string segment adds another set of partials from which to isolate overtone-derived harmonics. Although not readily discerned in *umakhweyana* traditionally pentatonic melodies and polyphonic approaches, the resulting derivative scale is a chromatic combination of whole and half tone intervals.

The pitch of the third fundamental is variable depending on the interval of stopping the bottom string segment relative to its open tone. The example in Figure 4.18 illustrates an unequal division of *umakhweyana* string to sound open fundamental notes of G and A. Stopping the open note A using an interval of a semitone yields notes G, A and Bb.[26]

A triradical tonal organization utilizing the third, fourth and fifth partials of the three fundamental notes above is reducible to three triadic chords: GBD, AC#E and BbDF.

The resulting octatonic scale (Figure 4.19) is composed of three whole tone and four semitone intervals as follows: G A Bb B C# D E F. The scale is a derivation of *amakhweyana* (harmonics) which are isolated using the technique of manipulating the size of the *igobongo (iselwa)* resonator opening relative to the player's body.

Figure 4.18 Transcription excerpt of 'Abantu Baphelile', *ugubhu* song by Princess Phumzile Mpanza of Mahlabathini – Zululand. Recorded by Fr Dave Dargie and Brother Clement Sithole (1982). Refer to Audio #3. Used by permission – courtesy of Prof Dr Dave Dargie.

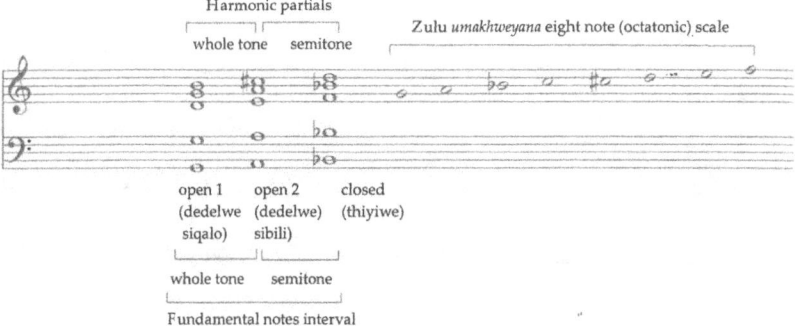

Figure 4.19 Triradical tonal organization – eight-note (octatonic) scale derivation on *umakhweyana* (see Rycroft 1967: 97).

Figure 4.20 An excerpt transcription of 'Kwasenza (It happened to us)' by Mama Bavikile Ngema – illustrating *umakhweyana* overtone voices. Refer to Audio Excerpt #4.

In the Zulu *umakhweyana* polyphonic tradition, overtone-derived voices – or *amakhweyana* (Figure 4.20) – progress in a consonant rhythmic relationship with respect to (1) the leading voice melody and (2) the ostinato pattern established in the fundamental note cycle. Within the cyclic antiphonal structure of *umakhweyana* songs, overtone-derived melodies typically substantiate the leader voice 'call' or the chorus-like response that is rhythmically closely related to the fundamental note ostinato pattern.

Inkohlisa[27] as performance context and inclusive category of Zulu musical bows

Reiterations of *inkohlisa* in influential references invariably include the term within an undifferentiated category of calabash-resonated musical bows.[28] Kirby categorized *inkohlisa* by (1) a calabash resonator 'permanently fixed to the lower end of the bow' and (2) the recognition of chords as a derivation of fundamental tones and their harmonics (1968: 201, 2013: 265 and 2013: 269). Kirby's first criterion clearly identifies the Zulu *ugubhu* (Swati: *ligubhu*), except for the inclusion of *inkohlisa* in the same category as *imvingo* and *umakhweyana*[29] (Rycroft 1985: 698). In the latter's understanding that *inkohlisa, imvingo* and *umakhweyana* are all calabash-resonated musical bows with their single string divided near middle, the two categorical attributions of *inkohlisa* are confusing. Besides contradictions apparent in similarly enduring descriptions of distinctions in their visual appearance, the existence of an assorted variety of Zulu calabash-resonated musical bows is not convincingly borne out in artefact, image or oral historical narrative.

Inkohlisa: Traditional performance of Zulu women's socio-individual entanglement

In view of existing contradictions, the following discussion considers the meaning of *inkohlisa*[30] in its reference to the functional, expressive context of Zulu women's bow music repertoires. A further significance of a sociocontextual understanding of *inkohlisa* is its inclusion (by default) in Kirby's (and Rycroft's) in both categories of calabash-resonated musical bows *with or without* a divided string, such as the Zulu *umakhweyana* and *ugubhu*.

Previous studies of Zulu musical performance have not considered bow songs as individual expressive responses to uniquely gendered female experiences within a culturally paternalistic society. Traditionally, although *umakhweyana* and *ugubhu* playing was only marginal as a male preoccupation,[31] Zulu females practised both musical bows and predominantly *umakhweyana*. Upon marriage, the performance of bow songs on *ugubhu* and *umakhweyana* became curtailed through a censorial socio-moralism, as Rosemary Joseph noted,

> The performance of the repertory of songs traditionally associated with the *umakhweyana* by middle-aged women is, however, something of a travesty as this is the instrument of the *izintombi* (unmarried girls) and the repertory consists largely of love songs.
>
> (Joseph 1989: 91)

In its affirmation of dominant Zulu paternal interests, the dictum legitimated censorship of married women's romantic memories of maidenhood. In the context of bow songs, the moralizing was a radical reversal of expressive independence of adolescent female musical socialization. Inevitable as women regarded it, betrothal was fate anticipated with fear, and well known to be one of burden and trial for womankind, as observed of the Zulu,

> []Neither should one underestimate the girl's sorrow at leaving her home, even though she anticipates this event all her life, and would not choose to do otherwise. In the early years of marriage, a young woman has an unenviable role in her husband's homestead. Subject to the *ukuhlonipha* code of behaviour mentioned previously, she is the victim of stringent restrictions on her freedom, in contrast to the carefree days in her father's homestead.
>
> (Joseph 1989: 75)

As a term *inkohlisa* is meaningful in a consideration of the role of Zulu calabash-resonated bows in their contextual performance accompaniment of specific repertoires. The name *inkohlisa* accurately describes Zulu women's self-accompaniment of bow songs about personal memories whose emotional gravity is willed forgotten. The socio-domestic institution of family expectations of the bride was 'to forget' (Zulu: *khohlwa*[32]) the romantic memories of her unconsummated past loves of maidenhood. Understanding the term *inkohlisa* equivalently positions both *ugubhu* and *umakhweyana* in the musical mediation of intransigent subjective conditions of their female practitioners. As critical and socially discursive voices, *ugubhu* and *umakhweyana* bow songs musically illustrate well both disjuncture and female subjective continuity experienced in Zulu traditional rites of passage.

Inkohlisa: Princess Magogo *ugubhu* 'love' songs of remembering

Self-accompanied *ugubhu* bow songs are understood to represent a serious, stately music of the Zulu royal court of Princess Constance Magogo kaDinizulu's paternal birth (Rycroft 1975). Prior to *ugubhu* virtually disappearing from everyday practice and its subsequent association with ceremonial musical repertoires, it was played by premarital Zulu females in self-accompaniment (Joseph 1989: 99). Traditionally, bow song themes related to women's experiences of love as an emotion of the individual subject's social entanglement.

As a royal, Princess Magogo kaDinizulu significantly identified with such traditional socializing experiences of Zulu girls. Some of her repertoires reveal the censorial bearing of Zulu paternalism on female memories of maidenhood, in this case her apparent romantic love for an 'unnamed' commoner youth. Dubiously attributed simultaneously to both traditional musical socialization *and* the Princess' memories of her attraction to her then adolescent future husband, the song *Ngibambeni Ngibambeni*[33] ('Hold me [back], Hold me [back]') illustrates this interpretation (Rycroft 1975: 49).

The song's traditional category of repertoire and performance context is that of an *isimekezo*[34] lament. It affirms *ugubhu* context as *inkohlisa* in a veiled remembrance of unrequited maidenly romantic love – as opposed to a widow's celebration of a departed husband – as evident in its last two lines of stanza:

> *Sengimuka nomoya ye mama!* I am being swept away with the wind, O mother!
> *Ngibambeni, ngibambeni, ngibambeni!* Hold me, hold me, hold me!

The patriarchal arrangement between Princess Magogo's brother, the Zulu monarch King Solomon kaDinizulu and Inkosi Mathole of the Buthelezi clan, that led to her betrothal were recently revealed[35] (Buthelezi 2019). Among both commoners and royalty, the exchange of cattle and women in *ukulobola*[36] custom effectively served political economic relations between powerful families and clans and involved. Women had little power to oppose a royal decree and disobeying it had previously resulted in Zulu warriors killing defiant maidens in 1878 during King Cetshwayo kaMpande's reign (Fuze 1979: 107). The attribution of 'Ngibambeni Ngibambeni' to a posthumous celebration of enamoured love for a young Inkosi Mathole Buthelezi is implausible since he was never Princess Magogo's maidenly *isoka* suitor. As a contemplation of elopement (from the prospect of an arranged marriage) however, the song's title alludes to flight, against which the fleeing maiden pleads to be restrained: *Ngibambeni Ngibambeni*' ('Hold me [back], Hold me [back]').[37] In this consideration the song is the matriarch's lament of maidenly love left unconsummated in deference to customary traditions of patriarchal power. In the gendered post-marital Zulu traditional context, the application of the term *inkohlisa* is apt in regards whereby calabash-resonated musical bows functioned as a discursive musical engagement with forgetting – in this instance – of romantic memories of maidenhood.

Umakhweyana as *inkohlisa*: Gendered age stratifications of traditional Zulu females

In their mapping of age and gender stratifications of Zulu traditional culture, certain bow repertoires substantiate the role and category of *umakhweyana* as *inkohlisa*. In traditional musical practices of female adolescence, the bow was a musical accompaniment to private expressions of maidenly love. However, following the female rite of passage of marriage, *umakhweyana* playing became disapproved of because of bow songs' thematic preoccupation with issues of love. In articulating to the customary bridal behaviour of *ukuhlonipha* ritual avoidance, the taboo against *umakhweyana* playing in marriage invariably culminated in a total relegation of musical bow performance. The silencing of *umakhweyana* in marriage contextualized its characteristic repertoires as that of *inkohlisa*, in a position of private, solitary pastime. For Zulu women musical bows occupy a mature role as *inkohlisa* in a meditative, individual context wherein music is made by performer for primary self-experiencing and only secondarily for appreciation by audience.[38] In their musical narratives of personal experiences of this singular condition, women accompanied their songs on *inkohlisa*, a musical bow named after that '[which] causes to escape memory' (Doke-Vilakazi 1990: 397). The term *inkohlisa* indicates to the centrality of the musical bow in mediating memory and experiences in love encountered by Zulu females. In defying cultural patriarchal dominance, Zulu married females who played *umakhweyana* demonstrated their subjective position in engagement with a traditional institution of power. In the *inkohlisa* context, bow songs map female experiences of the rites of passage as embedded in traditional practices of *umakhweyana* before and after marriage.

A premarital *inkohlisa* context of *umakhweyana*

Zulu women's premarital *umakhweyana* self-accompanied bow songs exceed their characterization by a preoccupation with love-engendered emotions (Impey 1983, Joseph 1983, and Joseph 1989). Bow songs of female adolescence were more than an engagement with subjective memory and emotional experiences of romantic affirmation and alienation in maidenhood. Their musical narratives of individual emotional entanglements were also significant mediations of the dominant social conditions of cultural tradition and change.

Performance of *inkohlisa* repertoires on *umakhweyana* brings attention to Zulu bow songs as ritual repertoires of remembering and forgetting, of familiarity and strangeness, as well as social institutional entanglements of traditional female subjects. At the height of South Africa's culturally disruptive processes of migrant economic labour in the latter half of the twentieth century, *umakhweyana* bow songs narrated the implication of social structure and conditions beyond the control of the subject. Beyond a musical engagement with history and structural power, the role of *umakhweyana* as *inkohlisa* is potent in expressing subjective desire to either remember (as in declaring and celebrating love) or forget (memories and feelings of rejection and unreciprocated love).

Umakhweyana bow song texts are remarkable in their structural implication of a uniquely South African political economic condition in a ritual performance of memory – in this case abandonment in love. Two such songs documented in 1955 by the late African ethnomusicologist Dr Hugh Tracey for the International Library of Music (ILAM) Sound of Africa audio archive are Akasangibhaleli' by Nomatheku Zungu (Figure 4.21) and 'EBloemfontein' by Cwayizile Shandu (Figure 4.22).

Lyrics excerpt of **Akasangibhaleli**	(He does not write to me anymore) by Nomatheku Zungu:
Asangibhalel' nencwad' encan'	He does not write to me even a little letter anymore
Kudala kangiziboni neyincwad' eyincan'	Long have I not seen even the little letters
Akasangibhaleli lomntanomuntu	He does not write to me anymore this Child of Man
Kudal' angizitholi yebuya ma!	Long I have not received *them O Mother!
Lyrics excerpt of **EBloemfontein**	(In Bloemfontein) by Cwayizile Shandu
EBloemfonteni wobuya nini?	When will he come back from Bloemfontein?
Kudal' angiziboni yelele ma!	Far too long, I do not see *them O Mother!
Ezindumeni yelele baba!	[Where there are] mounds of earth O Father!
Imal' ingaphela wemntanomuntu	Money can run out O Child of Man!

* Letters in the post

Akasangibhaleli (He does not write to me anymore) - excerpt

Figure 4.21 'Akasangibhaleli' (recorded in 1955 by Dr Hugh Tracey as performed by Nomatheku Zungu of Nongoma, Zululand). Refer to Audio #5. Permission to use by courtesy of The International Library of African Music (ILAM).

EBloemfontein (In Bloemfontein) - excerpt

Figure 4.22 'EBloemfontein' (recorded in 1955 by Dr Hugh Tracey as performed by Cwayizile Shandu of Nongoma, Zululand). Refer to Audio #6. Permission to use by courtesy of The International Library of African Music (ILAM).

The lyrics to both songs lament separation in love through physically unbridgeable distance and cessation of visual and literary communication of feelings between couples. For Nomatheku Zungu, not receiving letters in the post is evidence of love lost while for Cwayizile Shandu, the distant city of Bloemfontein and its mounds of mine dumps are to blame. Shandu contemplates love's worth against the depreciating value of money, in need of which her lover left Zululand to work in Bloemfontein.

Umakhweyana in a post-marital *inkohlisa* context

A significant rite of passage, marriage introduces a singularly intractable context for Zulu women's bow songs in their mediation of emotions associated with female entanglements in love. In marriage, the traditional travestorial regard for *umakhweyana* playing foreclosed not only the celebratory or the cheerful of love situations, but also the lamentable. Adversity anticipated in the texts of the ritual *izimekezo* bridal laments only manifested subsequently in everyday experience as a wife in a polygamous marriage. Despite the paternally determined exclusion, female experiences of the intransigence of love in Zulu married life add an urgent individual agency for the continuation and role of *inkohlisa* repertoires. From being laments of maidenly 'trials and tribulations' in love, post-marital *inkohlisa* repertoires adapt in defiance of traditional patriarchy and protest intolerable conditions imposed on Zulu women through polygamy. A post-marital *umakhweyana* tradition demonstrates the transformation of *inkohlisa* bow songs from youthful love laments to protest and resisting contestation of gender power relations within Zulu traditional marriage.

Self-accompanied on *umakhweyana* bow, 'Amadoda kashelani'[39] is a self-accompanied song by Delisa Sibiya who is among the most significant *umakhweyana* players from Zululand's Nongoma district at the turn of the 1980s. Recorded by the ethnomusicologists Veit Erlmann and Bongani Mthethwa on the field in Zululand in the early 1980s, the track's title in the Lyrichord LP album wrongly alludes to the taboo of homophobia.[40] In transcription (Figure 4.23) however, the correct title of the song is 'Madoda ngash' elangeni' (Men, I am burning in the sun), the phrase that is repeatedly sung as a leader's call, as well as being responsorially reiterated as a 'chorus' phrase together with the musical bow ostinato. The subject of the song's text laments the intolerable,

Figure 4.23 Transcription of 'Amadoda kashelani [Madoda ngash' elangeni]' by Delisa Sibiya. The 1982 field recording by Veit Erlmann and Bongani Mthethwa was subsequently included in *Zulu Songs of South Africa*, and LP released by Lyrichord in 1986. https://www.amazon.com/Africa-Namashizolo-Misimango-Delisa-Sibiya/dp/B006320ADQ/

outdoor working conditions that characterize domestic responsibilities for the least-favoured wife – and invariably the youngest – in a polygynous traditional household. In the song the title phrase functions as a chorus and is sung in a full line of text as *[m]adoda ngash' elangeni mnakweth' ungiyel' enyangeni*.[41] A literal translation of this is:

Figure 4.24 Delisa Sibiya, umakhweyana bow player from Nongoma, Zululand in 1981. Photo: Veit Erlmann.

Men, I burn in the sun
[Because] My co-wife consults a witchdoctor

The lament uses as a metaphor, the symbolic opposition between the sun and the moon. However, the isiZulu synonymy alludes to witchcraft and sorcery traditionally associated with practices of wicked *inyanga*.[42] Thus, the singer attributes her untenable circumstance to negative charms and spells cast upon her by a jealous co-wife with the assistance of the medicine man. Another layer of meaning is imbued to the lyric by its address to 'men' – who traditionally attend court to hear and decide upon cases. In Zulu customary law, it is the responsibility of *ibandla* – a ritual gathering court of mature adult males that hears and deliberates upon cases brought before the court of the tribal or village leader for arbitration. In this instance the appeal of the phrase to 'men' may well be a plea by the suffering wife to be rescued by being married by another man, hopefully more equitable in matters of household division of labour.

In contemporary Zulu culture, the ubiquity of widowed and female single parenthood strains against traditional patriarchy. The resulting condition opens

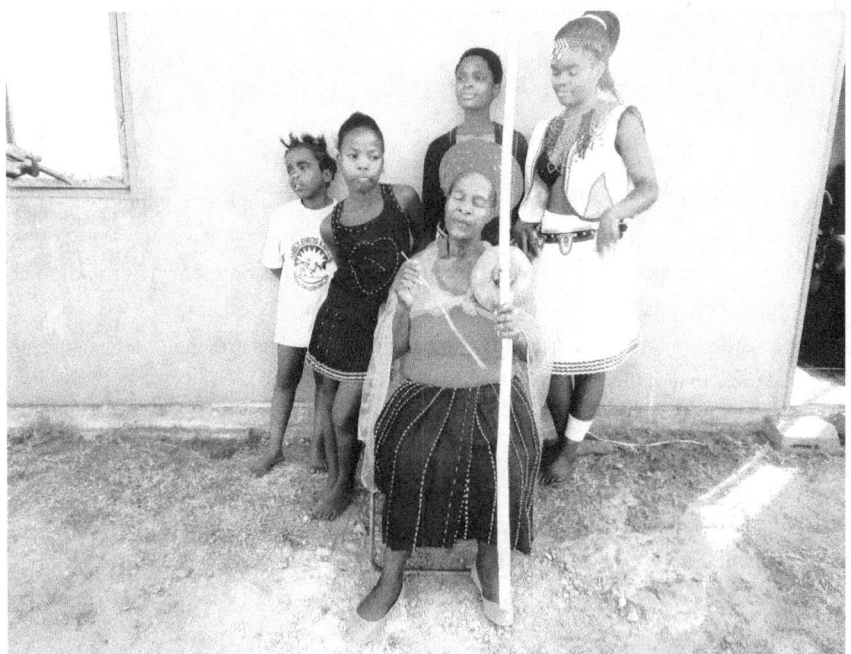

Figure 4.25 Mama Bavikile Ngema – *umakhweyana* bow player from Mbongolwane Mission near Eshowe, Zululand. Photo: Maria Cristina Giampietri.

space for female outspokenness and independence further transforming *inkohlisa* repertoires away from those of *ukuhlonipha* condescension and towards a vocal criticism of Zulu indigenous domestic order. In 'Alikho La[pha] Ekhaya' ([My grave] won't be in this homestead), Zululand *umakhweyana* bow player Mama Bavikile Ngema (Figure 4.25) of Mbongolwana (eShowe) disavows her ties to the family of her deceased husband [the Ngema] and expresses a rebellious wish to be buried instead in her parents' family homestead upon her death:

> Thuna lam' alikho la ekhaya   My grave will not be here
> Thuna lam' alikho kwaNgema   My grave will not be at the Ngema homestead
> Thuna lam' liseMandawe   My grave will be in Mandawe.

In a post-marital *umakhweyana* playing context, Delisa Sibiya's 'Madoda Ngash' elangeni [Amadoda kashelani]' and Bavikile Ngema's 'Alikho la ekhaya' both illustrate unique performances of the bow as *inkohlisa*. In the role of *inkohlisa*, the musical bow mediates ambivalent Zulu female experiences that articulate simultaneously to both memory and the present – as well as to remembering and forgetting. In the traditional context of a patriarchal disapproval of *umakhweyana* playing by Zulu married women, the two examples of songs discussed above illuminate *inkohlisa* repertoires as including songs of lament and radical protest.

Notes

1. Bracing here refers to the division of the musical bow's single string into two segments of unequal length.
2. One of the names by which both the Zulu and the Swati commonly refer to the mid-braced, calabash-resonated, mono-heterochord musical bow.
3. A musical bow with a single undivided string and calabash resonator attached near the lower end of the stave.
4. A Nguni term that is a synonym for *umakhweyana* – and is defined as a 'musical instrument consisting of a gourd with a "musical bow" attached above' – *imvingo* refers to 'a pile or bundle of chopped wood' (Doke-Vilakazi 1990: 835).
5. Also according to Doke-Vilakazi (ibid., 835), *imvingo* is a [m]usical instrument consisting of a gourd with 'musical bow' attached above [cf. *unkokha*].
6. In the Zulu indigenous building vocabulary, the commonly used term is *izintingo* [English translation: 'bows'] (Frescura 1981: 39, Nyembezi-Nxumalo 1966: 41, Msimang 1975: 5).
7. According to Franco Frescura, specialist in Zulu indigenous architecture: 'Traditionally the Zulu beehive dome consist of a series of saplings planted in

a circle on the ground, and bent into arches spanning from the one side of the circle to the other beginning with the great arch at the diameter of the circle and diminishing in size as the circle reaches its two extremities. A further and more closely spaced set of saplings is arched over this first dome at right angles to it, the two being bound together by means of woven grass ropes at every point where the second frame crosses over the first' (1981: 39). See Figure 4.4.

8   Heavy stones are sometimes used as weights to straighten the sticks during a curing period of about two weeks.

9   The noun *[i]nkokha* originates from *khokha* or *koka*, an Ur-Bantu verb meaning to 'draw out ready for attack, be prepared to strike' (Doke-Vilakazi 1990: 398). Understood as a physical state of energy harnessed to do work, *inkokha* recognizes tension force as a functional organological characteristic of musical bows.

10 A force that appears when an object is displaced from its equilibrium position and is always directed toward that position (Backus [1969] 1977: 23).

11 The dividing brace in *umakhweyana*, *ingono/ingona* is an isiZulu name for the stem by which a fruit attaches to the plant (Doke-Vilakazi 1990: 257). In deriving from the verb *gona*, meaning 'to embrace' or 'to hug', *ingona* refers to the bracing loop function of pulling the string closer to the *umakhweyana* bow stave.

12 See Bowsher (1975: 90).

13 Instead of *ngaphansi* used by Impey's informants (1983: 10), I prefer the term *ngenzansi*, for its connotation of the downward dimension in a vertical, human anatomical position (Doke-Vilakazi 1990: 888).

14 To stop the lower wire segment (Impey 1983:10).

15 Not to be confused with *isithontolo*, the braced mouth-resonated bow played by the Swati and the Zulu, which the latter people alternatively refer to as *isiqomqomana* (Dargie 1988: 42, Joseph 1987: 91).

16 Reiterated in other studies of Zulu music, this was subsequently attributed to the Zulu Princess Magogo kaDinizulu in a substantiation that, Princess Magogo can perform very ably on the *umakhweyana*, but she does not have as high a regard for it as for the *ugubhu*. She maintains that it is not truly a Zulu instrument, but was borrowed from the Tsonga, of Mozambique. This statement confirms Kirby's claim that it had been adopted in 'relatively recent times' (Rycroft 1977: 58).

17 Allusions to this orally documented Zulu prehistory include the following narrative from ethnomusicologist Angela Impey: 'The *umakhweyana* bow is said to have been adopted by the Zulu people from the Tsonga of Moçambique in the early nineteenth century. One informant suggested that *umakhweyana* was originally adopted by the [pre-Zulu] Qwabe people (the bow was then called uQwabe). The Qwabe clan was defeated by Shaka in 1819 and thereafter incorporated into the Zulu nation. It is possible that thereafter the bow was adopted by the Zulu people throughout Northern Natal' (Impey 1983: 1).

18 In her studies of Zulu women's music Rosemary Joseph recorded that:
    [] most women over the age of around forty had played the *umakhweyana* as young unmarried women, and, in the case of older women (above the age of around sixty), the *ugubhu* as well (Joseph 1983: 91).
19 Rycroft's conclusions in this regard are inconsistent with historical cultural traditions and socio-ethnic customary relations of the region. There are no other spheres of Tsonga-Zulu cultural exchange documented besides the 'borrowing' of *umakhweyana* alluded to in Rycroft's interviews with the Princess Magogo kaDinizulu. While the Tsonga/Thonga and Ndau-Shangana and Tshopi *xitende* are similar to *umakhweyana* in appearance, the former tradition's gendered contexts differ significantly from those of the Zulu. The intimacy suggested by the trans-ethnic 'borrowing' claimed between predominantly male Tsonga, Ndau-Shangana and Chopi *xitende* practitioners and adolescent female Qwabe[1] ancestors is not explicitly verified in historical accounts. Among other reasons for contestation, the alluded borrowing falls short in accounting for *umakhweyana* (and *ligubhu*) traditions among the Swati, which includes a common use of the name *umakhweyana* with the Zulu. It is however plausible to imagine the occurrence of the braced calabash-resonated bow that is traceable through much older, common Bantu genealogical relationships between present-day Swati, Zulu and Thonga cultural ethnicities over a *longue durée*.
20 As further noted by Joseph:
    The performance of the repertory of songs traditionally associated with the *umakhweyana* and *ugubhu*
    by middle-aged women is, however, something of a travesty, as these are the instruments of [] *izintombi* (unmarried girls), and the repertory consists largely of love songs. When a girl marries and goes to live in her husband's homestead, she no longer plays the bows as part of her observance of the *ukuhlonipha* code of conduct (ibid.).
21 Southern Bantu dialects of isiXhosa and isiZulu pronounce the consonant 'q' as a 'radical' palato-alveolar click (Doke-Vilakazi 1990: xvi).
22 'Rhythm in most African musics is built up on a basis of equal-spaced small units of time, often fast-moving. These have been given several longer names, but I prefer to call them simply PULSES. All parts in a piece of music share one system of pulses, but very often draw on it in different ways' (Tracey 1987: 44).
23 Of pattering, tapping, striking lightly (Doke-Vilakazi 1990: 705). The derivation of *uqwabe* (n.) from [uku]*q[h]wába* (v.) similarly relates to sonic patterns played on *umakhweyana* string using a dried *ubhaqa* grass-stalk (Doke-Vilakazi 1990: 705).
24 Triradical tonal organization was a term coined by David Rycroft in reference to three fundamental notes elicited from braced musical bows such as *xitende* and *umakhweyana* because of their divided string (see Rycroft 1967: 97).

25 In the plural, a diminutive form of the Nguni noun *ikhwelo/i(li)khwelo* (Eng. 'shrill whistle') is *amakhwelana* (English: 'little shrill whistles'). The noun *umakhweyana* derives from palatalization, a linguistic Zulu phonetic process for diminutive nouns, in this case an alteration of the palatal consonant 'l' in *amakhwelana* to 'y' in *amakhweyana* (Doke-Vilakazi 1990: xxiii). A synonym of *ikhwelo* is *umlozi* or 'soft whistling', a term also given to 'a whistling spirit', a 'spiritual being who manifests ... in whistling within the hut' or 'ventriloquist' (Doke-Vilakazi 1990: 464).

26 According to Kirby, 'when played upon, each of the two sections of the divided string yielded a fundamental note and a corresponding chord. A third fundamental elicited by stopping the lower (higher pitched) segment sounded a semitone higher than the second open fundamental. In pitch terms the three fundamentals were G, A, and Bb below middle-C for the Swazi *umakhweyana* and E, G, and Ab two octaves below middle-C in the case of the Thonga *nkokha*'. Nowadays the most common tuning interval between the two open fundamentals is a whole tone. During his time however, Kirby noted interval size variations, among different *umakhweyana* practitioners, between a whole tone and a fifth (1968: 206).

27 A description of *inkohlisa* is included in a statement that 'this type is widely distributed, being found among Chwana, Thonga, Sotho, Swazi, Zulu and Xhosa. [I]t was not used by the Hottentots, and is unknown to the Venda. (Kirby 1965: 196). The first type is given various names by the different people who use it: Chwana – *segwana*, Thonga – *thsitendje* or *dende*, Sotho (Transvaal) – *sekgapa*, Sotho (Basutoland) – *thomo*, Swazi – *ligubu*, Zulu – *ugubu*, *ugumbu*, *gubu olukhulu*, or *inkohlisa*, and the Xhosa – *uhadi*' (p197).

28 Kirby's typography is reiterated in other instances where different names for a calabash-resonated musical bow – including *imvingo*, *inkohlisa* and *ugubhu* – are all defined as 'a [large] musical bow with a calabash resonator attached' (Doke-Vilakazi 1990: 397, 1990: 835, Kirby 1965: 206). As criteria for identifying *ugubhu/ligubhu* and *umakhweyana* further uncertainties included (1) whether the position of the calabash resonator was in the middle or towards the end of the bow stave, and (2) the presence or absence of a divided string. Kirby had categorized *ugubhu* and *inkohlisa* among bows with undivided string and calabash resonators permanently attached near the lower end of the bow stave (1975: 201 and 2013: 265). However, by referring to *inkohlisa* as a 'complete form' of a type of bow played by the Angola San (to Dorothy Bleek in the early 1920s) Kirby had contradictorily regarded *inkohlisa* as, or similar to, *umakhweyana* (1975: 206 and 2013: 274).

29 *The Grove Dictionary of Musical Instruments* has an entry as follows:
  '**Umakhweyana** [imvingo, inkohlisa, isiqwemqwemana, uqwabe, unkoka,

unkokha, umakweyana]. Braced gourd-resonated MUSICAL Bow of the Zulu people of southern Africa. It is similar in construction and performing practice to the Tsonga *xitende* (or *nkoka),* Northern Sotho (or Pedi) *sekgapa,* Tswana *segwana,* Chopi *tshitendole* (or *chitende),* Swazi *makhweyane,* Venda *dende,* Ila and Tonga *kalumbu,* Humbi *mbulu-mbumba,* and the Cuban *burumbumba'* (Rycroft 1984a: 698).

30 In its derivation from *khohlisa,* an isiZulu verb whose primary meaning is 'to cause to escape the memory, cause to puzzle', *inkohlisa* (n.) points to the traditional use of musical bows as instruments for making time pass, 'to bring about forgetfulness' and 'as distraction' (Doke-Vilakazi 1990: 397).

31 The following accounts attest to this view:
'Among the Zulu ... [T]here are no specialist makers, though men make the instrument for the women, who are usually the players' (Kirby 2013: 269). Elsewhere Kirby is cited a description by Shooter (1857), of *ugub[h]u* that was illustrated with 'a drawing of a woman playing upon it' (ibid., 271). Regarding *umakhweyana,* '[a]mong the Zulu [*umakhweyana*] is played by both sexes, the larger sizes by men, single or married, and the smaller by maidens or newly-married women' (ibid., 277).
'While the tradition of playing *ugubhu* and *umakhweyana* had ceased to be active in the areas of my field-work, it became apparent from conversations with my informants (the majority of whom were women) that most women over the age of around forty had played the *umakhweyana* as young unmarried girls, and in the case of women above the age of about sixty, the *ugubhu* as well' (Joseph 1987: 91).

32 According to Zulu grammatical definition, the noun *inkohlisa* is a causative verbal derivative form of *khohlwa* (Eng. 'forget') and, in ending with the suffix *-isa,* indicates that the subject causes the action [of forgetting] to be done (Doke-Vilakazi 1990: xxi).

33 According to Rycroft's transcription note:
[*Ngibambeni, ngibambeni* (Hold me, hold me)] is a nostalgic love song, adapted by Princess Magogo in memory of her late husband, Chief Mathole Buthelezi. She first learned the traditional form of the song from relatives, in her youth, while staying at Ngenetsheni, the residence of Prince Hamu kaMpande. In the present rendering of the song, line 1 was sung twice, line 4 was sung three times, and line 15 twice.
Helele, helele! awu, helele   Oh, oh .... •
Way(e)muhle lomfana, yeyeni!   He was handsome, that boy, alas!
Ye mama, ye mama, ye mama!   O mother ... !
Ngibambeni, ngibambeni, bomama!   Hold me, hold me, my mothers!
Usebeyath' uyangibheka ngamthanda!   When he used to look at me, I loved him!
Yeyeni, yeyeni, ye mama!   Alas ... mother!
Wagibel' amahash' amfanela!   When he rode on horseback, it suited him!
Sengimuka nomoya ye mama!   I am being swept away with the wind, O mother!

34 *Isimekezo* songs are generally of a sorrowful character, lamenting the bride's estrangement from her family home and making mention of her father and other close relatives from whom she has been parted (Rycroft 1975: 45).
35 In his recent history lecture presentation at the University of KwaZulu-Natal on 9 February 2019, the Prince Mangosuthu Buthelezi confirmed the terms of this 'arrangement' as involving an order for the princess to 'abandon her boyfriend to marry my father, Inkosi Mathole of the Buthelezi clan' (Keynote Address – KwaZulu-Natal Global Musicians in Dialogue: 2019). This example of a traditional application of absolute patriarchal power of the Zulu royal clan order verifies the impossibility of the princess going against her brother's wishes at the time (Buthelezi 2019).
36 Part of the Zulu traditional wedding ritual ceremonial practice is the ceding of cattle by the bridegroom's family to the bride's family, as bride wealth.
37 https://www.amazon.com/songs-Princess-Constance-Magogo-KaDinuzulu/dp/B073XN9YJJ
38 'Holicipation' was a term coined by Andrew Killick to refer to practices of performing music primarily for the self, a concept of which he introduced in his provocative essay 'Holicipation: Prolegomenon to an Ethnography of Solitary Music-Making' as follows: 'Solitary music-making for personal satisfaction is a widespread form of musical behaviour that has hitherto been neglected by ethnomusicologists and other students of music. By analogy with 'participation' (taking part), this activity might be termed 'holicipation' (taking the whole), in that, as the only performer and listener involved, the solitary music-maker personally experiences the whole of the musical event. This paper assesses the treatment (or neglect) of musical holicipation in a wide range of literary and audio-visual sources, and argues that a number of recent developments in the study of music call for a more serious study of holicipation, especially by ethnomusicologists' (Killick 2006: 273).
See Stacey (2017) for an extended discussion of holicipation in the context of Swati *makhoyana* tradition.
39 https://www.amazon.com/Africa-Namashizolo-Misimango-Delisa-Sibiya/dp/B006320ADQ/
40 The title 'Amadoda kashelani' literally translates to 'men to not court each other' – thereby alluding to the contested traditional regard for same sex relationships as taboo. Upon transcription however, the repeated theme of the lyrics of Delisa Sibiya's song is 'Madoda ngash'elangeni' and clearly understood as a lament by a hard-working woman labouring under unequitable labour responsibilities of the least favourable wife in a polygamous marriage.
41 In isiZulu, the locative noun of 'inyanga' (moon).
42 The isiZulu noun *inyanga* refers to both the celestial moon and a sorcerer, witchdoctor or medicine man.

References

Angas, George F. (1849), *The Kaffirs Illustrated*. London.
Backus, John ([1969] 1977), *The Acoustical Foundations of Music*, London/New York: WW Norton & Co.
Bleibinger, B. (2017), 'How to Tune Modernised Versions of a Traditional Musical Bow, the *Umrhubhe*, from the Eastern Cape', in S. Dlamini (ed.), *First International Bow Music Conference Proceedings*, 85–93, Rhodes University, Grahamstown: International Library of African Music (ILAM).
Bowsher, J.M. (1975), 'Vibrations of Strings', in J. Bowsher and Alexander Wood, *Alexander Wood's The Physics of Music*, 90–109, London: Chapman and Hall.
Buthelezi, M.G. (2019), 'The Princess Magogo kaDinizulu Lecture on the Role She Played in Promoting and Preserving Indigenous Music', in *Keynote Address*, University of KwaZulu-Natal, Durban: KwaZulu-Natal Global Musicians in Dialogue.
Dargie, D. (1988), *Xhosa Music: Its Techniques and Instruments, with a Collection of Songs* (with accompanying cassette), Cape Town: David Philip.
Dargie, D. (1991), '*Umngqokolo*: Xhosa Overtone Singing and the Song Nondel'ekhaya', *African Music* 7 (1): 33–47. Available online: http://www.jstor.org/stable/30249985
Dargie, D. (2001a), 'Magical Musical Bows', *Talking Drum* 1 (16): 4–12.
Dargie, D. (2001b), *Magical Musical Bows* – An Article/Handbook with Accompanying CD, Fort Hare, South Africa: recording.
Dargie, D. (2003), 'Zulu Bow Songs: Songs with the Traditional Zulu Musical Bows *Ugubhu, Umakhweyane* and *Umqangala*', in *Rare Recordings Made by Dave Dargie during the Period 1981–1982 in the Nongoma District of Kwazulu-Natal*, Fort Hare: Dargie, Print.
Dargie, D. (2007), 'Umakhweyane: A Musical Bow and Its Contribution to Zulu Music', *African Music* 8 (1): 60–81. Available online: http://www.jstor.org/stable/30249999
Dargie, D. (2017), 'Bow Songs as Carriers of Heritage', in S. Dlamini (ed.), *First International Bow Music Conference Proceedings*, 1–13, Rhodes University, Grahamstown: International Library of African Music (ILAM).
Dlamini, S. (2004), 'The Role of the *Umrhubhe* Bow as Transmitter of Cultural Knowledge among the AmaXhosa: An Interview with Latozi 'Madosini' Mpahleni', *Journal of the Musical Arts in Africa* 1 (1): 138–60.
Dlamini, Sazi (ed.) (2017), *First International Bow Music Conference Proceedings*, Rhodes University, Grahamstown: International Library of African Music (ILAM).
Doke-Vilakazi, C., D. Malcolm, J. Sikakana and B. Vilakazi (1990), *English – Zulu/Zulu-English Dictionary* [First Combined Edition], Johannesburg: Witwatersrand University Press.
Frescura, Franco (1981), *Rural Shelter in Southern Africa : A Survey of the Architecture, House Forms, and Constructional Methods of the Black Rural Peoples of Southern Africa*, Johannesburg: Ravan Press.
Fuze, M. M. and A. T. Cope (1979), *The Black People and Whence They Came: A Zulu View*, Pietermaritzburg: University of Natal Press.

Gardiner, Allen F. (1836), *Narrative of a Journey to the Zoolou Country*, London: William Crofts.

Hornbostel, E. von (1933), 'The Ethnology of African Sound Instruments', *Africa* 6: 129–54; 277–311.

Hornbostel, E. von and C. Sachs (1961), 'Classification of Musical Instruments: Translated from the Original German by Anthony Baines and Klaus P. Wachsmann', *The Galpin Society Journal* 14: 3–29.

Impey, A. (1983), 'The Zulu umakhweyana Bow: Ndabisehlele Myeza and Her Songs', BMus Hon. diss., University of Natal, Durban.

Joseph, Rosemary M.F., and University of London. School of Oriental and African Studies (1989), *Zulu Women's Bow Songs: Ruminations on Love*, London.

Joseph, R. (1989), 'Zulu Women's Bow Songs: Ruminations on Love', *The Bulletin of the School of Oriental and African Studies* L (I): 90–119.

KaDinuzulu, C.M. 1973, 'Ngibambeni, ngibambeni (Hold me, hold me)', in H. Tracey (recordist), *The Zulu songs of Princess Constance Magogo KaDinuzulu*, Johannesburg: Gallo LP, Side A: Track #5. Available online: https://ukzn.on.worldcat.org/oclc/181940028

Khumalo, R. (1995), *Uphoko* (Roasted and Ground Millet) – *Umqulu 1*, Pietermaritzburg/Cape Town/Randburg/King Williamstown: Shuter & Shooter.

Killick, A. (2006), 'Holicipation: Prolegomenon to an Ethnography of Solitary Music-Making', *Ethnomusicology Forum* 15 (2): 273–99.

Kirby, P. (1968), *The Musical Instruments of the Native Races of South Africa* [Second Edition], Johannesburg: Witwatersrand University Press.

Kirby, P. (2013), *Musical Instruments of the Indigenous People of South Africa* [3rd Edition of *the Musical Instruments of the Native Races of South Africa*], Johannesburg: Witwatersrand University Press.

Kubik, G. (1975), 'Musical Bows in South-Western Angola, 1965', *African Music* 5 (4): 98–104. Available online: http://www.jstor.org/stable/30249727

Kubik, G. (1999), 'Dr. David Kenneth Rycroft, 7 December 1924–8 August 1997', *African Music* 7 (4): 3–5. Available online: http://www.jstor.org/stable/30249816

Mpanza, P. (2002), 'Abantu Baphelile' (Rec. D. Dargie), *Zulu Bow Songs: Songs with the Traditional Zulu Musical Bows Ugubhu, Umakhweyane and Umqangala; Rare Recordings Made by Dave Dargie during the Period 1981–1982 in the Nongoma District of Kwazulu-Natal, Alice*: Fort Hare University Archives: Dargie, [c. 2002], Music Recording.

Msimang, C. (1975), *Kusadliwa Ngoludala* (The Good Olden Times), Pietermaritzburg/Cape Town/Randburg/King Williamstown: Shuter & Shooter.

Ngema, B. (2017), 'Kwasenza (It Destroyed Us)', S. Dlamini (prod.), *Umakhweyana* [cd album Track #8], Durban: Rec. at The Headroom Studio.

Nyembezi-Nxumalo, S and O. Nxumalo (1982), *Inqolobane Yesizwe* (The Storehouse of the Nation) [Third Edition], Pietermaritzburg: Shuter & Shooter.

Rycroft, D. (1957), 'Zulu Male Traditional Singing', *African Music*, 1 (4): 33–5. Available online: http://www.jstor.org/stable/30250199

Rycroft, D. (1967), 'Nguni Vocal Polyphony', *Journal of the International Folk Music Council*, 19 (1967): 88–103. Available online: http://www.jstor.org/stable/942193

Rycroft, D. (1975), 'The Zulu Bow Songs of Princess Magogo', *African Music* 5 (4): 41–97. Available online: http://www.jstor.org/stable/30249726

Rycroft, D. (1981), 'The Musical Bow in Southern Africa', in *Papers Presented at the Second Symposium on Ethnomusicology*, 70–6, Grahamstown: Music Department, Rhodes University.

Rycroft, D. (1984a), 'Umakhweyana', in S. Sadie (ed.), *The Grove Dictionary of Musical Instruments* [Volume 3], 698, London: Macmillan Press Limited.

Rycroft, D. (1984b), 'Ugubhu', in S. Sadie (ed.), *The Grove Dictionary of Musical Instruments* [Volume 3], 695, London: Macmillan Press Limited.

Rycroft, D. (1985), 'Princess Constance Magogo KaDinuzulu – 1900 to 1984', *Africa Insight* 15 (4): 244–7.

Rycroft, D. (2001), 'Musical bow', in S. Sadie and J. Tyrrell (eds.), *The New Grove Dictionary of Music and Musicians* [Second Edition], 465–9, London: Macmillan Press Limited.

Shandu, C. (1955), 'EBloemfontein* (In Bloemfontein)', in H. Tracey (recordist), *The Sound of Africa – Sons d' Afrique Series TR-10*, Roodepoort: ILAM LP, Side A: Track #4. https://samap.ukzn.ac.za/emalomeniemgangaleni-southern-african *Wrongly labelled as 'Emalomeni … Emgangeleni'.

Sibiya, D. (1986), 'Amadoda kashelani', in Veit Erlmann, and Bongani Mthethwa (recordists), *Zulu Songs of South Africa*, New York: Lyrichord LP, Side A: Track #3. https://ukzn.on.worldcat.org/oclc/19056542

Stacey, Cara L, and Sylvia Bruinders (2017), 'The *Makhweyane* Bow of Swaziland: Music, Poetics and Place', PhD diss., University of Cape Town.

Treffry-Goatley, A. (2015), *Brother Clement Sithole – A Musical Biography*, Knysna: Outcomes Publishing.

Tracey, A. (1987), 'Workshop in Transcription of African Music', in *Papers Presented at the Sixth Symposium on Ethnomusicology*, 43–52, Grahamstown: International Library of African Music (ILAM).

Zungu, N. (1955), 'Akasangibhaleli (He does not write to me anymore)', in H. Tracey (recordist), *The Sound of Africa – Sons d' Afrique Series TR-10*, Roodepoort: ILAM LP, Side A: Track #5. Available online*: https://samap.ukzn.ac.za/ibikele-kangekauneshikhwele-southern-african *The track is wrongly labelled as 'Ibikele Kangeka ….Uneshikwele'.

Umakhweyana bow performance online

https://www.youtube.com/watch?v=JaEQFBvNZe4
https://www.youtube.com/watch?v=C5JDnI_GtsQ
Mama Bavikile Ngema performing in the University of KwaZulu-Natal's Elizabeth Sneddon Theatre at the First International Bow Music Conference, 27 February 2016.

For audio and visual examples, see https://www.bloomsbury.com/us/musical-bows-of-southern-africa-9781501346743/.

5

The social dynamics of three Zimbabwean musical bows: The *chipendani*, *mukube* and ground-bow

Jennifer W. Kyker

Abstract

Zimbabwe's large family of musical bows represents a rich field of musical practice, yet one that has largely been left out of conversations on the nation's music. Drawing on fieldwork with two elderly bow players, this chapter analyses the social dynamics of three Zimbabwean musical bows – the *mukube*, *chipendani* and ground-bow. In the process, it suggests new possibilities for researchers interested in bow music research.

Introduction

While the Shona *mbira dzavadzimu*, or 'mbira of the ancestral spirits', is Zimbabwe's most recognizable musical icon, many other indigenous instruments remain part of the nation's contemporary musical life.[1] Among them, Zimbabwe's large family of musical bows represents a particularly rich area of musical practice. Drawing on extended ethnographic fieldwork with two elderly bow players – Sekuru Compound Muradzikwa and Sekuru Tute Chigamba – I analyse the social dynamics of three of Zimbabwe's musical bows. These include two mouth-resonated bows, known as *mukube* and *chipendani*, as well as a ground-bow constructed around a resonating chamber dug directly into the earth.

There are at least a dozen Zimbabwean bows, each with its own particular morphology and playing technique. Most involve plucking or beating the instrument's single string; among these bows are the *chipendani* (Brenner 1997,

Maraire 1982), *mukube* (Hoffman 1895, Kauffman 1970), *chitende* (Ellert 1984), *wedsa* (Balfour 1899, Mason 1897), *chidangari* (Ellert 1984, Winter 1907), *dimbwa* (Snowden 1938) and *hugu* (Brown 1899).² At least two other instruments – the *chimwanikoda* and the *incanco* – were played with a bow (Snowden 1938).³ Demonstrating a third playing technique, the friction bow known as *chizambi* is played by rubbing a stick across notches carved into the instrument's stave (Ellert 1984, Jones 1992).⁴

In the literature, a single bow may be called by many names. The *chizambi*, for example, is variously referred to as *chinyamazambi*, *chinyamadzimbi*, *chimazambi*, *chitambe* and *mazambi*. Spellings likewise vary widely, particularly in colonial era accounts. Thus, a single bow may be referred to variously as *wedsa* (Mason 1897), *wedza* (Camp and Nettl 1955, Sachs 1913) or *widsi*.⁵ Together, these different names and alternate spellings make it difficult to trace various references to a single instrument, complicating bow musical scholarship.⁶

Readers will note that I use emic terms for two of the instruments described in this chapter, and the etic term 'ground-bow' for the third. This decision was influenced by several factors. Sekuru Muradzikwa and Sekuru Chigamba both play the chipendani (pl. *zvipendani*) and agree upon the instrument's name. Only Sekuru Chigamba played the *mukube* (pl. *mikube*), eliminating any potential conflict. The names *chipendani* and *mukube* are also established in the literature on Zimbabwean music, as well as in ethnographic and commercial recordings.

In contrast, Sekuru Muradzikwa called the ground-bow *dzikamunhenga*, while Sekuru Chigamba called it *kambuya-mbuya*. Unlike the *chipendani* and *mukube*, the ground-bow rarely appears in discussions of Zimbabwean music. When it does appear, the ground-bow is almost never called by the same name in different accounts. Furthermore, none of the names that appear in the literature – among them *zingaringi* (Huwiler 1995; Jones 1992), *zindingwandingwa* (Zimbabwe News 1979) and *dibukandinga* (Maraire 1982) – correspond to those used by either musician with whom I worked. As a result, I avoid settling on a single emic term for the Zimbabwean ground-bow.

Resurgent interest in bow music

For many decades, Zimbabwean musical bows have been deemed instruments 'of lesser importance and somewhat obsolete' (Zimbabwe News 1979: 18). Yet interest in musical bows is resurfacing across the African continent and in associated diasporic locations. This growing body of scholarship ranges from Cara Stacey's study of compositional techniques for the Swazi *makhweyane* bow (2017) to Suzanne Fürniss's analysis of the limitations of organological conventions in respect to Central African musical bows (2012).[7] At the same time, recent scholarship has shown particular interest in questions of cultural and environmental sustainability. Angela Impey, for example, demonstrates how musical bows mediate relationships between people and their environments in Maputaland (2018), while several scholars discuss the *makalapo* ground-bow's role in preserving historical memory and intangible culture in the Seychelles (Jeffery and Rotter 2018, Pallai 2017, Parent 2018).

In this chapter, I bring extended fieldwork with Sekuru Compound Muradzikwa and Sekuru Tute Chigamba into dialogue with various archival and scholarly sources. I also briefly refer to Sekuru Chigamba's grandson Brian Chigamba, who is likewise an accomplished bow player.[8] By examining musical bows in Zimbabwe, I suggest several potential lines of enquiry for the study of bow music throughout Southern African and beyond. At the same time, I observe that scholars of other musical traditions are likewise poised to benefit from serious consideration of musical bows.

I begin by observing that Zimbabwean bow musicians often play more than one type of bow. At the same time, they also frequently play other instruments, most notably the *mbira*. Similarly, musicians overwhelmingly report taking up musical bows relatively early in life, followed by other instruments. As I illustrate, these collective tendencies open space for important scholarly questions, approaches and insights.

I proceed to discuss the social dimensions of musical bows. Drawing on my interviews with Sekuru Chigamba and Sekuru Muradzikwa, I offer several accounts of occasions when bow music has facilitated moments of freedom between people whose interactions are normally more restrained, such as parents and children, youth and elders, and unmarried men and women. While these accounts are based in fieldwork with only two musicians, they offer preliminary evidence that bow playing offers performers and listeners alike the potential to circumvent certain social norms.

I conclude by reiterating an argument put forth in my article on the *chipendani* (Kyker 2019), but which bears repeating in the context of other musical bows. For over a century, musical bows have been portrayed as 'self-delectative' or intended only for the performer's own hearing. At times, bows are certainly played for a single musician's solitary enjoyment. However, most contexts for bow music are decidedly social in nature. Accordingly, scholars working on musical bows should turn renewed attention to the social dynamics of these instruments in a diverse range of performance contexts and abandon the outdated conception of bow music as 'self-delectative'.

Working with Sekuru Chigamba and Sekuru Muradzikwa

Figure 5.1 depicts Sekuru Muradzikwa and Sekuru Chigamba holding *zvipendani* mouth bows at Imire Game Park, a white-owned farm and wildlife sanctuary located near the town of Marondera (Figure 5.1).[9] Born in 1943, Sekuru Muradzikwa grew up in the rural region of Buhera located in the eastern part of Zimbabwe.[10] In 1992, he began working as a security guard at Imire Game Park, where he would remain employed for nearly three decades. In 2002, I learned of Sekuru Muradzikwa from friends who had visited Imire purchased one of his *zvipendani*. A few weeks later, I travelled to Imire to meet him. On this trip, I learned that Sekuru Muradzikwa likewise played the ground-bow, which he refers to as *dzikamunhenga*.[11]

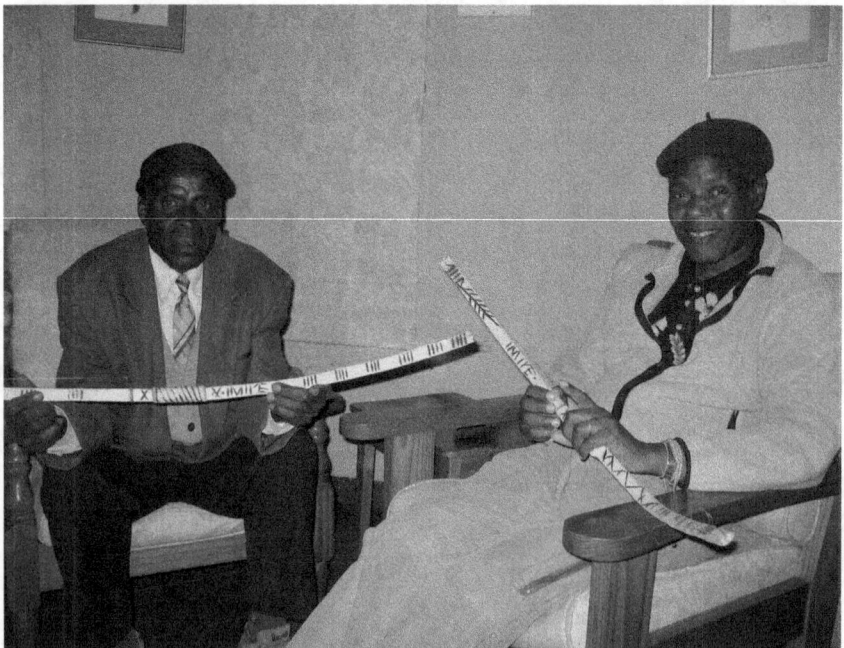

Figure 5.1 Sekuru Chigamba and Sekuru Muradzikwa. Photo: Jennifer W. Kyker.

Soon after this encounter I brought Sekuru Chigamba, with whom I have studied the *mbira dzavadzimu* since 1995, to meet Sekuru Muradzikwa at Imire. Born in 1939 in the north-eastern region of Guruve, Sekuru Chigamba has played all three of the musical bows discussed in this chapter. A multi-instrumentalist, he is also a renowned *mbira dzavadzimu* musician, teacher and instrument maker. Sekuru Chigamba and Sekuru Muradzikwa have since met on several other occasions, often accompanied by Sekuru Muradzikwa's son Polite. The resulting conversations between these elderly musicians have significantly influenced my own understanding of Zimbabwean musical bows.

Over the past several years, Sekuru Chigamba and I have worked together to produce *Sekuru's Stories*, a public digital humanities project that presents Zimbabwean musical and cultural heritage in an interactive format. At the heart of the project are Sekuru Chigamba's extended first-person narratives, or *nhoroondo*, which are available in both Shona and English versions. Audio examples, video footage, additional photographs and short descriptive essays accompany his accounts. All three of the musical bows discussed in this chapter appear in *Sekuru's Stories*; to access these materials, please visit sekuru.org/learn

Three Zimbabwean musical bows

For readers unfamiliar with Zimbabwean musical bows, I offer a brief overview of each instrument in this chapter. I begin with the *chipendani*, which both Sekuru Chigamba and Sekuru Muradzikwa were actively playing at the time of my fieldwork (Figure 5.2).

The *chipendani* features a single string, divided into two parts by means of a thread. The 2:3 ratio of the string's division enables the instrument to produce two separate fundamental pitches, separated by an interval of a fifth. By pinching the string between the thumb and index finger, players can produce an additional fundamental pitch. Using the mouth as a resonating chamber, *chipendani* performers can also produce a series of amplified, isolated harmonics above these three fundamental pitches.[12]

The *chipendani* has been described by ethnomusicologist Robert Kauffman as 'probably the most widespread' Zimbabwean musical bow (1970: 36). It is also the most widely discussed, from passing mentions (Chikowero 2007, Kahari 1981) to general overviews (Jones 1992, Matare 1992, Snowden 1938), and from

Figure 5.2 Sekuru Chigamba plays the *chipendani*. Photo: Jennifer W. Kyker.

technical analyses (Brenner 1997, Kauffman 1970) to ethnographic accounts (Kyker 2019, Maraire 1982). Given the relative prominence of *chipendani*, I spend less time discussing its basic characteristics than those of the other bows featured in this chapter.

The *chipendani* has largely been portrayed as the musical domain of solitary herdboys. While herding is indeed among its many performance contexts, the *chipendani* musical and social identity extend far beyond its conventional portrayal as a herdboy instrument. As I illustrate in a recent article, the *chipendani* has historically been played by a diverse group, including women as well as men, and elders as well as youth (Kyker 2019). At the same time, I observe that the *chipendani*'s social role extends into diverse contexts, ranging from domestic interactions such as socializing and courtship to Shona ritual events, including ceremonies featuring spirit mediumship (ibid.).

The second musical bow discussed in this chapter, known as the *mukube* (Figure 5.3), is made of a 'one-piece stave of very slightly curved river reed' (Camp and Nettl 1955: 67). Like the *chipendani*, it is also mouth-resonated. Yet both its construction and playing technique differ markedly, leading Klaus-Peter

Figure 5.3 Sekuru Chigamba plays the *mukube*. Photo: Jennifer W. Kyker.

Brenner to describe the *mukube* as 'organologically, acoustically, technically and musically completely different' than the *chipendani* (personal communication 15 October 2015).[13]

The mukube is part of a family of closely related bows that include the Zulu *umqangala*, the Nyasa *mtangala*, the Sotho *lekope*, the Tswana *lengope*, the Pondo and Xhosa *inkinge*, the Korana Khoe *gabus* and the Venda *lugube*. All of these instruments share nearly identical organologically features, including a single, undivided string. By 'pressing the fingers against the string to change its effective length', players are able to produce multiple fundamental pitches (Jones 1992: 60).

In 1970, ethnomusicologist Robert Kauffman called the *mukube* 'rather uncommon' in Zimbabwe and suggested it was most commonly played in the district of Murewa (1970: 38). Yet both ethnographic and historical accounts suggest the instrument's range extended far beyond Murewa. In this chapter, for example, Sekuru Chigamba recalls his father Chigamba Tavasika playing mukube in the north-eastern region of Guruve in the 1940s.[14]

Written records illustrate that the *mukube* has been played in Zimbabwe since at least 1891, when Theodore Bent observed residents near Masvingo playing 'a sort of Jew's harp, made out of a reed and string, giving forth a very faint and ineffective sound' (1895: 82). Although Bent did not record the instrument's name, his description strongly suggests that it was a *mukube*. The following year, Bent obtained a similar instrument, which he described as a 'bow of pale jointed cane ornamented with patches of incised triangle'.[15] This instrument, which is now held at the British Museum, appears in Balfour's history of bow (1899: 14).[16]

In 1895, German missionary Carl Hoffman likewise heard the *mukube*, which he identified by name:

> The Makaranga also have, amongst others, a musical instrument in the shape of a so-called toy crossbow, only that it is made from reed. The one end of the instrument is taken into the mouth while the other rests between the thumb and index finger of the left hand. The right hand strikes the bowstring close to the mouth with a splinter of wood, while the left-hand fingers that are still free are pushed along the bowstring as one does with a violin, thus producing the different notes. *O no liza mochube*, they say, i.e. that's the way the mochube plays.
>
> (1981: 79; my translation)

Together, these accounts suggest that the *mukube* has been played across a wide geographic area in Zimbabwe. Yet scholars have generally treated the *mukube* as unworthy of serious consideration, reflecting a more general disregard for musical bows. As Zimbabwean academic George Kahari put it, 'the *chipendani* and the *mukube* are not worth talking about as they are personal and individual instruments. They are regarded as anti-social instruments which require no audience participation' (1981: 87).

Even in comparison to the *chipendani*, the *mukube* remains particularly marginalized. In regard to the well-known twentieth-century bow player Frank Gomba, for example, ethnomusicologist Tony Perman has observed that Gomba's *mukube* recordings 'have not been influential' in comparison to his *chipendani* recordings (2007: 36). Apart from the analysis of two *mukube* songs in Robert Kauffman's dissertation on multi-part relationships in Shona music, this particular bow has rarely received little more than a passing mention, mainly in the context of general surveys of Zimbabwean musical instruments.

The ground-bow is unique among Zimbabwean bows in that its resonating chamber is constructed by digging a hole directly in the earth (Figure 5.4). On Sekuru Muradzikwa's instrument, a sheet of scrap metal is then secured over this resonating chamber with bricks. The ground-bow's single string, for which Sekuru Muradzikwa used a length of wire, is then affixed to a young sapling or

Figure 5.4 Sekuru Muradzikwa plays the ground-bow. Photo: Debby Chen.

tree branch at one end, and to the underside of the sheet of metal at the other. The resulting tension bends the tree branch into a quarter-arch shape.

The ground-bow has been documented across much of sub-Saharan Africa, making it one of the most widely distributed instruments on the African continent (see Kyker, forthcoming).[17] While scholars have posited that it is played mainly in equatorial regions, however, the ground-bow's range extends at least as far north-west as the Fouta-Djallon region of Guinea, and as far south as the Northern Transvaal. It is also widespread throughout eastern Africa, including many islands in the Indian Ocean. In addition, the ground-bow reaches over the Black Atlantic, where it is played in diasporic locations such as Colombia, Cuba and the Dominican Republic.

Many writers have suggested that the ground-bow is either quickly disappearing or has already vanished in certain areas where it was formerly played. As Sekuru Muradzikwa was the only musician I was able to identify who was still actively playing the ground-bow, the instrument indeed appears endangered – possibly critically so – in Zimbabwe. At the same time, there is evidence that the ground-bow is still actively played in several countries. This includes written accounts, photographs and online videos from within the past few decades, which depict both children and adults playing ground-bows in places such as

Uganda, the Central African Republic, Cameroon, Gabon, Mauritius, Colombia and Haiti. Many decades after Sekuru Muradzikwa first played the ground-bow while herding cattle in the 1940s and 1950s, he reconstructed the instrument just outside his modest brick security post at the entrance to Imire's Sable Lodge. As Sekuru Muradzikwa demonstrated his playing technique, he took particular care to identify exactly how to pinch the instrument's single string in order to produce the desired pitch:

> When you are playing, now, if you make your own and are playing it, the tune, you pinch it here, if you pinch it here, you hear the right sound, if you pinch it here, you'll see that it is square, that's where the tune is.
>
> (Interview, 29 July 2006)

Sekuru Muradzikwa's attention to pitch was mirrored by a concern for timbre, leading him to place jacaranda flowers and leaves in the resonating chamber of his ground-bow in order to subtly temper the instrument's sound (Figure 5.5).

Figure 5.5 Jacaranda leaves fill the resonating chamber of Sekuru Muradzikwa's ground-bow. Photo: Debby Chen.

Reflecting Sekuru Muradzikwa's early experiences, the ground-bow is nearly universally described as a children's instrument and is specifically associated with cattle herding across much of sub-Saharan Africa (see Kyker, forthcoming). In our interviews, Sekuru Chigamba similarly recalled playing the ground-bow as a young herdboy, telling me, '*Kambuya-mbuya* was played by people who went with the cattle. Even girls who went with the cows, herding cattle, they could also play. It is something for young children' (Interview, 1 March 2016). With its unique construction, distinctive timbre, complex bent pitches, and widespread associations with children, herding and the forest, the ground-bow possesses both a fascinating sound and a rich social identity.

Bow musicians as multi-instrumentalists

Although the sources remain sparse, the literature on Zimbabwean musical bows regularly describes bow musicians as multi-instrumentalists. Like Sekuru Chigamba, many of these musicians specialize in a particular combination of instruments, involving the *chipendani* and the *mbira dzavadzimu*. Among these musicians are Ephat Mujuru, Chris Mhlanga, Sydney Musarurwa Nyandoro, Mondrek Muchena and Golden Nhamo. Other musicians, such as Chaka Chawasarira and Jacob Mhungu, have played *chipendani* and at least one other type of *mbira*, such as the *njari*, *karimba* or *matepe*.[18] Yet other accounts refer to bow musicians playing instruments such as the *ngoma* drums and the acoustic guitar. Sekuru Chigamba's father Chigamba Tavasika, for example, played both *mukube* and *ngoma*, specializing in a type of drumming known as *mangwingwindo*.[19] Similarly, Klaus-Peter Brenner describes the *chipendani* player Green Tamanikwa Mususa as the organizer of a *ngoma* group in Mabvuku township.[20] Like Sekuru Chigamba, some bow players are versed in multiple instruments. Thomas Turino, for example, describes Jacob Mhungu as playing *chipendani, njari* and guitar.[21]

At the same time, bow musicians frequently play more than one type of musical bow. During my fieldwork, for example, Sekuru Muradzikwa was actively playing both *chipendani* and ground-bow, while Sekuru Chigamba had experience playing the *chipendani, mukube,* and ground-bow Sekuru Chigamba's grandson Brian Chigamba further played both ground-bow and *chipendani*. Other examples in the literature include the noted bow musician Frank Gomba, who played *chipendani, mukube* and *chizambi*, as well as Sydney Musarurwa Nyandoro and Ephat Mujuru, both of whom played *chipendani* and *mukube*.

Together, these examples suggest that the many instruments within Zimbabwe's large family of musical bows should be treated as related, rather than separate. While this conclusion may seem self-evident, it has important organological implications. Among them, for example, I argue that the ground-bow should be classified as a bow, rather than a harp (Kyker, forthcoming).[22] The tendency for bow musicians to play multiple instruments also suggests exciting possibilities for further research. For example, scholars interested in locating bow musicians might begin by determining whether *mbira* musicians also play musical bows. While bows are generally considered to be rare, endangered or disappearing, this approach may well reveal that musical bows are more commonly played than previously assumed, opening space for more detailed ethnographic fieldwork. On the other hand, it may reveal bow musicians who are no longer actively playing, opening space for bow music revival efforts.

By approaching musical bows in relation to other instruments, scholars may also develop important new questions, insights and perspectives bridging wide fields of musical practice. For example, musical bows appear to constitute an initial point of entry that facilitates the performance of other musical instruments, with implications for the study of children's music, musical transmission and the cross-fertilization of musical genres. In Zimbabwe, specific links between *chipendani* and *mbira* dzavadzimu playing also offer ethnographic evidence strengthening Klaus-Peter Brenner's analytical work, which suggests that the deep structures of *mbira dzavadzimu* songs were likely derived from *chipendani* music. At a regional level, this approach may lead to remapping the geographic distribution of individual bows, and analysing relationships between regional variants of a single bow type.

The social dynamics of bow music

In his study of Basotho migrant poetry, David Coplan reminds us that expressive forms are produced, received and interpreted in locally determined contexts, imbuing them with 'an inherent potential for social critique' (1994: 27). As one among many forms of what Coplan calls 'African auriture', bow music has frequently been mobilized in the service of social criticism, opening space for historically grounded analyses of evolving social forces. Zimbabwean chipendani player Green Tamanikwa Musasa's song 'Murungu', or 'White Man', for example, illustrates how bow musicians have responded to colonial oppression (see condensed transcription and analysis in Brenner 1997: 42–3). Recalling his interactions with Mususa, Klaus-Peter Brenner told me:

> Mususa gave the following information: This song was composed by an elder brother of his in the 1950s, while – according to the then legal regulations of the *chibaro* system of forced labour – being compelled to work on a white man's farm. This meant that he was not free to quit that job by himself. Only if the employer would agree to release the worker by formally signing his worker's passport he would be free to leave and move away in search of another job ... Mususa's brother hated being trapped in that exploitative situation and subversively used to cheer up himself and his co-workers and fellows-in-misery by playing and singing this *chipendani* song, containing lyrics like 'Hey boss, sign my worker's passport, I want to leave', especially funny when performed in the presence of that – addressed, but unsuspecting – white 'boss'.
>
> (Brenner, pers comm)

In this account, we see an example of the type of direct musical protest that emerged as Zimbabweans confronted settler colonialism.[23]

At the same time, I argue that bow music is caught up in more subtle forms of ongoing social negotiation, enabling musicians to secure certain freedoms in contexts that are otherwise governed by considerations of age, gender and classificatory kinship relations. Drawing on fieldwork with Sekuru Muradzikwa and Sekuru Chigamba, I illustrate how musical bows have enabled children to engage in normally prohibited forms of verbal expression, facilitated communication between unmarried men and women, and opened space for relaxed, informal interactions between parents and children, whose relationships are normally characterized by distance, formality and respect.

The ground-bow: Children making fun of elders

As elsewhere in Africa, the Zimbabwean ground-bow has been played primarily by young children and is specifically associated with herding. As Sekuru Muradzikwa told me, 'I used to herd cattle, so I came up with this' (Interview, 12 October 2003). Although the ground-bow's construction is site-specific, the instrument can easily be moved from place to place, as its various components are easily taken apart, transported and reassembled. As Sekuru Chigamba told me:

> The way we played, it would happen that when you are really into it, your cattle wandered off. Yes. Because you would be enjoying it, as your cattle are on their way. So, what we would do is, once you play and play, you would go after your cattle, and bring them back nearby, then play some more. If you saw that there was no longer sufficient pasture for your cattle there, you would detach it, and go with it. You would get to a place where you see that there is enough pasture, and dig another hole there. You would reassemble it there, and start to play again.
>
> (Interview, Chigamba, 1 March 2016)

As herding often took children quite some distance from the family's home, ground-bow playing constituted a strikingly autonomous sphere of children's musical practice.[24] Far from the watchful gaze of their elders, ground-bow playing enabled children to indulge in forms of musical expression that were otherwise strictly prohibited. Indeed, Sekuru Chigamba's name for the ground-bow, *kambuya-mbuya*, comes directly from lyrics he recalled singing while playing the ground-bow as a child. As he told me:

> We called it "*kambuya-mbuya*" – it's embarrassing! This is what we used to sing:
>
> | | |
> |---|---|
> | *Panyo pambuya-mbuya* | From grandmother's anus |
> | *Panobva mukonde mukuru* | Comes a big heap of dung |
> | *Panyo pambuya-mbuya* | From grandmother's anus |
> | *Panobva mukonde mukuru* | Comes a big heap of dung |

Sekuru Chigamba explained these lyrics quite literally, saying:

> When grandmother goes to the forest to do her business, when she needs to defecate, her waste is very big, bigger than that of young children. Yes, that's why we played it in the forest, because that's what we were talking about! Imagine. That's why we called it "kambuya-mbuya." And that's why we played it in the forest, rather than playing it at home. Because our grandmother would beat us! So, we weren't allowed to play it at home. They used to say, "Go and play there, in the forest!" Yes, so, it was so embarrassing when we started to sing. You could also sing other songs, but they told us not to bring it home because they know that we would end up singing that one anyway. Maybe we start off singing something else, but we'll end up singing that! Because that's *kambuya-mbuya*. So that is what we used to play, as young children.
>
> (Interview, 31 May 2017)

In a similar vein, Sekuru Muradzikwa associated the ground-bow with children's herding games. Among them, he described inciting children to fight by building mounds of sand, which represented their mothers' breasts. As he told me:

> When we sat down I would take the other children and mound the soil into breasts, saying, 'Sarudzai and Chipo, come here. This is Sarudzai's mother's breast, and this is Chipo's mother's breast, so come and destroy them.' So Chipo would destroy Sarudzai's mother's breast, and Sarudzai would run and destroy her mother's, until they would end up fighting. You see? Now they would begin to fight. After they fought and fought, when I saw that one of them was getting hurt, I would say, 'Stop, stop, stop'. And they would stop. They would be crying, and I would shush them. (Interview, 12 October 2003)[25]

Like Sekuru Chigamba's ground-bow song, these games were prohibited by adults. Relating her own memories of playing this game, Zimbabwean author Tererai Trent has observed, 'This kind of talk excites every adolescent cattle herder because it is taboo. In my culture, a mother's breast is not something with which you play around! Mothers are well respected and their reproductive parts are generally not discussed' (2017: 99). Just as Sekuru Chigamba's grandmother would beat her grandchildren for playing the ground-bow, Sekuru Muradzikwa's headmaster would thus beat him for these herding games:

> Now, at school one day, that is when I was beaten by the headmaster, who said, 'Every day you are taking other children and making them fight ... ' That is when I stopped. You see? I never did it again. But those children grew up to be shrewd. Yes, because, if they beat you, you become shrewd. You won't be naïve.
> (Interview, 12 October 2003)

In these accounts, the ground-bow emerges as part of a constellation of related activities with close links to cattle herding, through which children found space to engage in otherwise prohibited forms of social expression.

The Chipendani: Opening space for courtship

In contrast to the ground-bow, which Sekuru Chigamba describes as an instrument for 'young children', the *chipendani* is associated with older children, adolescents and adults. Performed by men and women alike, the *chipendani* is played in diverse social contexts (Kyker 2019). Among them, however, the instrument appears to have particular associations with courtship, marriage and relations between agnatic kin. As Sekuru Chigamba told me:

Chipendani was for people who were mature, who were grown, such as boys who were becoming young men, about whom it was said, 'Let him go look for a girl.' Yes, that is when he would play *chipendani*. Walking along, going wherever he was headed.

(Interview, 1 March 2016)

In a previous article, I have suggested that chipendani songs often revolve around issues of agricultural labour, gender, cattle, courtship and marriage (Kyker 2019). Furthering these associations, Sekuru Chigamba suggests that *chipendani* performance created opportunities for young men and women to communicate in an environment where their interactions were otherwise tightly controlled. As he explained to Sekuru Muradzikwa's son Polite:

One of the *chipendani's* uses was for courtship. If you noticed that the girls at a particular house were not allowed to come outside, you would take your *chipendani* as you passed by, walking very slowly, and playing your *chipendani*. Then she would have come out to ask, 'What is it that you are playing?" You would answer, and that is how you would have the chance to speak to her. Because parents were so strict with their child; they wouldn't want to see her talking to a boy. So to speak to a boy – if you are passing by while playing she will ask you what it is. She is asking you about it. That is when you find time to speak to her of those things, of loving each other. You would play and play. During the time you are playing, she would be listening. And when asked, 'Hey, who was that you were talking to?' she would reply, 'He was playing *chipendani*, and it was very exciting.'

(Interview, 29 February 2016)

In this account, Sekuru Chigamba brings walking, bow playing, and courtship together in ways that resonate strongly with Angela Impey's recent scholarship on women's music in Maputaland. In her work, Impey illustrates how walking, bow playing, and singing have mediated relationships between people, environments and political histories of belonging and displacement (2018).[26] Yet Sekuru Chigamba's narrative retains distinctly different contours. Featuring male rather than female bow musicians, his account illustrates how young men strategically linked walking and bow playing in order to produce a particular form of musical mobility as they traversed public areas located in close proximity to the domestic spaces where young women dwelled. Through the practice of walking-while-playing, young men rendered themselves uniquely able to broadcast their presence in an unthreatening way as they sought to approach young women who would otherwise be prohibited from speaking with them.

Mukube: *Light-hearted interactions between avoidant relations*

As I have discussed in the previous section on bow musicians as multi-instrumentalists, Sekuru Chigamba's father, Chigamba Tavasika, was an accomplished musician who played both *mukube* and *ngoma*, specializing in the ritual drumming style of *mangwingwindo*. Furthering his ritual ties, he also served as a *mutapi*, or interpreter, for an ancestral spirit known as Dumbu in the nearby village of Kamuchanyu. After the colonial state seized their land following the Land Apportionment Acts of 1930 and 1941, the Chigamba family was forced to destroy their houses and relocate within an increasingly crowded 'native reserve', while their old village was sold to a white settler. Out of economic necessity, Sekuru Chigamba's father worked on a series of white-owned commercial farms. As a result, Sekuru Chigamba lived with both his paternal and maternal grandmothers for several years.

Despite these extended absences, Chigamba Tavasika's musical activities were particularly important in shaping his relationship with his son. Many years later, for example, Sekuru Chigamba recalled his father's mukube playing with exceptional fondness:

> When my father came home after drinking beer ... he would take his *mukube* and play. This was so exciting, because my father never talked much; he was very quiet. He was so quiet that if you sat with him, there wasn't ever much to talk about. If you told an interesting story and he so much as smiled and said, 'Oh', that was enough – at least he had smiled. So, he was someone who didn't talk much. So, whenever he ended up picking up his *mukube* when he was drunk, oh, we had to smile. He would be telling us all kinds of interesting things, and we wondered, was this our father? He would play his *mukube*, finish playing, and go to bed. That was the end of the evening.
>
> (Interview, 31 May 2017)

While Sekuru Chigamba describes his father as particularly reserved, relationships between parents and children are normally characterized by deference, respect and a certain degree of social distance in Zimbabwe. In contrast to grandparents, who are treated as *vasekedzani*, or 'those between whom there is laughter', parents are treated as *vanyarikani*, or 'those between whom there is shyness' (Fortune 1974: 28). Accordingly, children are expected to follow 'complicated rules of address and deportment, whereby a child must address a whole range of persons as *baba* (father) and *sekuru* (uncle) or *amai* (mother) and *ambuya* (grandmother) and behave with appropriate respect towards these people' (Pearce 1990: 148). Sekuru Chigamba's account illustrates how his father's *mukube* playing loosened these strict rules of deportment, creating moments of exceptional intimacy between them.

Several years ago, Sekuru Chigamba made his own mukube in order to play the songs he remembered hearing his father play. As he told me:

> The *mukube* is good. I have a *mukube* mainly so that I can maintain my father's instrument, and keep one in my home with me. So, that is how I came to seek one out, and stay with it. And now, it is being recorded; my father has come back!
> (8 March 2016)

Like his father, Sekuru Chigamba selected a length of river reed for the stave of his *mukube*. While the single string on his father's instrument was of cow sinew, however, Sekuru Chigamba's was made of nylon.[27]

The *mukube* is played with a plectrum made of cow horn. At the time of my research, however, Sekuru Chigamba did not have a plectrum, rending his instrument unplayable. The first step in recording his mukube playing, then, was to visit a local slaughterhouse in search of a suitable horn. After wandering

Figure 5.6 Cow horn plectrums made by Sekuru Chigamba. Photo: Jennifer W. Kyker.

the grounds for over an hour in search of the manager, we met one of Sekuru Chigamba's maternal cousins named Muriro, who worked at the slaughterhouse by sheer happenstance. With Muriro's assistance, Sekuru Chigamba obtained two horns, carved thin plectrums (Figure 5.6) and began practising his *mukube*. During our recording sessions Sekuru Chigamba performed two songs, both of which he remembered hearing his father play as a child. As he told me:

> There is one about horses running, and then there is 'Paraffin, Chinyemwere'
> *You've poured paraffin on me, Chinyemwere*
> *You've poured paraffin on me, Chinyemwere*
> That is the second one. That is what my father used to play. Those are the only two that I know. But I will look for my own songs to play on it. (8 March 2016)[28]

While Sekuru Chigamba's repertory was limited to these two songs, simply possessing a *mukube* was important in keeping alive his memories of the exceptionally intimate moments associated with his father's bow playing. At the same time, Sekuru Chigamba's mukube playing constituted tenuous space for an instrument that appears to have largely disappeared from the Zimbabwean musical landscape.

Abandoning the term 'self-delectative'

In a previous article, I have argued against conceptions of the *chipendani* as 'self-delectative' or intended solely for the performer's own enjoyment (Kyker 2019).[29] I conclude this chapter by revisiting this argument, which has significant implications for bow music scholarship writ large. The term 'self-delectative' rose to prominence largely through the work of Hugh Tracey, who used it to describe a great number of the bow songs he collected throughout Southern Africa.[30] While musical bows have certainly been played in solitary context, their categorization as 'self-delectative' has produced certain conceptual distortions. Among them, the rich frequencies of musical bows have been described as 'almost inaudible' to anyone but the performer (Kauffman 1970: 31). As a result, these instruments have been rendered 'not worth talking about', leading to the erasure of their complex social dynamics and diverse performance contexts (Kahari 1981: 87).

My work strongly refutes established conceptions of musical bows as 'self-delectative'. As I have illustrated, Zimbabwean musical bows have participated in the creation, maintenance and ongoing negotiation of social relationships at several levels. Whether played to express irreverence towards elders, to attract a life partner or to entertain children and grandchildren, bow music is fundamentally geared towards an audience. The literature is similarly full of accounts describing bow music played in beer-halls, at funerals, and by wandering musicians soliciting money (Malamusi 1996), as well as at wrestling matches, for dancing, and even to announce the arrival of guests (Ballgobin and Antoine 2003).

By privileging 'self communication' as the primary purpose of bow playing throughout Southern Africa, Tracey's work heavily influenced subsequent readings of musical bows. For too long, however, the term 'self-delectative' has silenced the diverse range of social contexts in which musical bows have historically been performed. Particularly in light of the current resurgence of interest in bow music, scholars must treat solitary performance as one among many contexts, actively resist stereotypical portrayals of musical bows as 'self-delectative' instruments and critically interrogate the social dynamics of bow music.

Conclusion

The *chipendani*, *mukube* and ground-bow are but a few of Zimbabwe's many musical bows. In turn, Zimbabwean bows belong to the large family of musical bows found throughout Africa and associated diasporic locations. In their detailed oral narratives, both Sekuru Chigamba and Sekuru Muradzikwa call attention to the social dynamics of bow music performance. Whether played by children singing vulgar songs about their elders, by young men hoping to entice marriageable girls outside for a few moments of stolen conversation or by fathers sharing intimate moments with their children, musical bows are deeply engaged in producing moments of autonomy, intimacy and freedom.

My discussion of musical bows in Zimbabwe suggests several lines of enquiry for scholarship on bow music throughout Africa and beyond. As I have illustrated, bow musicians often report playing other instruments, with particularly strong connections between musical bows and various types of mbira. Frequently, a single individual also plays more than one type of musical bow. As I have suggested, these combined tendencies offer new possibilities for researchers interested in locating contemporary bow musicians across a wide area in sub-Saharan Africa. In turn, further scholarship with these musicians is likely to reshape our understanding of the geographic distribution both of individual bow and of relationships between various instruments within the bow music family.

At the same time, I suggest that scholars of other musical traditions are likewise poised to benefit from serious consideration of musical bows. Given the social dimensions of bow music, for example, I have argued against labelling musical bows as 'self-delectative'. Yet many other African instruments, vocal traditions and individual songs have likewise been described as 'self-delectative', including music played on various types of *mbira,* harps, lutes, zithers, flutes, ocarinas and xylophones. The import of my argument thus extends well beyond the study of musical bows, for the numerous recordings, instruments and practices currently labelled 'self-delectative' similarly deserve critical reassessment.

Notes

1   Among them are other types of *mbira,* such as the *matepe, njari* and *mbira dzaVaNdau;* aerophones such as the *chigufe, mutoriro* and *nyanga* panpipes; and idiophones such as the *kavembe* shaker. Zimbabwean drums, collectively known as *ngoma,* represent an exceptionally wide area of musical practice, encompassing drums such as *mhito, dandi, mutumba, mhiningo, usindi* and *mbete-mbete* (Kyker 2016).
2   The mukube is also referred to as *chimukubhe, chimukube, kamukubhe* or *mochube,* and is similar to the South African *umqangala.* The chidangari is also referred to as *chimadangari* or *kambuko,* and the wedza as *wedsa* or *widsi.* The *dimbwa,* an unbraced bow with a gourd resonator affixed quite near one end of the stave, is also referred to as *dimbga, katimbwa, kalumbo* or *kalumbu, and* is similar to the Zulu *ugubu.* The chitende is also variously referred to as *chinyamatende, chimatende, chimadandari, chidandari* or *chitandari,* and is similar to the South African *umakhweyane.* The gourd-resonated hugu is also referred to as *mahuga* and is a likely relation of the Angolan *hungu.*
3   The chimwanikoda is also referred to as *chimvokomvoko* and is similar to the *ximbvokombvoko* (Mucavele 2018). The incanco is also referred to as *ichacho* and is similar to the Chwana *segankuru.*
4   The chizambi is also referred to as *chinyamazambi, chinyamadzimbi, chimazambi, chizambi, chitambe, chizambe* or *mazambi,* and is similar to South Africa's *isizenze.*
5   https://research.britishmuseum.org/research/collection_online/collection_object_ details/collection_image_gallery.aspx?partid=1&assetid=176957001&object id=604896 (accessed 25 November 2019).
6   For a detailed analysis of this problem as it pertains to the ground-bow, see Kyker (forthcoming).
7   For further discussion see Kyker (forthcoming).

8   For more on the challenges of working on endangered instruments for which only a small number of musicians may be identified, see Kyker, (forthcoming).
9   Imire was founded in 1948 by Norman and Gilly Travers, and continues to be run by the Travers family. Because of Imire's black rhino breeding programme, the property was exempted from former President Robert Mugabe's chaotic land redistribution programme.
10 Illustrating the type of humorous banter that often accompanies his chipendani songs, Sekuru Muradzikwa frequently refers to Buhera by the acronym 'BBC', or 'Buhera, Beautiful Country'.
11 For more on Sekuru Muradzikwa's chipendani playing, see Kyker (2019).
12 For a detailed discussion of the chipendani, see Brenner (2019).
13 Among these many differences, Kauffman suggests that the mukube 'differs from the chipendani in the use of fewer harmonics' (1970: 38).
14 The Chigamba family has lived in Guruve for at least seven generations, according to an oral genealogy recounted by Sekuru Chigamba. See https://sekuru.org/familytreepaternal/ (accessed 25 November 2019).
15 https://research.britishmuseum.org/research/collection_online/collection_object_details/collection_image_gallery.aspx?partid=1&assetid=176957001&objectid=604896 (accessed 25 November 2019).
16 Despite Balfour's inclusion of this bow, Charles Camp and Bruno Nettl overlooked the mukube in their subsequent discussion of the umqangala and related bows, stating, 'Nowhere between South Africa and Nyasaland were references to this particular instrument found' (1955: 67). As I discuss in a forthcoming article on the ground-bow in Africa, research on musical bows remains particularly marked by similar failures to identify, acknowledge and analyse existing sources (Kyker, forthcoming).
17 In this article, I argue that certain disciplinary orientations have led ethnomusicologists to overlook the groundbow. While several factors have contributed to the ground-bow's marginalization, a long-standing scholarly disregard for children's music is foremost among them. At the same, the site-specific nature of the ground-bow's performance has eluded conventional approaches to musical collection and archiving, further contributing to its neglect.
18 Chaka Chawasarira specializes in *chipendani, matepe* and *karimba*, while Thomas Turino speculates that Jacob Mhungu likely played *chipendani* and *njari* (2000: 238).
19 https://sekuru.org/interpreting-for-the-spirits/
20 Among the four musicians with whom Klaus-Peter Brenner worked, Musasa was the only one who played neither another type of musical bow nor the *mbira*.

21 As Turino reports, 'The well-known guitarist from Masvingo Province, Jacob Mhungu, for example, told me that he had been a *chipendani* (bow) and lamellophone (probably *njari*) player in his rural home, but in 1949 was inspired to take up the guitar after he had seen movies with country and western performer Tex Ritter at a mission school' (2000: 238).

22 Among other considerations, the term 'harp' renders this monochord instrument exceptional within an organological family that primarily includes instruments with multiple strings. As a monochord instrument, the ground-bow's playing technique and musical sound share important commonalities with that of other musical bows. With these considerations in mind, I argue that while the term 'ground harp' may be technically correct according to the rigid demands of Western organology, it is in fact a misnomer that misdirects ground-bow scholarship by obscuring the instrument's multivalent relationships to other African musical bows. The term 'ground bow', on the other hand, places it firmly within an established world of musical practice.

23 For more on musical protest in Zimbabwe, see my chapter in the *Oxford Handbook of Protest Music* (Kyker, forthcoming).

24 Sekuru Chigamba, for example, recalls herding cattle as far as Chihwe Mountain, located at least three miles away from the family home.

25 Similarly, Tamanikwa Mususa 'used to closely associate the playing of *chipendani* music with some other – though non-musical – rural pastime activities with homemade toys such as throwing spears or whipping spin tops.' Brenner (pers. comm. 15 October 2015).

26 Beyond the Zimbabwean context described by Sekuru Chigamba, connections between musical bows and courtship are evident throughout Southern Africa. In neighbouring Mozambique and South Africa, for example, Thomas Johnston has reported that the Shangana-Tsonga xipendana, a close relative of the chipendani, is played mostly by young girls. Johnston directly links xipendana playing to courtship, suggesting 'the girl who plays the bow has generally manufactured it, with help from a suitor' (1980: 264). Similarly, Percival Kirby has described the lekope, a close relative of the Zimbabwean mukube, as integral to Pedi marriage negotiations, stating, 'A girl will not marry a youth who is not a performer, as she fears that she might not be allowed to go to her husband' (1965: 233). More recently, Tandile Mandela has asserted: 'There is no doubt that the umakhweyana played a special role in Zulu courtship processes, which involved young girls and young men' (2005: 46).

27 In a previous article, I have argued that the *chipendani* is closely associated with cattle (Kyker 2019). Sekuru Chigamba's description of the *mukube*'s construction extends some of these associations to the *mukube*.

28 With respect to these lyrics, Sekuru Chigamba said, 'It means, "You have provoked me, and now that you have provoked me, we will fight." To say, "You have poured paraffin on me" is to say that you have provoked me.'
29 Among the scholars who use the term 'self-delectative' or depict bow music as nearly inaudible to all but the performer are Tracey (1957), Brenner (1997) List (1971), Kauffman (1976) and Joseph (1983).
30 The largest single collection of Tracey's recordings is held in the audio archive of the International Library of African Music.

References

Balfour, Henry (1899), *The Natural History of the Musical Bow. A Chapter in the Developmental History of Stringed Instruments of Music*, Oxford: Clarendon.

Ballgobin, D. Veena and Antoine Marchaline (2003), 'Traditional Musical Instruments from Oral Tradition: Folk Music in Mauritius', *Revi Kiltir Kreol* 3: 69–82.

Bent, Theodore (1895), *The Ruined Cities of Mashonaland: Being a Record of Excavation and Exploration in 1891, with a Chapter on the Orientation and Mensuration of the Temples by R. M. W. Swan*, London: Longmans.

Brenner, Klaus-Peter (1997), *Chipendani und Mbira: Musikinstrumente, nichtbegriffliche Mathematik und die Evolution der harmonischen Progressionen in der Musik der Shona in Zimbabwe*. Abhandlungen der Akademie der Wissenschaften in Göttingen, Philologisch-Historische Klasse, 3rd Series, 221. With 2 companion audio CDs, Göttingen: Vandenhoeck & Ruprecht.

Brown, William Harvey (1899), *On the South African Frontier: The Adventures and Observations of an American in Mashonaland and Matabeleland*, New York: Charles Scribner's Sons.

Camp, Charles and Bruno Nettl (1955), 'The Musical Bow in Southern Africa', *Anthropos* 50 (1–3): 65–80.

Chikowero, Mhoze (2007), 'The State and Music Policy in Post-colonial Zimbabwe, 1980–2000', *Muziki* 4 (1): 111–28.

Coplan, David (1994), *In the Time of Cannibals: The Word Music of South Africa's Basotho Migrants*, Chicago: University of Chicago Press.

Ellert, H. (1984), *The Material Culture of Zimbabwe*, Harare: Longman.

Fortune, John (1974), 'Nhango and Ndyaringo: Two Complimentary Poetic Genres', *Zambezia* 3 (2): 27–50.

Fürniss, Susanne (2012), 'Morphologies et usages: Laharpe-en-terre d'Afrique Centrale face à la classification universelle des instruments de musique', in Ignace de Keyser (éd.), *Annual Meeting of the International Committee of Musical Instruments Museums and Collections*, Coll. Documents de Sciences humaines et sociales, 9–20, Tervuren, MRAC.

Hoffmann, C.A.G., D.E.H., Neitz and H.G.C.M., Neitz 1981, *Das Tagebuch des Missionars Carl Hoffmann – The Diary of Missionary Carl Hoffmann*. Volume 2: 18 July 1894–7 April 1895. Available online: http://uir.unisa.ac.za/handle/10500/5249

Huwiler, Kurt (1995), *Musical Instruments of Africa*, Harare: Mambo Press.

Impey, Angela (2018), *Song Walking: Women, Music, and Environmental Justice in an African Borderland*, Chicago: University of Chicago Press.

Jeffery, Laura and Rebecca Rotter (2018), 'Safeguarding Sega: Transmission, Inscription, and Appropriation of Chagossian Intangible Cultural Heritage', *International Journal of Heritage Studies* 25 (10): 1020–33.

Johnston, Thomas (1980), *The Mqangala and Xipendana Musical Bows of the Shangana-Tsonga*, Afrika und Übersee: Sprachen, Kulturen 63 (2): 257–68.

Jones, Claire (1992), *Making Music: Musical Instruments in Zimbabwe Past and Present*, Oxford: Baobab Books.

Joseph, Rosemary (1983), 'Zulu Women's Music', *African Music* 6 (3): 53–89.

Kahari, George P. (1981), 'The History of the Shona Protest Song: A Preliminary Study', *Zambezia* 9 (2): 79–101.

Kauffman, Robert (1970), 'Multi-Part Relationships in the Shona Music of Rhodesia', PhD diss., University of California, Los Angeles.

Kirby, Percival (1965), *The Musical Instruments of the Native Races of South Africa*, Johannesburg: Witwatersrand University Press.

Kyker, Jennifer (2018), 'Reassessing the Zimbabwean Chipendani', *African Music* 10 (4): 40–66.

Kyker, Jennifer (forthcoming). '*Music under the Ground: Ethnomusicological Approaches to the Ground-Bow in Africa*," Ethnomusicology 65 (2).

List, George (1971), 'On the Non-Universality of Musical Perspectives', *Ethnomusicology* 15 (3): 399–402.

Malamusi, Moya (1996), 'Stringed Instrument Traditions in Southern Malawi', *African Music: Journal of the International Library of African Music* 7 (3): 60–6.

Mandela, Tandile. (2005), 'The Revival and Revitalization of Musical Bow Practice in South Africa', MMus diss., University of Cape Town.

Maraire, Dumisani (1982), 'The Position of Chipendani (bow instrument) in Shona Music Culture and Tradition', MA diss., University of Washington, Seattle.

Mason, Otis (1897), 'Geographical Distribution of the Musical Bow', *American Anthropologist* 10 (11): 377–80.

Matare, Joseph (1992), *Tawanda. Wie ein afrikanisches Kind Musik und usikinstrumente kennenlernt /Music and Musical Instruments in the Life of an African Child*, Zürich, Switzerland: Hug Musikverlag

Pallai, Károly Sándor (2017), *Subjectivités seychelloises:Identité et insularité dans la poésie seychelloise contemporaine*. Pécs: Presses de l'Université de Pécs.

Parent, Marie-Christine (2018), 'Le moutya à l'épreuve de la modernité seychelloise : Pratiquerun genre musical emblématique dans les Seychelles d'aujourd'hui (océan Indien)', PhD diss., Université Côte d'Azur.

Pearce, Carole (1990), 'Tsika, Hunhu, and the Moral Education of Primary School Children', *Zambezia* 17 (2): 145–60.

Perman, Tony (2007), 'Building Bridges: The Creative Processes of Chartwell Dutiro', in C. Dutiro and K. Howard (eds.), *Zimbabwe Mbira Music on an International Stage: Chartwell Dutiro's Life in Music*, 27–40, London: Ashgate.

Sachs, Curt (1913), *Real-Lexikon der Musikinstrumente, zugleich ein Polyglossar fur̈ das gesamte instrumentengebiet*, Berlin: J. Bard.

Snowden, A.E. (1938), 'Some Common Musical Instruments Found among the Native Tribes of Southern Rhodesia', *Native Affairs Department Annual (NADA)* 15: 99–103.

Stacey, Cara (2017), *The Makhweyane Bow of Swaziland: Music, Poetics, and Place*, PhD diss., University of Cape Town.

Trent, Teererai (2017), *The Awakened Woman: Remembering & Reigniting Our Sacred Dreams*, New York: Atria/Enliven Books.

Turino, Thomas (2000), *Nationalists, Cosmopolitans, and Popular Music in Zimbabwe*, Chicago: University of Chicago Press.

Winter, Julia Flora (1907), 'Home Life in Mt. Selinda', in *Life and Light for Woman*, Boston: Woman's Board of Missions.

'Zimbabwe News' (1979), Central Bureau of Information of the Zimbabwe National Union.

6

The *sitontolo* mouth bow of eSwatini: Embodiment, stories and music

Cara Stacey and Vusi Sibandze

Abstract

This chapter presents a profile of the *sitontolo* mouth-resonated musical bow from the Southern African kingdom of eSwatini (formerly Swaziland). It introduces this country and its cultural and musical environment and discusses the music of this rare instrument. Though there are few musicians who still make and perform with the *sitontolo*, it forms part of a network of other mouth-resonated musical bows across the Southern African region. The *sitontolo* songs performed by these musicians serve as rich texts filled with personal, artistic, moral and community-related information. This chapter draws upon the work of two contemporary musicians who play *sitontolo*: Bhemani Magagula and Solomon Shongwe. ESwatini provides an interesting case study of how nationalism and a traditionalist cultural construct can often both serve and neglect indigenous instrument performers. The *sitontolo* provides an example of how an indigenous instrumental tradition can be fluid and diverse while holding cultural and personal messages.

Introduction – The kingdom of eSwatini

This chapter draws upon research completed between 2014 and 2016, and additional ethnographic research completed in 2019 with two of the only contemporary musicians who continue to play *sitontolo*: Mkhulu Bhemani Magagula and Mkhulu Solomon Shongwe.[1]

ESwatini is a small landlocked country in eastern Southern Africa, situated between South Africa and Mozambique. This kingdom was known as Swaziland until 2018 when King Mswati III, the current monarch, renamed the country 'eSwatini' – the original SiSwati name for the kingdom. The national languages of eSwatini are siSwati and English. According to the local Central Statistical Office and projected from 2016 figures, the population of eSwatini is currently 1,132,700 with estimated unemployment at 41.7 per cent.[2] Seventy-five per cent of the population live in the diverse rural areas of the country and many urban-based people are closely connected via family to these regions.[3] ESwatini is a monarchy and is jointly ruled by King Mswati III, son of King Sobhuza II, and his mother, Queen Regent Ntfombi. The two royal leaders, along with a parliament and the current Prime Minister, Absalom Mandvulo Dlamini, rule the country with limited opposition in the form of trade union leaders and small political parties such as Pudemo and Swayoco.

Because of its geographic position, eSwatini has a rich and dynamic political and cultural history. As a nation, people in eSwatini were unified after the Mfecane wars under Ngwane III (who lived in the mid-1700s). They subsequently experienced colonial contact first through trade and land concessions in the eighteenth and nineteenth centuries, and then finally rule as a British protectorate during the twentieth century (Kuper 1963: 7). ESwatini was given independence in 1968 and the initial independence-era elections were won by the Imbokodvo National Movement, led by King Sobhuza II (Davies et al. 1985: 9). After King Sobhuza II's passing in 1981, his son Makhosedive (Mswati III) became king. Because of its location, eSwatini has been affected by regional events such as apartheid in South Africa and the independence and civil wars in Mozambique – from the participation and support of the Queen Mother Labotisbeni in early black South African opposition politics (MacMillan 1985: 647/8) to the housing of anti-apartheid activists notably at 43 Trelawney Park or KwaMagogo in Manzini. More recently, eSwatini served as a refuge for Mozambicans the civil war in their country. Regional events have affected eSwatini both positively and negatively since people first settled in the area.[4]

ESwatini is known internationally for its homogenous nationalism and large-scale performances of culture such as the Umhlanga and Incwala. As a small and relatively monocultural country, these ceremonies are important spaces for the kingdom to perform its identity. The cultural calendar in the country has significant events throughout the year from the Buganu ceremony in February to Umhlanga in August or September and Incwala in November or December. Many of these and other national and smaller local events and festivities integrally involve the performing arts and so these artistic practices are often used to represent national identity.

Music in eSwatini

Music and dance are interwoven into all of the large mass-participation ceremonies and festivals. Outside of these contexts, small scenes of diverse musicking exist in and around the urban hubs of Mbabane, Matsapha and Manzini. Though most young learners do not have access to formal arts (and specifically music) education in school, recent years have seen a growth in small, private music education programmes and opportunities. Beyond these, many young people learn to play instruments or to sing in the numerous churches active within the country, either in collaborative services or as a part of gospel choirs and bands. The Swaziland National Council of Arts and Culture oversee various artistic associations and support local traditions through these: such as the *a capella* choral tradition of *umbholoho*, music of local traditional instruments, local pop and hip-hop, and gospel. Increasingly, house music and other electronic dance musics are being produced locally through software and home studios and these genres are performed regularly on local radio. Through these informal and formal musical learning spheres, eSwatini is producing slowly growing numbers of individual visual artists, musicians and other performers.

Within indigenous music (referred to as 'traditional music' within eSwatini), the two prominent musical instruments performed in contemporary times are the *makhweyane* or *makhoyane* gourd-resonated, braced musical bow and the *sitolotolo* mouth harp or jews harp.[5] Similar to the Zulu *umakhweyane* and the xiTsonga *xitende*, the *makhweyane* is a large musical bow, usually played as accompaniment to songs about life, courtship and local news (Stacey 2017). Other instruments performed in eSwatini are the *inkhositina* or concertina, the *bhelebane/imfiliji* or harmonica, the *sikhelekehle* monochord bow and the guitar. Most of these instruments are performed by rurally based elderly men and women across the country. Although the guitar is commonly played across musical styles and so is played by many, the rest of these instruments is rarely performed with few or no young learners currently. Most of the performers of these instruments compose their own music and perform this music for themselves, their families and onstage when opportunities arise.

Despite their rarity, these indigenous instruments can be heard performed at events where what is deemed 'traditional' culture is performed and celebrated. In certain areas of the country, local organizers have created ensembles or 'teams' to perform this type of music, for example, Make ('mother') Cathrina Magagula and her fellow musicians in the Shewula region. Cathrina Magagula is a singer and *makhweyane* and *sitolotolo* player who has organized numerous large and small ensembles for ad hoc performances or tours. Gogo Khokhiwe Mphila, a *makhweyane* player based in the north-western Hhohho region of the country, is a notable composer and musician and plays with fellow traditional musicians in her locale. In recent years, both authors of this chapter have been involved in the ensemble Bashayi Bengoma – a fluid group of traditional musicians who have had numerous public performances.

The *sitontolo* mouth bow (Figure 6.1), is a rarely performed traditional instrument within eSwatini, with only two performers known by the authors, but due to these ensembles and ad hoc public performance opportunities, it still holds a position within a network of elderly but vibrant traditional musicians and their instruments.

Figure 6.1 Mkhulu Solomon Shongwe with his *sitontolo* bow at his home. Photo: C. Stacey.

The *sitontolo* mouth bow

The *sitontolo* is a mouth-resonated musical bow of approximately 70 – 110 cm in length. It is constructed out of a wooden stave with a cylindrical handle piece at its centre and a wire or nylon line that is drawn into the stave and braced at an off-centre position. Where the wire is drawn into the stave, it is done with a wound piece of string connected to the top of the stave (from the perspective of the performer's playing position) and to the right of the performer's handgrip. This brace creates two lengths of wire and so two different fundamental tones from which rhythmic and harmonic patterns are generated. When wire is preferred to the more modern nylon line, the wire can be burnt in ashes to increase its resonance and create a preferable tone quality (ibid.).

Historical writing on the *sitontolo* places it within a network of numerous regional organological bow variants, from the Karanga *tshipendani*, tshiVenda *tshigwana*, xiTsonga *isitontolo*, sePedi *lekope* and isiZulu *sitontolo*. Among this family of mouth-resonated, braced bows, Kirby describes three types:

> The first is the true Sotho type […] which is made in three pieces. The second imitates this externally, the barrel consisting of a length of hollow reed through which a suitable length of flexible wood is thrust, the projecting ends forming the two curved sections when strained by the string of ox-tendon. The third is made, like the *tshigwana* of the Venda, in one piece.
>
> (Kirby 2013: 311)

In eSwatini, the *sitontolo* is an example of the third type of braced mouth bow: one created from one piece of wood. The wood used to make it can be sourced from two different types of local trees: the *umnunu* or *liphambo* (Torchwood or small Torchwood tree, *balanites maughamii or balanites pedicellaris*), and the *lugagane* (Flamethorn, *acacia ataxacantha*). Prominent musician and instrument maker, Solomon Shongwe, describes the process of making a *sitontolo*:

> *Sitontolo ngikhandza lesihlahla similile lenje, hhayi lesikhulu nje lesilingene. Besengiyasigawula. Tehlukene ke letihlahla eh emagamato. Lona nje ngumnunu* [pointing at his instrument]. *Eh, labanye batsi liphambo. Ukhetsa tihlahla lotawutsi ungatibata bese tibalula. Tingabi deki. Nelugagane luningi nje lugagane la. Uyakhetsa lokutakhela sibesikhulu kanje* [pointing at his instrument] *nale livi laso libalikhulu.*
>
> (Shongwe 2019)

I find the mature tree that has germinated on its own, not a big one but moderately sized. Then I chop it down. They have got different names. This one is *umnunu* [pointing at his instrument]. Eh, others call it *liphambo*. You choose trees that, when you have planed [filed] them, become light in weight. It shouldn't be thick. Of *lugagane*, we have a lot here. You choose your preferred size [pointing at his instrument] and the voice is bigger.

(Shongwe 2019)

As the quote demonstrates, the length of the bow stave can vary depending on the performer's preference and larger bow staves create bigger sounds.

Like other mouth-resonated musical bows, the *sitontolo* is a quiet instrument and so tends to be performed alone without accompaniment. The natural amplification of the produced tones comes from the player's mouth, making the sound-producing capabilities of the instrument inherently related to small muscular movements within the throat and mouth and the player's body more broadly. The instrument is generally played as a solo instrument. The player will hold the cylindrical handle of the stave in his or her left hand while striking the wire with the right hand. The wire is struck with a small piece of metal, stick or hard wire – a plectrum or striker. The wooden stave is held so that the mouth of the player can be placed on the stave to the right of the handle. While the right hand strikes out a rhythmic pattern on the lower and upper portions of the wire (producing two different tones), the left-hand forefinger can be used to pluck the lower portion of the wire as an additional tone-producing technique. This finger-struck tone is used to create faster, interlocking tones between the broader struck patterns. This technique can be seen in Figure 6.2.

Tuning and hence the tonality of the *sitontolo* bow is variable. Shongwe (cited above) stated that he prefers the key of D, with his two *sitontolo* notes tuned to the interval of a perfect fourth, though Bhemani Magagula is less specific in his tuning preferences and with the instrument picture in Figure 6.2, played and sang for us with his *sitontolo* tuned to a diminished fourth.

A key aspect to the performance practice of this bow and its tonal identity emerges from the fundamental tones created by the struck wire portions and their resulting overtones. While playing the underlying rhythmic pattern of any song, the performer is able to highlight different overtones by opening and closing his or her mouth to different degrees while holding the bow stave in position, as Shongwe stated that

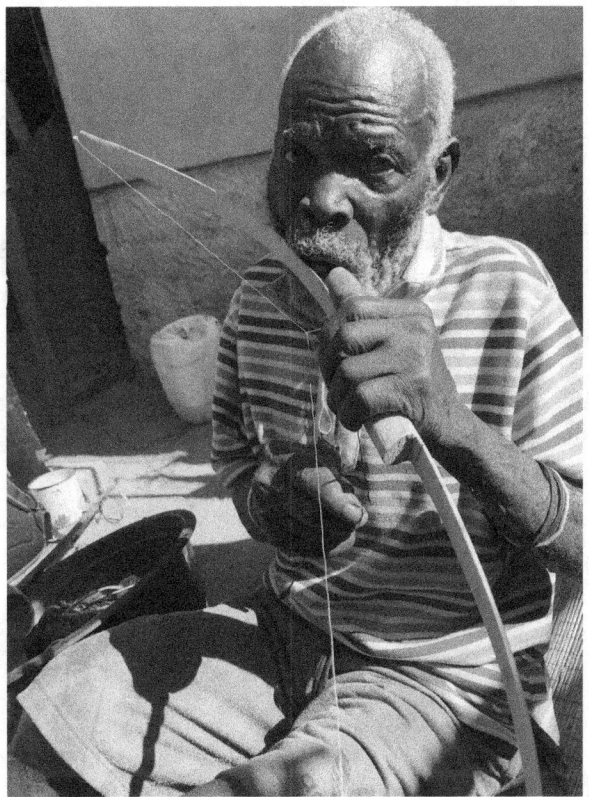

Figure 6.2 Mkhulu Bhemani Magagula playing *sitontolo* with a short, wire plectrum and left-hand forefinger. Photo: C. Stacey.

"*Uyawuvula lomlomo langekhatsi uphindze njalo uvale beseke lomsindvo uyancipha, uyakhula, njalo njalo*" ["The more you open the mouth inside, the sounds becomes lower (in pitch) and when you close it, the sound becomes high, again and again (in pitch)"].

(Shongwe 2019)

The following notated extract shows how overtone melodies are constructed from the struck pattern of the *sitontolo*. It is an instrumental composition by Shongwe and is titled '*Sawubona maguj'endlini*' which translates as 'Hello, the one who likes staying in the house'. In the transcription, one can see how the struck melody outlined by the *sitontolo* wire alternates down strikes on the strong beats (where the plectrum or striker hits the wire from above) and shorter interlocking strikes are created by the Shongwe's forefinger (indicated by the triangular *marcato* accents). The rhythmic profile of this song is lilting and the

Figure 6.3 An excerpt from Solomon Shongwe's *sitontolo* song 'Sawubona maguj'endlini'.

overtone melody highlights this with its prominent off-beat notes. The extract shows the overtone melody outlining the melodic structure implied by the struck pattern but also shows a variant effect created by Shongwe, where he creates a low overtone on the final quaver of each beat and, by opening his mouth quickly, creates a short glissando effect aspirated by a 'wa' vocal sound.

Learning and living: Performers of the *sitontolo*

As stated earlier, this research centres around two key *sitontolo* players. While Kirby writes that the *sitontolo* is only played by men within eSwatini, the performers did not acknowledge any gender division, and due to the small sample size of current performers, it is hard to identify any gender preference trends in players. Magagula is the older of the two players and is a prominent performer of indigenous instruments and musics in eSwatini. Magagula is unsure of his age but believes himself to be in his late eighties at the time of writing. He currently lives alone in the northern part of the country, where he plays his instruments for himself. Despite living alone in the rural areas, Magagula is a well-respected, traditional musician within the country. He has been recorded numerous times and most of the other traditional musicians within this musical community know his musical work well.

Mkhulu Shongwe is slightly younger and is based in the Shewula area of eSwatini, in the Lubombo ridge near to eSwatini's eastern border with Mozambique. Shongwe lives in this area with his family and works as a mixed-crop, subsistence farmer. Shongwe's introduction to playing the *sitontolo* is similar to that of many indigenous instrument performers in the country: most male and female musicians learned to play while minding livestock (*kulusa* in siSwati). He described the experience of learning from his older brothers:

> *Sitontolo ngasicala ngisengumfana kusukela nga-1968. Ngiselusa tinkhomo ngakhulake totimanje ngidlala sona. Bebabaningi [lebebasidlala] ngoba nami ngasifundza kubobhuti.* And *ukhandze kutsi bayasifundzisa nasibafana le – esigangeni sibanengije kakhulu. Bekulula [kudlala] sitontolo ngekucala kwetfu usicala kanje* [demonstrating putting *sitontolo* in his grandchild's mouth] *lokukuva kutsi sitontolo. Uyambona nje lomntfwana nangim'shayela ke lomsindvo awuve naye umtfwana kutsi uyakhala lapha. Umnandzi lomsindvo. Sekelengcondvo ke ikhula ufuna kutentela. Sekenami sebaya ngibatela lesilingane mine sitontolo. Sebaya nginika nami ngiyashaya ke. Yona ayisiyo intfo lemetima kakhulu. Kulula nangabe utimisele kutsi ukufundze.*
>
> (Interview, Shongwe, 16 June 2019, Shewula)

> I started playing *sitontolo* when I was a boy, around 1968. Since minding cattle, I grew until now still playing it [*sitontolo*]. There were many other people who were playing it because even I learned it from my brothers. And then you find that they teach us as boys – at the field, we were many. It was easy to play *sitontolo* according to our beginning, you start like this [demonstrating putting *sitontolo* in his grandchild's mouth] to feel that it is *sitontolo*. You see this child, I hit for him to feel the sound and the child hears the sound made and realises it is nice. Then the mind starts growing and the child is willing to do it himself. Then as a boy, the brothers made a *sitontolo* for me. Then they give it to me. It is not a very difficult thing. It is easy when you are serious about learning.
>
> (Shongwe 2019)

This quote highlights the field, where young people mind livestock, as a site of musical learning and *sitontolo* performance. The quote above shows the important link between feeling and hearing when learning *sitontolo*. While a young child may not be able to hold a bigger bow and strike it him or herself, a young learner's first experience of playing is by creating overtones with his or her mouth. In interviews, Shongwe demonstrated to us how he is teaching one of his grandchildren in the same way that he learned (Interview, Shongwe, 16 June 2019, Shewula). Young players learn by experimenting with the creating overtones with mouth and throat muscular manipulations, and then by watching the movements of the older players and mimicking these. Like with other mouth-resonated instruments, it is difficult to describe the techniques used to create various overtone sounds and so, learning and feeling within one's body are crucial to playing *sitontolo*.

In most parts of the world, musicians who play indigenous or folk musics rarely earn their living by their practice. In eSwatini, most musical bow players live in the rural areas and so survive as subsistence farmers. Both Magagula and Shongwe now live as farmers in their respective areas but both spent periods of time working on the mines in South Africa like many male musicians of older generations. Magagula spent a short period working on a mine in the South African province of Mpumalanga but returned to eSwatini due to a health ailment. Having played music as a young man, Shongwe stopped performing *sitontolo* music as he spent much of his life working on various mines in and around Johannesburg, South Africa. He only returned to eSwatini in 2013. He stated:

> *Ngikengakuyekela esikhatsini lesinengi nangisebentela etimayini. Ehh ngingasahlali nako ngakuyekela nje. Lesekutsi nyalo nasekunale-team yaboMake Magagula. Uyangibona ke Babe Mahlalela uyangicocela kutsi sebase thimini yendlovukazi uyangicela kutsi kute umuntfu wesitontolo. Sengiyasho kutsi sitontolo ngiyasati. Sengiyashaya ngiyati vusetela tingoma tami. Letindzala lengitatiko sengiyengetangeta nje letimbijana nyalo loku sengimdzala. Impala Mine eRustenberg, Vare Reef Klerksdorp, East Breefontein Carltonville, Randfontein, Springs Jongengozi. [...] Toti ke ngigugele khona.*
>
> (Shongwe 2019)

> I had stopped [playing] previously, most of the time when I was working in the mine. I wasn't with it then I just stopped. And then now that there is the team of Make Magagula. Babe Mahlalela saw me and then told me about them being in the Indlovukazi's team and asked me to play as no-one plays *sitontolo*. Then I told him that I know how to play *sitontolo*. Then I started playing, reminding me of my old songs. The old songs I knew and then I added a few new songs. [...] Impala Mine in Rustenberg, Vaal Reef Klerksdorp, East Breefontein [sic] Carltonville,[6] Randfontein, Springs Jongengozi.[7] Until I grew old, I worked in there [in the mines].
>
> (Shongwe 2019)

In this quote, Shongwe makes reference to other active indigenous instrument players, Cathrina Magagula and John Mahlalela. He describes physically playing *sitontolo* as a way of remembering songs from his youth.

Text and poeticism in *sitontolo* music

Sitontolo music exists with and without sung text. Despite this, poeticism is woven into the music in song titles and in associated lyrics inferred by the performer's overtone melodies. Mkhulu Solomon Shongwe's instrumental pieces of music are given titles with rich, interpretative meaning. His song titled '*Sawubona magujendlini*' teases and entices out the figurative protagonist who hides indoors, possibly healing from an injury or retreating from society for personal reasons. Another one of his songs '*Matjatjayela*' (translated as 'The child abuser') is about a man who abuses young girls. The song can be interpreted as being sung by the girls who call the man out as he approaches and is a warning song for his community. While instrumental *sitontolo* songs take on moral and other meanings through their assigned titles, some songs have articulated and sung lyrics which can communicate a variety of messages.

Both Magagula and Shongwe perform instrumental pieces and songs, where they alternate playing melodic overtone melodies using their mouth and throat cavities (or *lesipika*, 'speaker') and singing lyrics. When a song contains sung lyrical material, the performer moves the bow slightly away in order to sing and then seamlessly places it back at the mouth position, so ensuring a smooth transition between overtone melodic material and sung vocal material within the song structure. The song below, composed by Mkhulu Bhemani Magagula, is a *sitontolo* song with sung lyrics. The song is not formally titled and is formed from alternating cycles of few sung, lyrical ideas and instrumental overtone-laden interludes. This song was performed by Magagula at his home in eBuhleni in June 2019.

> *Balele eMalalane* – They are sleeping in Malalane
> *Ngibuye eMalalane, babe* – I am from Malalane, my father
> *Maye bangibulele, babe* – They have destroyed me, my father
> *Ngabuye eMalalane, babe* – I was from Malalane, my father
> *Bangibulele, babe* – They have destroyed me, my father
> *Ngisemahlathini impela* – I am in truly in the bush
> *Ngiyawuchacha tinkinga* – I am going to solve problems
> *Ngiyawuchacha tinkinga* – I am going to solve problems
> *BoMatsenjwa balele* – Matsenjwa has died
> *Balele emhlabeni Nkosi eSwatini* – They have left this world, King of eSwatini
> *Hawu!* [exclamation vocable]
> [overtone-based melodic interlude]

Yebo eMbabane – Yes, Mbabane
Ngibona Goje – I see Goje (the author Vusi Sibandze's praise name)
Ngibona Goje – I see Goje
Maye ngikhwehlele – I have coughed
Hawu! Ngiyawulala kabani? – Hawu, at whose house will I sleep?
Ngiyawulala kabani? – Hawu, at whose house will I sleep?
Ngiyawulala kabani? – Hawu, at whose house will I sleep?
Live libuyile – The country is back
Tinkhomo tingibulele – The cattle have destroyed me
Indlu ifile yebabe – The house has died, my father
Buka lapha endlini – Look in the house,
Utawubona, babe wam' – You will see, my father
Sivalo siwile – The door is down
Bangibulele ngihlala ngedwvane – They have destroyed me, I live alone
Ngihlala ngedwvane – I live alone
Ngihlala ngedwvane– I live alone
Maye babe – Oh dear, my father
Maye babe – Oh dear, my father
Maye babe – Oh dear, my father
Ngibuy'ezitheni – I am from the royal palace
Nkosi'khulile iNkhosi eSwatini – The King has grown, King of eSwatini
Mswati ukhulile – Mswati has grown
Utsi angidlale letisha letingoma – He says I must compose new songs
takaNgwane – of eSwatini
Ngintjintje letingoma – I must change the songs
Ngintjintje letingoma – I must change the songs
Live libuyile – The country is back
Live libuyile, babe– The country is back
Live libuyile, babe– The country is back
Malindane ungilulekile – Malindane advised me [possible reference to the King]
Utsi angishaye tingoma maye babe – He said I must play songs, my father
Bantfwana abalaleli – The children are not listening
Badle bhanana – They ate bananas
A ha ha! [vocables]
Labantfwana laba – These children
Labantfwana laba – These children
Labantfwana laba – These children
Badle bhanana – They ate bananas
Badle bhanana– They ate bananas

Abalaleli leleli – They are not listening
Abalaleli, babe – They are not listening, my father
Hhoowee [vocables]
[overtone-based melodic interlude]
Bajube dalada – They cut the fence
Bangene mahlatsini lalalabantfwana – They went into the forest, the children
Sebadle bhanana – They have eaten bananas
A haha [vocables]
Abafuni kulalela boyise – They don't want to listen to their fathers
Bomake bayabatfuma boyise – Mothers send the kids, fathers
Batele emakhilayoni – They have given birth to crayons
Yebabe – My father
Yebabe – My father
Yebabe – My father
Live libuyile – The country is back
Live libuyile, babe – The country is back
Basokile bonkhe labantfwana – All the kids are circumcised
Praise:
Yayi Ngibone bantfwana babasokile bonkhe – I have seen all the kids circumcised
Ngiyamangala nebakitsi – I am wondering, oh dear
Maye babe – Oh dear, my father
Maye babe – Oh dear, my father
Maye babe – Oh dear, my father
Maye babe – Oh dear, my father
Ngilele eMalalane – I slept at Malalane
Ngilele eMalalane – I slept at Malalane
Eh, Ngilele eMalalane – I slept at Malalane
Eh, Ngilele eMalalane – I slept at Malalane
Oh, lele babe – Oh dear, my father
Oh, lele babe – Oh dear, my father

The *sitontolo* music that accompanies and underlies the lyrics from the song above is notated in Figure 6.4. The tuning for this song shows Magagula's preference for a wide interval between the two wire portions. In this case, he tuned the lower note to a D flat and the upper note to a G natural, creating a diminished fourth between the two. As can be seen in this transcribed excerpt, the down strokes of the struck melody are alternated with faster semiquaver notes created by the left-hand forefinger (indicated by the triangular *marcato* accents). Because of the decay of these sounds and the muscular action of the

Figure 6.4 An excerpt from Bhemani Magagula's untitled *sitontolo* song.

mouth when playing, the overtone melody follows the rhythmic framework of the struck pattern but does not replicate its rhythm exactly. In the second bar, the high D notes in the overtone melody are created through a short glissando effect as Magagula opens his mouth cavity again and again in quick succession.

In Mkhulu Bhemani Magagula's untitled song above, we can see a lyrical structure with short phrases, much repetition and a series of stories and scenes represented. He begins the song by outlining biographical information from his past – as a young man, he had worked on a mine near to Malalane in Mpumalanga province of South Africa. He sings out, 'Ngiyawuchacha tinkinga' which translates as 'I am going to solve problems'. This resonates with the lyrics of many of his *makhweyane* and *inkhositina* songs which directly address community and moral issues such as HIV/AIDS, looking after the elderly and various political concerns Magagula has expressed. Magagula has spoken about his *makhweyane* bow being a 'radio' with which he 'broadcasts' contemporary community issues. In this way, his untitled *sitontolo* song has a societal and moral function, though it draws upon many themes.

Magagula makes mention of Elias Matsenjwa, a *sikhelekehle* monochord player who passed away more than a decade ago. As two musicians of the same generation, Magagula may be referring in his lyrics to his now sole responsibility to speak and advise through his music from this perspective. The repetition of the phrase '*Ngiyawulala kabani?*' (at whose house will I sleep?) speaks to a theme that emerges in *makhweyane* repertoire by other elderly musicians as well, where the player expressly worries about how he or she will survive, poetically worded referring to where one would find shelter or sometimes where the performer may find their final resting place. An example of this theme can be heard in the archival recording of *makhweyane* player Sitandi Mabuza's song

'Umbiliphi' (1972/3) in the David Rycroft South Africa Collection in the British Library sound archive.[8] As the song continues, Magagula goes on to bemoan the physical state of his house. At the time we visited him in 2019, the door of his house had been damaged and Magagula believed that young boys from the surrounding areas had tried to steal from him, causing the damage. This distressing event was woven into his *sitontolo* performance as he mournfully repeats the lines 'I live alone' (*Ngihlala ngedwvane)* and 'Oh dear, my father' (*Maye babe*).

The next section in this song deals with an important event in 2013 when King Mswati III had called for all musicians to create new repertoire and not rely on or merely re-arrange old music.[9] In earlier interviews, Magagula made special mention of this event and noted how he had responded by creating new songs on his various instruments (Magagula 2014). In this song, after describing his response to the king's call, Magagula circles back to the traumatic experience of theft and his suspicion that local children were the perpetrators. In this section of the song the lyrics embrace a moralistic tone, concerned that children do not listen to their parents anymore. He sings out a comical insult that parents are now giving birth to *yemakhilayoni* or crayons and seems to question whether the recent policy of medical circumcision (implemented as part of HIV prevention attempts in eSwatini) is a good idea.

This song is divided into sections with numerous repeated phrases within each section. Thematically, it is clear from the transcription that the song has an almost through-composed feel to it and Magagula weaves together different moral and community-related messages through this use of repetition. He does so directly through his siSwati lyrics but, as mentioned earlier, musicians can embody their instrumental *sitontolo* compositions with lyrical and moral meaning through the use of with poetic and poignant titling as well.

Sonics and performance in *sitontolo* music

In stage performance settings, the quietness of the *sitontolo* is hard to balance with other amplified instruments. Numerous sound-related challenges emerge and often audiences are unable to hear clearly the overtone engagement of the *sitontolo* in performances. Public performances on this scale are rare for these musicians and so the *sitontolo* is often an instrument performed for the performer him or herself, or their family.

Despite the natural quietness of the plucked and overtone tones produced by this instrument, the sonic experience of this music can be dynamic. In the case of Magagula and Shongwe, both can integrate sung lyrics and also recited praise into their *sitontolo* performances. In a rehearsal for a performance at a large arts festival in eSwatini, Solomon Shongwe alternated a quiet *sitontolo* composition with a loud moment of praise, sung out at speed and with great virtuosity, before turning back to his bow:

> *Tibambe Jomba Majaketi usuka ligonso nawuy'etjitjini, thambo letjitji bufacafaca, usuka ligonso nawuye etjitjini, thambo letjitji bufacafaca. Jomba Majaketi uphuma pansi kaShewula eLubonjeni, aludle lubombo lufukutse. Jomba Majeketi usuka ligonso nawuy'etjitjini, thambo letjitji bufacafaca. Zonke ingane ziyafacazela usomalenhle iyotjela unina. Elubonjeni aludle lufukutse. Bhatata ngamumba nge-AK47.*
>
> (Interview, Shongwe, 16 June 2019, Shewula)

> On it, Jomba Majaketi [praise name], you take a long jump when you go for a beautiful young woman, the beautiful body a young woman, the beautiful body a young woman, the beautiful body a young woman. Jomba Majaketi, you come from down at Shewula in the Lubombo region, let the region eat and enjoy. Jomba Majeketi, you take a long jump when you go for a beautiful young woman. All the young women are beautiful; you propose to a beautiful one and go tell her mother. Let the region eat and enjoy. I dug a sweet potato using an AK-47.
>
> (Shongwe 2019)

Within Swazi traditional performance, one person can collect numerous praises as one's life progresses. In the praises above, Shongwe compliments himself by describing himself as a man who is able to entice beautiful young women. He poetically interlaces his own proclaimed courting prowess with acknowledging the area he comes from (Shewula) and asks for blessings for that region. His praise is brief but filled with poetic, sexual innuendo and performative ego, perhaps from his younger years, as he is now a husband to two women and a grandfather to numerous grandchildren.

In the final festival performance for which this moment was a rehearsal, Shongwe performed a different praise. He did so with a knobkerrie raised while he shouted out to an appreciative audience of mostly foreign tourists. He began his performance with this bombastic and poetic performative moment and immediately followed the praise with a quiet and still *sitontolo* performance as he hovered close to his microphones (depicted in Figure 6.5). In this stage

Figure 6.5 Solomon Shongwe performing with the Bashayi Bengoma ensemble (May 2019). Photo: Lesedi Rudolph.

performance, his bodily expression was separated into distinct moments – the enthused regimental dancer-warrior and then the still, introspective musician, positioned so that every overtone could be picked up by the microphones.

Conclusion

The kingdom of eSwatini forms a particular cultural background for musical practices with its political and societal struggles and mass-participatory festivities. It is within this context that we find a musical bow practice that is both vulnerable and well-integrated into musical ensembles of similar music. Though this research is based on the testimony and praxis of the two musicians who still perform on this instrument, there has been a recent increase in interest in traditional or indigenous instruments in eSwatini. This can be seen in the programming of the Bashayi Bengoma ensemble at the large, local arts festival twice in recent years and various other performance and compositional opportunities that have come up. Recently, numerous traditional musicians were hired to contribute to the soundtrack for the critically acclaimed film *Liyana* and this has led to additional exposure for *sitontolo* and other musics from eSwatini. Some younger musicians such as Thobile 'Makhoyane' Magagula and Sibusiso Nkambule have been learning different indigenous instruments with elderly players and integrating these sounds into their individual music. While it is common to bemoan the lack of interest in these types of instruments by players and audiences, Mkhulu Solomon Shongwe's experience of learning to play sitontolo as a boy some decades ago shows that perceptions around these instruments have, until recently, generally been negative. He stated about his long life with the *sitontolo*: 'Abasanendzaba' ('People don't care anymore') (interview, Shongwe, 16 June 2019, Shewula). It has been some time since there was an engaged interest in these musical instruments and more than a handful of actives players.

This chapter has presented a profile of this *sitontolo* mouth bow of eSwatini despite there being so few players. In it, we have described the artistic praxis in *sitontolo* music and the mechanics of producing tones and overtones with wood, wire, hands and mouth. Text can be integrated into a *sitontolo* performance. This chapter has outlined how lyrical meaning can be brought into the music through compositional titling, melodic and lyrical inference and praise poetry. While this is the case, there is much about the resultant ephemeral sounds of the *sitontolo* mouth bow that cannot be tied to a page or to text. The *sitontolo* music of these two musicians is evanescent, diverse and fluid, as they tell stories and respond artistically to their personal experiences and to the societal and environmental happenings around them.

Notes

1. 'Mkhulu' is a siSwati term of respect for older men.
2. http://www.swazistats.org.sz/
3. https://population.un.org/wup/Country-Profiles/
4. Further details regarding the history of anti-apartheid activists in eSwatini can be found in the 2011 publication by Elias Masilela.
5. Both spellings are acceptable.
6. It is unclear what mine Shongwe is referring to here but possible that it is the Blyvooruitsig gold mine in Carltonville, Gauteng.
7. These are names of current and historic mines in the Gauteng, Free State and Mpumalanga provinces of South Africa.

8   The spelling of 'Sitandi' Mabuza should be Sithandi in siSwati but has been documented by Rycroft without the 'h'. 'Umbiliphi' by Sitandi Mabuza. Recorded by David Rycroft. British Library Sound Archive. [http://sounds.bl.uk/World-and-traditional-music/Rycroft/025M-C0811X0059XX-0400V0].
9   Dlamini (2013).

References

Davies, R.H., D. O'Meara and S. Dlamini (1985), *The Kingdom of Swaziland: A Profile*, London: Zed Books Ltd.

Dlamini, S. (2013), 'King Urges Regiments to Compose New Songs', 21 May 2013. Available online: http://www.times.co.sz/news/87571-king-urges-regiments-to-compose-new-songs.html (accessed 15 August 2014).

Kirby, P.R. ([1934, 1968] 2013), *Musical Instruments of the Indigenous People of South Africa*, Johannesburg: Witwatersrand University Press.

Kuper, H. (1963), *The Swazi: A South African Kingdom*, New York: Holt, Rinehart and Winston Inc.

MacMillan, H. (1985), 'Swaziland: Decolonisation and the Triumph of "Tradition"', *The Journal of Modern African Studies* 23 (4): 643–66.

Masilela, E. (2011), *Number 43 Trelawney Park: KwaMagogo*, Cape Town: New Africa Books.

Stacey, C. (2017), 'The Makhweyane Bow of Swaziland: Music, Poetics and Place', PhD diss., University of Cape Town.

Umbiliphi (n.d.), [Song] Perf. Sitandi Mabuza, Rec. David Rycroft, British Library Sound Archive. Available online: http://sounds.bl.uk/World-and-traditional-music/Rycroft/025M-C0811X0059XX-0400V0

Interviews

Bhemani Magagula, interview, eBuhleni, 6 May 2014.
Bashayi Bengoma rehearsal, Matsapha, 24 May 2019.
Bashayi Bengoma rehearsal, Matsapha, 25 May 2019.
Bashayi Bengoma performance, Bushfire International Arts Festival-Malkerns, 25 May 2019.
Bhemani Magagula, interview, eBuhleni, 15 June 2019.
Solomon Shongwe, interview, Shewula, 16 June 2019.

7

Musical bows of the amaXhosa

David Dargie

Abstract

The most important of the four musical bows in use isiXhosa traditional music is *uhadi*, a calabash-resonated percussion bow, indigenous to isiXhosa music for many centuries. The other three bows were adopted from other South African peoples. IsiXhosa musical style developed largely from *uhadi* playing techniques. In 1979, in the remote Eastern Cape village of Ngqoko, the author found a wonderful preservation of traditional music and a number of skilled bow players. In 1989 musicians of Ngqoko founded a performing group which brought Ngqoko music to many people, in South Africa, Europe and America. The chapter focuses on the way the bows are made and played, who are the bow players and the role of the bows in music as perceived by the musicians, and a brief introduction to isiXhosa bow music theory. The chapter includes photography, drawn illustrations and music score transcriptions.

Introduction

In 1979 I began working as a church ethnomusicologist for the Catholic Lumko pastoral institute, situated then at old Lumko Mission, 12 kilometres south of the Eastern Cape town of Lady Frere (no. 4 on the map (Figure 7.1)). To prepare for the work I began to research and record the local Thembu Xhosa music. I found an area of remarkable preservation of traditional music in the villages of Ngqoko and Sikhwankqeni very close to Lumko. Having heard recordings of the *uhadi* calabash-resonated musical bow on Hugh Tracey's *Sound of Africa Series* (International Library of African Music, Grahamstown), I began looking for the bow around Lumko. With the help of colleague Fritz Lobinger at Lumko, we

PART OF THE EASTERN CAPE PROVINCE OF SOUTH AFRICA
Showing Places of Special Musical Interest

Sites marked with *:
1. Ntsikana's Grave and Bell Stone. 2. Ngqika's Great Place and Tyhume Mission.
3. Mackay's Nek. 4. Old Lumko Mission. 5. Ngcuka Village. 6. Ngqoko Village.
7. Sikhwankqeni Village. 8. University of Fort Hare, Main (Alice) Campus.

Figure 7.1 The above map shows the part of the Eastern Cape Province referred to most in the accompanying article. Source: D. Dargie.

found *uhadi* and also the mouth bow *umrhubhe* at Sikhwankqeni. In 1980 I met the remarkable musician Nofinishi Dywili of Ngqoko village, at a celebration at Lumko. She was one of the main song-leaders of the village, and a master *uhadi* player (Figure 7.2, left). I made many recordings of her, and from her learned much about *uhadi* and other local music.

The people of the area are Thembu Xhosa. During the period about 1835–50 there was close contact between them and San people under their Chief Madoor, who had settled at a mission near Lady Frere.[1] During this time there was much contact, including intermarriage, between the Thembu and Madoor's people, which ended when the Thembu drove away the San as a result of disputes over cattle.

Of all the isiNtu (Bantu) language peoples the amaXhosa had the most contact with the Khoi and the San. KhoiSan influence brought not only the click consonants but also many words into isiXhosa language. The amaXhosa also absorbed a great deal of musical influence from the KhoiSan, including the use of certain musical bows. These were especially Kirby's 'string-wind instrument', the *gora*, which was called *ugwali* in isiXhosa,[2] and the mouth bow called *umrhubhe*, *umqunge* and *umqangi* (Figure 7.2, middle-left). Unfortunately *ugwali* was already extinct when I went to Lumko, only the name still being known. The names *umrhubhe*, *umqunge* and *umqangi* contain KhoiSan consonants (the clicks *c*, *q* and *x*, and the fricative *rh* [= Scottish *ch* and Afrikaans *g*]). This gives clear reason to believe that mouth bow also came to the amaXhosa from the KhoiSan.

P. R. Kirby on musical bows of the amaXhosa

Kirby's monumental study of the musical instruments of South Africa (Kirby [1934], 1968) identifies four musical bows used by the amaXhosa. These are: *Uhadi*, a large bow with attached resonator (1968: 197 and Plate 55); an instrument constructed by thrusting a bow stick into a 5 litre oil tin, called '*uhadi*' (1968: 215 and Plate 59), but also called *isankuni* in isiMpondo[3] (Plate 59); a mouth bow played by plucking called *inkinge* (1968: 225 and Plate 62); and a mouth bow played by friction called *umrhubhe* (and *umqunge* in isiMpondo) (1968: 239 and Plate 68).

The names of the isiXhosa bows

Kirby cites the name *uhadi* for two different musical bows. Undoubtedly this was the word used by players of the instrument. Kirby further mentions that the word *uhadi* 'is now applied to modern instruments such as the American organ' (1968: 202). Kropf's dictionary (Kropf 1915: 146) quotes the term as being used for a piano or harmonium. In Ngqoko village, 2 kilometres from Lumko, the instrument called *isankuni* by Kirby was called *inkinge* and also *ikatari* (Figure 7.2, middle right). *Inkinge* is another instrument, the plucked mouth bow. But *ikatari* is clearly a Xhosa adaptation of the word *sekatari* used for the instrument by the Sotho of Lesotho (Kirby 1968: 215). Seeing it is extremely likely that the instrument came to the amaXhosa via Lesotho, I prefer to call the instrument, as used in the Lumko area, *ikatari*. I have found the word *inkinge* also used for other instruments. For example, the mouth bow called *umrhubhe*, whether played by friction or by percussion, was called *inkinge* by the player, Mrs Eveline Mokwena of Hogsback. For the sake of clarity, I use the following bow names:

> *Uhadi* is the name of the large bow with attached resonator, played by percussion.
> *Ikatari* here means the instrument constructed by thrusting a bow into a tin as resonator, played by friction.
> *Umrhubhe* is the mouth bow played by friction, and by percussion – tapping the string. This bow is also called *umqunge* in isiMpondo in Kirby. The name *umqangi*, very close to the term *umqunge*, is known in Ngqoko. As will be explained below, I prefer to refer to this mouth bow as *umrhubhe* when played by friction, and as *umqangi* when played by percussion.
> *Inkinge* is the mouth bow played by plucking (Figure 7.2, right).

There are indications that *uhadi* was seen among the amaXhosa as early as the first decade of the nineteenth century.[4] *Umhadi* in isiXhosa means a 'deep pit',[5] and it seems only logical that the bow name *uhadi* is derived from the 'deep pit', the 'singing hole' in the calabash resonator from which the sounds of the overtones emerge. The *uhadi* bow type exists in West Africa, and it seems reasonable to think that this bow came with the ancestors of the amaXhosa on their long trek to the Eastern Cape, where they arrived more than a thousand years ago. Not only the amaXhosa, but the other isiNtu language peoples of South Africa all had this type of bow when Kirby did his research,[6] though sadly only the amaXhosa and possibly the Basotho of Lesotho still use this bow.

It seems clear that the mouth bow *umrhubhe/umqangi* came to the amaXhosa through their contact with KhoiSan people, possibly on the way south but more likely after their being settled in south-east Africa. *Ikatari* almost certainly came to them in recent times. As for *inkinge*, the instrument type was known to many peoples in Southern Africa, including South Africa and Namibia. This might indicate that it was known to isiNtu language people for a long time. The most influential bow was undoubtedly *uhadi*.[7] The Xhosa method of playing *uhadi*, using overtone patterns of two fundamental tones a whole tone apart, as will be described below, clearly determined the isiXhosa use of scale and harmony, even for unaccompanied singing.

Bow materials in the Lumko area

In Ngqoko and other villages of the area bows are made of a wood called *ulizi*. This is a tree-shrub which grows on the mountainsides. It is similar to hazel, but without the nuts, with long straight stems ideal for making bows. In the deep past, bow strings were made of gut or leather or twisted animal hair. With the coming of European traders, brass wire became available. This wire was carefully twisted and was used for the bangles which Xhosa women liked to wear on their ankles. To make bow strings, Nofinishi and company would throw an anklet into the fire, heat it, and then when it was cool, draw it out into bow wire. These days brass wire is either very scarce or unobtainable in South Africa. Brass bangles can no longer be obtained. The brass wire of 0.6 mm from Europe or America is ideal. Calabashes grow well around Ngqoko, when there is enough rain. A calabash of the right size (about the size of a human head) is dried, then cut and hollowed out for use as a resonator for *uhadi*. The construction of the bows, and how they are played, is shown in the photographs and illustrations below. All use overtones to follow the melody. Each sounds different from the others, but all use the same system of fundamentals, scale and harmony.

The bow is a singer

Bow players in Ngqoko regard their bow as a singer taking part in the song, rather than as something with which they accompany a song. '*Ihadi liyahlabela ingoma, ndilandela ngomlomo*' (*Ihadi* leads the song, I follow with the voice). All traditional Xhosa melodies grow out of the tones of speech. So the bow is not playing a melody – the bow overtone melody follows the tones of speech, so the bow is 'singing' the words, just as a 'talking drum' sends messages by imitating the tones of speech. All the songs of Ngqoko are in call-and-response form. The song line of a solo singer will usually be a combination of the leader and follower lines. This is also the case with someone playing a mouth bow: the bow melody is a composite of leader and follower parts: see the transcriptions below under *umqangi* and *inkinge*.

    The primary role of a musical bow is to lead a song by 'singing' either the leader or follower voice parts. If the bow starts with an ever-repeated follower chorus, then a singer using the normal leader voice parts is still considered to be following the song. It is also possible for a bow, especially *umrhubhe*, to follow a song which is being led by another bow or a singer. In Ngqoko it is also customary to play duets with two *imirhubhe*, with one bow leading and the other following. Both bows are first carefully tuned together. Examples of this may be seen in the DVDs 'Concert at Ngqoko' and 'Performance at the Home of Nofinishi Dywili' in the *Dave Dargie Collection* (Dargie 2000 to Present).

The 'Ngqoko Group'

As a result of my researches around Lumko, the music of the area began to be known to other musicologists, and musicians of the area began to be invited to perform, first at musicology conferences in South Africa, and later further afield. In 1989 nine musicians of Ngqoko performed at the Autumn Festival in Paris, France. In 1989 leading musicians of Ngqoko formed a performance group. They called themselves the 'Ngqoko Cultural Group', but I preferred to make them known as the 'Ngqoko Traditional Xhosa Music Ensemble'. Now they are known simply as the 'Ngqoko Group'.

Mrs Matiso's Maxim: Add the salt to the song

One of the early members of the group was retired schoolteacher Mrs Amelia Nosilence Matiso. She performed with the Group. She and schoolteacher Mr Tsolwana Mpayipheli, also a performer, were the only two in the Group who knew English. One day in 1985, after I had been recording songs at the home of Group Doyenne Mrs Nofinishi Dywili, Mrs Matiso said to me: 'Xhosa people like to put salt in their songs.' Perhaps this is the only 'rule' of Xhosa music. It is not enough just to perform: one must 'add the salt'. It is no easy matter to play any of the bows up to Thembu standards. With *uhadi*, it is not an easy task to follow a melody by opening and closing the calabash against the breast, while at the same time singing with the bow. It is even more demanding to bring in the use of more developed rhythm while playing *uhadi* – but the 'rhythm salt' brings very special life to the music. With *umrhubhe*, the most striking 'addition of salt' is to use the whistling technique. With *ikatari*, it is extremely difficult to control the overtones. The only control the player has, apart from the use of two fundamentals, is through the bowing method. And yet some players can astound one. Methods of spicing up the playing of the various bows will be discussed below.

Who plays the bows, and for what purposes

It is mainly women who play *uhadi*, but some men also play. Mr Mpahlolo Manisi (Figure 7.3, left) of Ngqoko became quite incensed when I told him, in 1983, that musicologists said only women play *uhadi*. He borrowed an *uhadi* from me, took it home to practise, then returned and recorded two songs for me.[8] When he came to me at Lumko he brought a friend who had also played *uhadi* at one time. He showed me his technique, but would not allow me to record him because he felt out of practice. Mr Tontsi Pintshana of Hogsback, who recorded a song for me with *inkinge*, told me he had also played *uhadi*, but had to stop due to arthritis in his hands. *Umrhubhe* is played by women and girls, but there is no reason why men should not play if they wish. *Ikatari* was the herd-boys' instrument. In my early days at Lumko one could still occasionally see a lad standing on an anthill, playing *ikatari* while watching the cattle. Unfortunately now it has been difficult to find someone who could play *ikatari* for the performances of the Ngqoko Group, so Mrs Nofirsti Lungisa (Figure 7.3, right) added playing *ikatari* to her skills with other bows and overtone singing for performances by the Group (Figure 7.3).

Bows are used more for non-ritual performances of songs, but may also be used in some rituals as well, and even important ritual songs may be sung with a bow outside the actual ritual. I believe it is the quiet nature of the bows which discourages their use for singing with large groups, but this can be done: I have made a number of such recordings. The *uhadi* player may sing with a group, or quietly on her own beside the small fire in her house. *Umrhubhe* may be used as a solo instrument or with a group, as also *ikatari*.

The four Xhosa bow types

Here follow descriptions and playing information on the bows *uhadi*, *umrhubhe/umqangi*, *inkinge* and *ikatari*. In each case the question is also raised – what contribution has this bow made to the amaXhosa people?

Figure 7.2 Four isiXhosa bows. Top left: Nofinishi Dywili with *uhadi*, Lumko 1981 (Photo: D. Dargie); Top right: Nogcinile Yekani with *umrhubhe*, Ngqoko, 1996 (Photo: D. Dargie); Bottom left: Two boys with *iikatari*, Lumko, 1979 (Photo: F. Lobinger); Bottom right: Tontsi Pintshana with *inkinge*, Hogsback, 1997 (Photo: M. Schmidinger-Dargie).

Figure 7.3 No restrictions on who may play bows. Left: Mr Mpahlolo Manisi playing *Uhadi*, Lumko, c. 1983 (Photo: D. Dargie). Right: Mrs Nofirsti Lungisa leads the Ngqoko Group with *Ikatari*, Cintsa School, 2002 (Photo: D. Dargie).

Uhadi

Uhadi is a large bow with attached resonator. The stick is usually about 1.5 metres long. Traditionally the resonator is a calabash. There are two photos of *uhadi* in Kirby's (op. cit.) Plate 55. One has a calabash resonator, the other has a Golden Syrup tin.[9] In former times the string was gut or twisted animal hair, but ever since traders brought brass wire into the Eastern Cape brass wire has been preferred. The beater is a light stick or reed. The calabash is tied to the bow stick, with some padding between.[10] In Figure 7.2, left here), the photo shows the *uhadi* master and song leader of Ngqoko village, Mrs Nofinishi Dywili, on the occasion when the author first recorded her in 1981. The playing method is shown in the illustration and described in the text below the illustration.

The player holds *uhadi* as shown (Figure 7.4, right) with the opening in the calabash towards the breast. The string is held by the forefinger against the thumbnail to obtain the upper fundamental tone, and released to use the lower fundamental. The beater is a light stick or reed. The player opens and closes the calabash against the breast to damp or release the overtones: the more open the calabash, the higher the audible overtone. The player follows the melody in this way – the highest audible overtone will be the melody tone, either of the original melody or of a parallel melody, whichever can best be used. The other audible overtones enable *uhadi* to produce harmony with the melody tones.

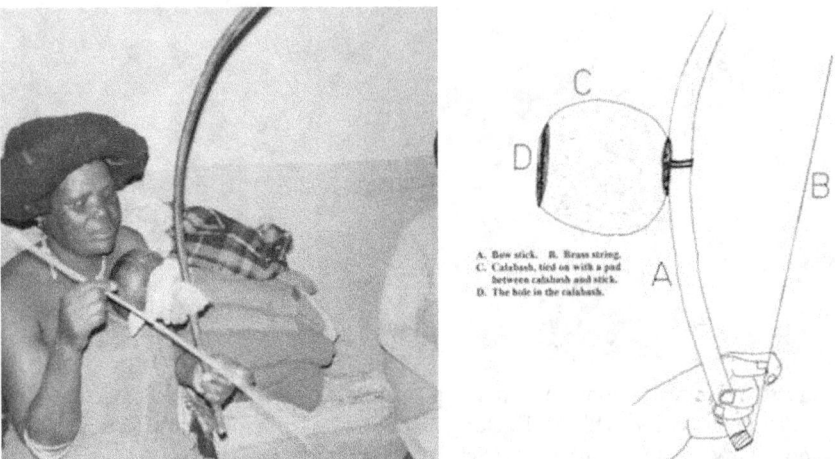

Figure 7.4 Playing *uhadi*. Left: Nofinishi Dywili plays *uhadi* at her home in Ngqoko (1981). Right: Playing *uhadi*. Photo and drawing: D. Dargie.

IsiXhosa bow music theory

Nearly all musical bows are overtone instruments. The vibration patterns of the bow string are amplified by a resonator, and the amplified sounds can be controlled to produce melody and harmony. With *uhadi* the player uses two fundamental tones a whole tone apart. In Figure 7.5 these are written as F and G. The usable overtones (written in black in the figure) make up two major chords, and these combine to produce the hexatonic scale shown.

This scale and the two-chord system of bow harmony have played a major role in Xhosa traditional music. Zulu music, for example, has several different bow scales,[11] so does Kavango music.[12] But isiXhosa traditional music is based almost totally on the hexatonic scale shown in Figure 7.5. This holds for unaccompanied singing, and also for the way the other Xhosa musical bows are played.

Figure 7.5 A. *Uhadi* bow overtones; B. *Uhadi* overtone chords; C. IsiXhosa bow scale. (In A, overtones are blacked in, fundamentals hollow).

AmaXhosa history in *Uhadi* songs

Naturally such a contribution comes not from the bow itself, but through and from the people who play and have played the bow. The ones who play *uhadi* are nearly all mature women. They are the ones who take part in the main rituals, the initiations of girls and boys, the dances at the beer gatherings which are actually ancestor rituals – because where alcohol is being consumed the ancestral spirits gather. The women are the educators of the girls in their initiation schools, preparing them for marriage. The women see their sons undergoing the process of initiation into manhood.

As in many societies it is the women who carry the loads, not just the physical burdens of working the fields, carrying water and firewood and so on, but the role of building the family and keeping it together. These are the concerns which have given rise to some of the most important songs which they sing with *uhadi*. For the women *uhadi* is not just an instrument of 'self-delectation' or self-amusement. Through *uhadi* they can give voice to those matters which deeply concern them, either singing alone or with other women. Through *uhadi* they reflect events in the history of their people; through *uhadi* they meditate on their culture and on many things which affect their lives.

Nofinishi Dywili squats by the side of the fire in her house and sings of the sufferings of women. In *Inxembula*, her great personal song, she recounts the suffering caused by the migratory labour system imposed by the British under Governor George Grey in the mid-nineteenth century, a system which still bedevils the lives of rural Xhosa women. 'December is coming,' she sings, '*Inxembula* – the ugly man – is coming in, and my friend Nomadambe becomes a whore.' When the men return from working in the mines and in the Cape, then the women who could not find husbands because of their enforced absence resort to prostitution to survive. Nosinothi Dumiso, called by the ancestors through her affliction of blindness, sings the song of the Christian Ancestor, Ntsikana the Prophet, the first Xhosa Christian, who died in 1821. In Ntsikana's song she and her friend Nomawuntini Qadushe sing 'Alas! For this War of Mlanjeni' – 200 local Xhosa people died in a battle in that war not far from their village of Mackay's Nek. Ntsikana's Prayer Song becomes a Freedom Prayer Song. In Hogsback, a vacation village for the white people but a place of deep significance to the amaXhosa, Nofetyu Tukani sings '*Yakayaka* – You ragged thing!' And the ragged thing answers '*Ndemka nehlungulwana* – I depart with the scavenger crow.' With the help of Dr Cecil Manona (anthropology) and Dr

Figure 7.6 Three bows playing the song *Nontyolo*.

Jeff Peires (history) of Rhodes University, I tried to unravel this most unusual text. It seems to be a re-enactment of the casting out of a small-pox victim from a village. Dread of the highly contagious disease caused villagers to drive out victims of the disease – 'to depart with the crow'. This is a Xhosa idiom meaning to die. Smallpox, along with guns, money and alcohol, came with the colonists from Europe. The epidemic of 1770 decimated the amaXhosa, but the many amaXhosa who sing this song today know nothing about that epidemic any more, just as Nosinothi and Nomawuntini did not know the real story of the War of Mlanjeni. It was the songs rather than the singers which carried the history. It is not only the historical content of these songs which is significant. The music itself is relevant for studying *uhadi*.

Musical Bows of the AmaXhosa 215

In the transcriptions below the vertical pulse lines indicate the beats, thick lines for main beats. The layout renders the rhythm plan visible, through the pulse lines and the spacing, without the use of tails and flags. The songs are cyclic, the transcriptions usually showing one (or two) cycles. The cycles of each part begin after the double line.

Nontyolo (Figure 7.6), is a song for the boys' and girls' *umtshotsho* dances. The original rhythm of the voice part was undoubtedly the rhythm used by *ikatari* in the transcription. The *umrhubhe*, however, adopts the equalized rhythm used by many young singers, including the leader line H 1 in the score. The *uhadi* master Nofinishi Dywili combines the rhythms of *ikatari* and *umrhubhe* into a single pattern. So whichever pattern any singer may choose, Nofinishi has it covered. While this is going on the singers clap and dance a three-against-four rhythm pattern shown in the two lowest lines of the score, with the additional use of clap/step delay. No trouble to Nofinishi!

The transcription shows the overtone patterns of three different bows playing the song. It shows the leader melody, played by each of the bows, in

Figure 7.7 Excerpt from the *uhadi* song *Inxembula*.[13]

black notes, and other audible overtones as hollow notes. I was able to test this with *umrhubhe* by playing the recording at half speed. This brought the pitch down an octave and made the recording sound like an organ playing five-note chords. This may be heard on the CD '*Umrhubhe wemimangaliso*' in the *Collection* (Dargie 2000 to Present). The score shows how the bows can easily produce parallel melodies of the sung melodies, which is what players do when sung tones are outside the bows range. It also demonstrates the basis of the system of parallel harmony used by singers (see comments on the transcription in Figure 7.7).

Nofinishi Dywili's *uhadi* song *Inxembula*

This song has been discussed above, under the aspect of its historical value, documenting the sufferings of rural Xhosa woman because of the migratory labour system. The score in Figure 7.7 demonstrates its musical sophistication. The first point to note is the complex rhythm of the bow part. In order to analyse the rhythm I videoed Nofinishi, singing the song not only with *uhadi*, but also without the bow, while clapping. The clap, in the top line of the score, shows that the rhythm is based on a 2 x 4 beat pattern. This allowed me to identify the bow beat pattern as 2 x [(1½+½+1) + (1½+½) + (1½+½+1)], which adds up to a normal (3+2+3 = 8 beats additive rhythm) x 2, to give a cycle of 16 beats. The performance with and without bow may be seen on the DVD 'Xhosa Music introduced by Dave Dargie' (in the *Collection*, Dargie 2000 to Present). Regarding the bow use of parallel melodies, this is shown clearly in the way the bow (lines 2 & 3 in the score) interprets the humming melody (line 2 in the score).

The historical importance of the version of the Song of Ntsikana, performed with the bow by Nosinothi Dumiso and Nomawuntini Qadushe (Figure 7.8, left), was also discussed above. Figure 7.9 is an excerpt from their performance.

The first line sung by the leader, Nosinothi Dumiso (line H 1), has the words 'Alas, alas, this War of Mlanjeni'. It was remarkable to find a survival of the song (Ntsikana died in 1821), but it was almost shattering to record the text about the War of Mlanjeni (1851–3). As regards the music, however, the performance style was normal. Nosinothi played a 'straight' 3+3+2=8 additive rhythm. Two years later, in 1983, Mrs Nowizine Mandumbu of Ngqoko came to Lumko with three friends to record another *uhadi* version of Ntsikana's Song (Figure 7.8, right). Apart from some small changes in the text, there were no surprises in the

Figure 7.8 *Uhadi* players who performed Ntsikana's song. Left: Mrs Nomawuntini Qadushe and Mrs Nosinothi Dumiso (with *uhadi*) with Father Arnold Fischer of Mackay's Nek Mission, 1981 (Photo: D. Dargie). Right: Mrs Nowizine Mandumbu at Lumko, 1983 (Photo: D. Dargie).

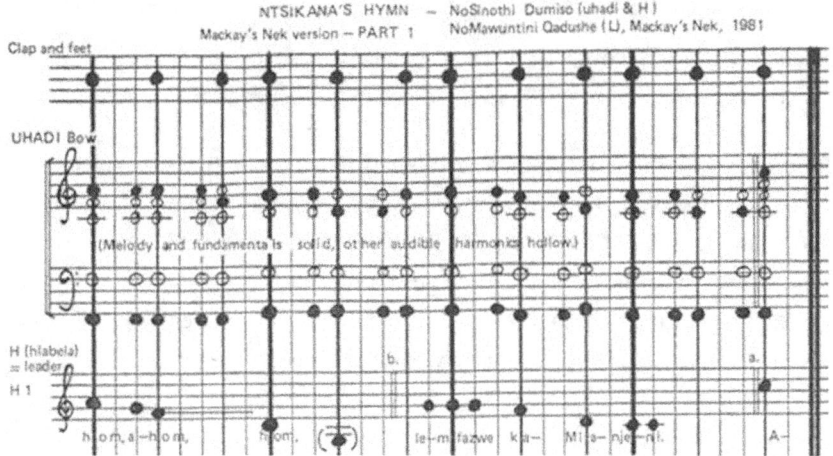

Figure 7.9 Ntsikana's song as performed with *uhadi*, by Nosinothi Dumiso and Nomawuntini Qadushe, Mackay's Nek Mission, 1981.

performance – except for the remarkable transformation of the rhythm. The usual rhythm of 3+3+2=8 beats is changed by equalization to 1½+1½+1½+1½+2=8 beats. This appears, perhaps, to be a 5 beat rhythm. However, I was able to video Mrs Mandumbu with three other ladies in 1985. While they sang the apparent

Figure 7.10 The 'Ngqoko *Uhadi* Version of Ntsikana's Song'.

5 beat rhythm, they moved in 4 equal beats. This is clearly visible in the video recording.[14] Part of the transcription of this 'Ngqoko' version of the song is shown in Figure 7.10. The layout enables one to 'see' this typical but nevertheless remarkable Thembu Xhosa use of disguised rhythm.

The transcriptions in Figures 7.7, 7.9 and 7.10 show different ways of 'adding the rhythm salt' in Xhosa *uhadi* bow technique. Note the parallel harmony in line L 1.

Umrhubhe/umqangi (umqunge)[15]

Umrhubhe is a very simple construction – just a small bow (stick c. 70 cm), strung with brass wire. It is held to the side of the mouth, which acts as resonator. The bow stick is held (in the illustration) with the left hand so that the thumbnail can be pressed to the string to obtain the higher fundamental tone (Figure 7.11, left). The player bows (scrapes) the string with a cleaned

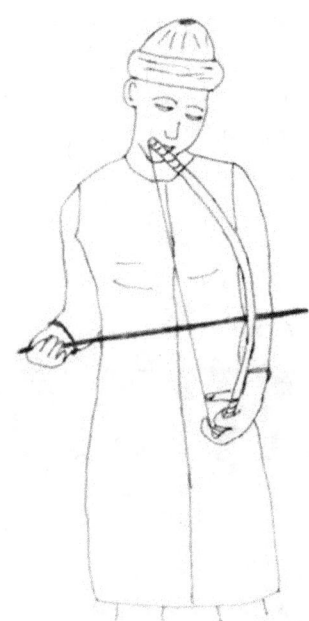

Figure 7.11 Playing *umrhubhe*. Left: A young girl plays *umrhubhe* at Sikhwankqeni village near Lumko, 1979. Right: Illustration based on the photo – playing *umrhubhe*. Photo and drawing: D. Dargie.

stick or reed and shapes the mouth to amplify the desired overtones. In this way the melody can be followed clearly, but with it the overtone chords can be heard. Skilled players may use the bow overtones to follow the melodies of the lead singer, while at the same time whistling the melodies of the followers' song lines. The CD (with accompanying handbook) '*Umrhubhe wemimangaliso – The Amazing Umrhubhe Mouth-bow*', in the *Collection* Dargie 2000 to Present, brings together many recordings of *umrhubhe* performances by musicians of Ngqoko, including the song in Figure 7.12. This song, *Nomkangaye*, has long been a favourite with Ngqoko musicians. Nomkangaye was a lady who pursued other women's husbands – an irresponsible person, perhaps, but also a victim of the migratory labour system inflicted upon the amaXhosa (and other peoples in South Africa). Figure 7.12 is a transcription of an *imirhubhe* duet performance, a performance illustrating a number of facets of *umrhubhe* technique and isiXhosa song structure.

In the performance transcribed (Figure 7.12), the master Nogcinile Yekani and her pupil Nopasile Mvotyo, with bows carefully tuned together, both play the same leader part (the top two lines in the score) in unison. Members of the

Ngqoko Group sing with them. Several of the sung melodies are shown in the bottom four lines of the score. The most extraordinary part of the performance is the whistling by the two bow players, shown in the four 'whistle' lines in the score. Note how, although they play the same overtone melody, the bow players answer one another in the whistling. Note also how the whistling melodies relate to the sung lines.

Figure 7.12 *Nomkangaye* as an *umrhubhe* whistling duet, performed by Nogcinile Yekani and Nopasile Mvotyo, together with (singing) the other members of the Ngqoko Group.

Playing the same mouth bow as *umqangi*

The method for playing the bow as *umqangi* is the same, except that the string is not scraped or bowed but tapped with a light stick. The only opportunity I had to record the bow played in this way was by Mrs Evelina Mokwena of Hogsback, in the middle 1990s, playing the remarkable historic song shown in Figure 7.13 (see photo in Figure 7.14). Her friend Mrs Nofetyu Tukani played the same song with *uhadi*, and Mrs Mokwena played it using the bow both as *umrhubhe* and as *umqangi*. The song dates from the dreadful smallpox epidemic of 1770. It re-enacts the casting out of a small-pox victim (the 'ragged thing') from the frightened village. In isiXhosa usage to depart with the crow means to die. Smallpox was such a terrible disease that victims were driven out of villages in the 1770 epidemic, in an attempt to protect those still healthy. The song is sung for beer dances, and also as an *uhadi* bow song. *Yakayaka – ndemka* is sung in many places in amaXhosaland, but I doubt very much that any of those who sing it know what it signifies. I traced the song back to its roots with the help of Dr Cecil Manona, anthropologist, and Dr Jeff Peires, historian, both of Rhodes University.

Figure 7.13 No. 2. *Yakayaka – ndemka nehlungulwana* – Beer Song = Ancestor Song. **Leader:** You ragged thing! **Answer:** I have departed with the scavenger crow. The score immediately below shows how the leader (H) and follower (L) parts are combined in mouth bow performance, simply absorbing the overlap of the voice parts.

Figure 7.14 *Umqangi* and *inkinge*. Left: Mrs Evelina Mokwena of Hogsback plays *umqangi* – 1997. (Photo: D. Dargie). Right: Mr Tontsi Pintshana of Hogsback plays *inkinge* – 1999 (Photo: M. Schmidinger-Dargie).

Yakayaka – ndemka: The basic song parts

Inkinge

Inkinge is a bow made of bamboo – see the photograph in Figure 7.14, right. The illustration shows *inkinge* (with the bow curvature slightly exaggerated, for clarity), and the inset at lower right shows how the string is attached, with protruding V-notches just beyond the nodes in the wood at either end (Figure 7.15). There must be a gap between the string and the bow so that the player – Mr Pintshana in the photo – can press down the string with the middle finger of his left hand to obtain the upper fundamental tone. However, bamboo is not easy to bend except when freshly cut. I was able to have some examples of *inkinge* made for me by an elderly man in Queenstown in the 1980s. When I went to collect the bows the man had left the bows for me but was away himself. I was not able to find him again, so could not record him. The bows were strung with brass wire, the same bangle wire as used for bows in Ngqoko. Because of the unbendable quality of the bamboo I found it very

Musical Bows of the AmaXhosa 223

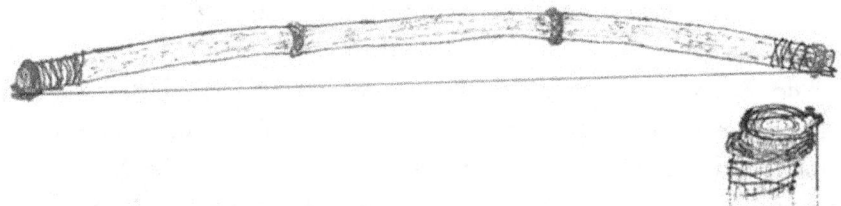

Figure 7.15 *Inkinge*. Illustration: D. Dargie.

difficult to bring sufficient tension into the wire to play the bows, except by forcing pieces of wood under the string near one end. Mr Pintshana, shown in the photo, made an *inkinge* strung with wire to show me in the mid- 1990s, but he too was unable to play it. Finally in 1997 he strung the bow with nylon fishing line.[16] He could then play it, and allowed me to record him. However, he found it very difficult to overcome his shyness about performing and allowed me to record only one song, *Icamagu livumile*, which he practised carefully for the occasion. Figure 7.16 shows a leader and a follower line from this song (Figure 7.17), one of the two most important diviners' songs. It is sung joyfully, proclaiming the success of the divination, and confidence therefore in the help of the ancestors. The word *camagu* refers both to the ancestors and to the acceptance of the divination by them.

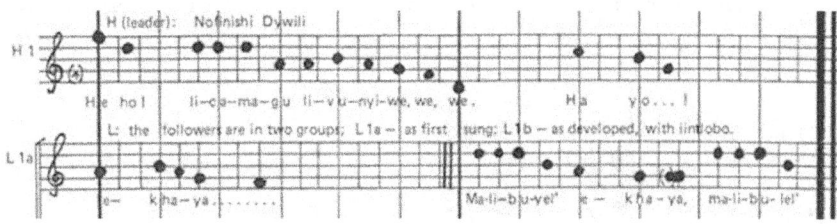

Figure 7.16 No. 14. *Icamagu livumile*. Text: Mayibuyel' ekhaya – licamagu livunyiwe! (The other texts are exclamations.) Translation: 'May the blessing of the ancestors come back on the homestead – the divination has been accepted by them!'

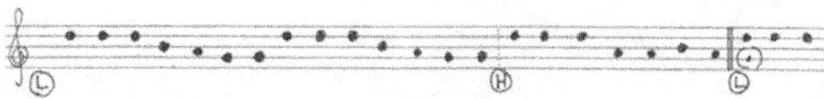

Figure 7.17 Shows how the bow can combine both leader and follower parts of the song.

Ikatari (also called *Isankuni, Isigankuri*, etc.)

Ikatari (Figure 7.18), is made by thrusting a bow stick (c. 1.25 metre in length) into the pouring hole of a 5 litre oil tin. The string, of brass wire, is tied to the protruding end of the stick and then fastened to the far end of the tin through a hole in the tin. A hole is cut in the side of the tin so that the sound can emerge. The player holds *ikatari* as shown, bowing the brass string with a small bow strung with animal hairs or agave fibre. He touches the string with the thumb of the hand holding the tin to obtain the upper fundamental tone. He can control the audible overtones only by pressure and bowing direction of the small bow. Despite the difficulty of this players may develop great skill in following melodies. A lump or smear of resin from a plant called *ulwapes'* (from the Afrikaans word *harp-ys* = resin) is put on the edge of the tin for use on the small bow.

In the 1980s the faith-healer of Cancele, a village in the deep rural area near Mount Frere in the Eastern Cape, drew people by the busload from Northern KwaZulu-Natal, Botswana and even further north. Even people from Ngqoko went there, to the amusement of the boys. For this recording of their song Mlamli Dlangamandla played *ikatari*. He was a real expert, drawing a flow of melody and harmony from his rough instrument. Note the tricky rhythm, the use of parallel harmony (imitating the bow) by the singers (Figure 7.19).

There is another playing style for *ikatari/isankuni*. Professor Luvuyo Dontsa of Walter Sisulu University is an expert in this style, in which the player plays melody tones very clearly, while minimizing the unwanted overtones. This is not

Figure 7.18 Playing *ikatari*. Left: Noted musician Dizu Plaatjies observes a boy playing *ikatari*, Lumko, 1979 (Photo: F. Lobinger). Right: Playing *Ikatari*. Illustration: D. Dargie.

Figure 7.19 *Siphum' eCancele*. Text: We come from Cancele – Greetings, Nomama!

at all easy with the instrument, seeing that the only control of the overtones open to the player is the method of bowing. Prof Dontsa is an acknowledged expert with the instrument, in both performance and academically.[17]

In conclusion

Professor Dontsa is a performer with, and also teaches students, *uhadi* and *umrhubhe*, as well as *isankuni/ikatari*. The *uhadi* type of bow is extinct among most peoples of South Africa, but the amaXhosa are fortunate still to have a number of noted *uhadi* players. The most famous of these is the remarkable Madosini. Madosini Manqina is also an extraordinary exponent of *umrhubhe* whistling songs. When the LP disc Marks 1975 came out, the name *umrhubhe* was not given on the record sleeve. Andrew Tracey of the ILAM urged people to find the instrument, because of the fine sound of her mouth bow songs. People in Ngqoko identified it for me as *umrhubhe nomlozi* – *umrhubhe* with whistling. Dizu Plaatjies and his colleagues in the Group Amampondo went one better – they found Madosini and brought her to the Cape.[18] For some time she taught the bows at Cape Town University. Since then she has continued to perform, in South Africa and in Germany.

Another fine *uhadi* and *umrhubhe* player, Mantombi Matotiyana of the Tsolo district in the Eastern Cape, was also discovered by Plaatjies, who made her known. She performed in the *Bow Project* with the Nightingale String Quartet on tour in South Africa. She performs with Dizu Plaatjies and his Ibuyambo Ensemble on the CD 'African Kings', Mountain Records no. 7575 (2009).

Academics are working to keep bow playing alive at a number of universities in South Africa. The survivors of the Ngqoko Group have also begun teaching in Ngqoko itself, with seven girls from ages seven to twelve learning the bows.

A final word: perhaps the most extraordinary way of adding salt to singing is the amazing Xhosa overtone singing, especially the type called *umngqokolo ngomqangi*. In *umngqokolo ngomqangi* the singer imitates the *umrhubhe/umqangi* bow, producing deep fundamental tones and high, clear overtones by the use of the vocal chords and vocal cavities. Going into *umngqokolo* is beyond the scope of this chapter, but there is plenty of other material on the topic in the *Collection Dargie 2000 to Present*, and in other publications (including the internet).

Notes

1. See Dargie (1988: 22–8).
2. 2 See Kirby ([1934], 1968: 171–92).
3. The amaXhosa are divided into the population groups originally in the Xhosa area (including the amaRharhabe, the amaGcaleka and others) and the intrusive peoples who entered the area later (including the abaThembu, the amamPondo and others). The languages or dialects of the different groups are indicated by the prefix *isi-* so isiMpondo is the amaMpondo dialect of isiXhosa, and isiThembu is that of the abaThembu. The prefix *isi-* also refers to culture. The term *iingoma zesiXhosa*, for example, means songs of Xhosa culture.
4. See Kirby, *Musical Instruments,* 204; Dargie (1988: 90).

5   Kropf (1915: 146).
6   Kirby, *Musical Instruments,* 196–204.
7   In the Lumko area, and certain other areas among the Xhosa, the prefix (affecting the noun class) *i* – is used for this bow – *ihadi* rather than *uhadi*, with plural *amahadi*.
8   The recordings are on the CD *Nguwe lo* in the *Collection* Dargie (2000 to Present).
9   In Germany a 2½ kilogram Sauerkraut tin will also fit the bill.
10 Traditional players tied the string directly onto the stick, used brass wire to attach the calabash and padded it against the stick with cloth – see Nofinishi's bow in the photo. Learning from a Zulu *umakhweyane* bow maker, I use string for attaching the string and the calabash, and, wound around the calabash tie, for the padding.
11 See Dargie (2007).
12 See Dargie (2013).
13 Most of the transcriptions in this chapter are taken from the book Dargie (1988).
14 See 'Ntsikana Music Collection 2000', a CD and handbook set, and the DVD 'Versions of Ntsikana's Song', in the *Collection*, Dargie (2000 to Present).
15 Regarding *umrhubhe* and *ikatari* (aka *isankuni, isigankuri*), see also Rycroft (1966) and (2014).
16 The same bow in Kavango, where it is called *rugoma*, is also strung with nylon fishing line – see Dargie (2013).
17 See the article Dontsa (2007). I did not come across this style of playing in Ngqoko, but examples of it from other areas of Southern Africa may be heard on the CD 'New World, Ancient Harmony', in the *Collection* Dargie (2000 to Present).
18 See the CD Madosini (1998).

References

Dargie, D. (1987), *Techniques of Xhosa Music*, PhD diss., Rhodes University, Grahamstown.

Dargie, D. (1988), *Xhosa Music, Its Techniques and Instruments, with a Collection of Songs*, Cape Town: David Philip.

Dargie, D. (2000 to Present), The 'Dave Dargie Collection', series of CDs, DVDs and Handbooks, Grahamstown: International Library of African Music (ILAM).

Dargie, D. (2003), *The Genius of Nofinishi Dywili*, handbook accompanying the CDs *Dargie 2002b*, Grahamstown: International Library of African Music (ILAM).

Dargie, D. (2007), '*Umakhweyane*: A Musical Bow and Its Contribution to Zulu Music', *African Music* 8 (1): 60–81.

Dargie, D. (2011a), 'The Xhosa *Umrhubhe* Mouthbow: An Extraordinary Musical Instrument', *African Music* 9 (1): 31–55.

Dargie, D. (2011b), 'The Redoubtable Nofinishi Dywili, *uhadi* Master and Xhosa Song Leader', *SAMUS* 30/31: 1–30.

Dargie, D. (2013), 'Kavango Music', *African Music* 9 (3): 122–50.

Dontsa, L. (2007), 'The Tonalities of the "*Isankuni*"', *The Galpin Society Journal* 60: 161–6.

Kirby, P.R. ([1934], 1968), *The Musical Instruments of the Native Races of South Africa*, Johannesburg; Witwatersrand University Press.

Kropf, A. (1915), In R. Godfrey (ed.), *A Kafir-English Dictionary* [Second Edition], Alice: Lovedale Mission Press.

Madosini, Madosini with Amampondo. (1998), 'Power to the Women', audio CD: MELT 2000.

Marks, D. (1975), 'Iimbongi: The Poet and the Minstrel', 12 inch vinyl long-playing disc, no. TBH 2000: Durban, Third Ear Music.

Rycroft, David. (1966), 'Friction Chordophones in South-Eastern Africa', *The Galpin Society Journal* 19: 84–100.

Rycroft, David. (2014), 'Isigankuri', in Laurence Libin (Hrsg.), *The Grove Dictionary of Musical Instruments*. Bd. 3, 55, Oxford/New York: Oxford University Press.

For audio and visual examples, see https://www.bloomsbury.com/us/musical-bows-of-southern-africa-9781501346743/.

8

Eastern Kalahari bow music

Jürgen Schöpf

Abstract

This chapter discusses several music bow playing techniques with reference to field work data obtained in 1997 in central Botswana by the author. Among the styles in question are two mouth bow techniques, both from the overtone series of the fundamental frequency of the bow called *N!oma* and played with a wire string: one for which the middle of the bow stave is held to the open mouth, and a second for which one end of the bow is pushed into one corner of the mouth. A further technique called *N!oma jieu* ('springhare music bow') is enjoyed by several players gathered around a hunting bow with sinew string that is held to a basin as a resonator. It is excited by different means at the same time. A closer look reveals that most bow music pieces have animal titles and their asymmetrical rhythms, or beat patterns, were derived from the stumbling of animals which have been hit by poisoned arrows. An acoustical analysis of the wire bow sounds reveals that the sound created hitting a wire bow is highly non-linear in its sonic content so that multiple partials can be filtered from this signal, not only the ones to be expected.

Introduction

In 1997, I spent seven months conducting fieldwork in Botswana, researching music in the Gaborone area. During that time, I had the chance to assist the cultural NGO Mambo Arts (in the year of its unfortunate collapse) in a few journeys to support local craftspeople in the Ghanzi and Central District. Then Mambo Arts Field Officer and well-known drummer Myizer Matlhaku had many contacts there, especially to musicians, and some of the craftspeople associated with Mambo Arts were producing lamellaphones, locally known as *setinkane*. In the course of these trips to central Botswana, I have been able to record several musicians; most of them young women playing said *setinkane* lamellaphones as well as young men playing four-string guitars, both drawing on a repertoire of popular tunes. Besides this musical mainstream, I also met a few elderly men who, at our request, were able to make music bows and perform on them in two distinct styles: as mouth bow in solo performances (*N!oma*)[1] and as group enjoyment with an external resonator (*N!oma jieu*).[2] These two styles and the related instruments and playing techniques are discussed in the present chapter.

Acknowledgements

I write this in appreciation of the art of !Xayee Moko and Meya Galotsa of Khwee settlement,[3] Kei Bi Tree of Bai,[4] Sekere Kiema from Xade (in the Central Kalahari Game Reserve)[5] and Lorry Tao Morris and Yohne of Karee cattle post.[6] I am very grateful for their engagement with my interest in their music. Besides the performers I am indebted to the people who I enjoyed company with during my travels in central Botswana: Myizer Matlhaku, Enjo, Makgona Marago, Pae Moeketsane, Limphitetse 'Chibuku' Sechuriti, Batho, and to Gordana Cavric in Gaborone. Many thanks also to my academic teacher and organologist Klaus-Peter Brenner of the Musical Instruments Collection of the University of Göttingen, Germany. My stay in Botswana was financed by a stipend of German Academic Exchange Service (DAAD) and during my research, I enjoyed the privilege to be Affiliate Researcher of the National Institute of Research (NIR) of the University of Botswana in Gaborone.

People

I was introduced to !Xayee Moko in Khwee.[7] He could not speak Setswana, the national language of Botswana and general *lingua franca* for linguistic minorities in the country. Therefore, communication was very limited for me, speaking English, or my fragments of Setswana, to other members of our changing travelling party, including Myizer, Pae, Limphitetse or Batho, they, in turn, speaking Setswana to Makgona or Sekere, and one of them, in turn, speaking

Figure 8.1 !Xhayee Moko playing *N!oma*. Photo: Jürgen Schöpf.

Figure 8.2 Meya Galotsa playing *N!oma jieu*. Photo: Jürgen Schöpf.

to !Xhayee in a language that is likely a variant of G/ui or G//ana. I guess he was certainly beyond sixty years of age when we met.

He chose a bow with a wire string and held it with his left hand close to the string-dividing noose and beat the string with his right hand by means of a strong stalk or small twig. The position of his left hand, palm facing downwards, allowed him to also use his left forefinger to pluck, or rather kick, the longer part of the divided string to articulate a rhythmical counterpoint to his otherwise regular beating of the string with the right hand and twig (Figure 8.1).

Meya Galotsa, apparently a friend of !Xhayee, was perhaps a bit younger than the latter. He made a mouth bow on my request and played a single piece on it while being more engaged with the music bow technique called *N!oma jieu* (Figure 8.2), to be explained in detail further below.

Keibi Tree (or K. B. Tree) was introduced to me as a traditional doctor. His residence was in Bai, a cattle post in the hinterland of Malatswae and Khwee. I met him a few times, once in his home when he built a wire-string music bow for me and we recorded him playing it, but we also met in Khwee where I recorded a longer session with him playing his main instrument, the lamellaphone *setinkane*, but also mouth and music bows. His preferred playing technique of the mouth bow worked by placing one end of the bow in his mouth, far up his right cheek.

Figure 8.3 Lorry Tao Morris playing *N!oma*. Photo: Jürgen Schöpf.

Lorry Tao Morris's home was the cattle post by the name of Karee (my orthography). He also played both, *setinkane* and music bow (Figure 8.3). His neighbour Yohne made a braced wire bow on our request, but he only played *serankure/segaba* for me and my recording machine.

I have not found any women playing mouth bows in Botswana, although Elizabeth Wood has reported Basarwa as well as Tswana women to have played the mouth bow called *lengope* in Setswana in the past (Wood 1975: 195, 1983: 2 and 1985: 24f). Makgona Marago of Kukamane near Malatswae, a distinguished lamellaphone player, enjoyed playing *N!oma jieu*. Given the few people I was able to meet my corpus of recordings is too limited to allow for any gender-based generalizations.

Places

My regional focus on the 'Eastern Kalahari' in the title is roughly concordant with what Hitchcock calls the 'Western Sandveld' (Hitchcock 1979). For me, it is the area between the Central Kalahari Game Reserve and the A14 highway that connects Palapye to Letlhakane. In other words, a virtual line encompassing the towns or settlements of Serowe, Mmashoro, Molapo (CKGR), Gope (CKGR), Lephephe, Shoshong and back to Serowe again. Within this area, to the best of my knowledge, are only two officially recognized settlements, Malatswae and Khwee, none of them reaching more than a thousand inhabitants, but providing some infrastructure such as primary schools and small shops. However, such geographical descriptions are of limited use in describing musics of a very sparsely populated area. People were – and quite likely are still – mobile within the wider area. I have met, for example, Keibi not only at his home in Bai, but also in Khwee, as was the case with other people in other places, sometimes people moved away for months. Generally, I believe the area is adequately described by Hitchcock in his brief note of 1979. Although his paper is forty years old by now, his notes have been valid for the time I travelled the area under consideration in 1997. Things may and will have changed since. In this respect, my contribution has to be read as history.

The economic basis of this area has been livestock and its socio-economic structure comes from the traditional Setswana institution of the *meraka,* or cattle post, where cattle are bred around sources of water. Another part of the economy is of course (diamond) mining (in Orapa and Letlhakane); however, whereas most old men I met had some past association with mining jobs (e.g. wearing branded clothes of mining companies), it seems mining already back then rarely recruited locals because the companies required certain skills. Passing the Letlhakane excavation once by car a local woman said and was translated for me as having said something like, 'We never saw any diamonds with our own eyes' (1997). I understood her in the sense that 'we are aware of the importance of mining for our nation, but to us, it is rather elusive.'

Fences cut through this landscape. Some were built by government institutions to tackle Foot-and-Mouth Disease (FMD), some by private landowners to keep their cattle separate from those of their neighbours. The cattle posts are usually operated by local people, known as *Basarwa,*[8] for a small salary or provisions. The Basarwa, or Bushmen, San, Khoisan, including the Bakgalagadi, are descendants of people who have been in the area for a very long time and have come in touch with the livestock economy slowly over perhaps the last millennium. The most recent expansion into more arid areas to the west became possible when borehole-drilling technology arrived in the 1940s (see Barnard 2019: 87). Since then, their hunting and gathering grounds have been gradually taken over by cattle post owners.

The people I have been able to record playing music in this area are considered as Basarwa in mainstream Batswana society, but they themselves have not expressed an ethnic identity or names for their native languages. From memory I recall that Sekere Kiema has been a native speaker of G//ana, and was able to communicate with !Xayee and Meya, although language differences were observed and expressed by Sekere. Chebanne (2014: 2) summarize current linguistic knowledge of the people in the Western Sandveld. He used the designation 'Eastern Kalahari Khoe' and wrote:

> These languages are spoken in North-Central Botswana, to the east towards the Shashe River in the north-eastern part of the country, and even in Eastern Zimbabwe (Cashdan 1979). Historical accounts of these ethnic communities indicate that they have lived there for thousands of years (cf. Dornan 1917, Cashdan 1979, Dowson and Lewis-Williams 1994) (Chebanne 2014: 2). He also acknowledges that there is clearly a geographical overlap in the distribution of these ethnic communities in the identified locations.
>
> (Chebanne 2014: 3)

From his conclusion I learned the glossonyms in the area under consideration are Kua, Cua, Tsua and Shua, and he regards Kua as 'a G‖ana sub-lect', thus supporting my tentative observation of mutual intelligibility between Sekere and !Xhayee above. None of these terms have been brought up in my conversations with local residents.

Instruments of the Eastern Kalahari

The dominant musical instrument of the area under consideration has been the *setinkane* lamellaphones of at least two different types (see Schöpf 1999: 162ff). The Khama III Memorial Museum in Serowe has a fair quantity of specimens in their storerooms. Also prominent was the *sekatare*, a four-string guitar made from 5-litre oilcans with local timbers as neck. The music bows, however, were not available generally. When we asked about them and supplied some material (wire or sinew for the string), elderly men were ready to go for a branch of *moretlwa* (Setswana; botanical name probably *grewia flava*) growing close by, and made one. As is good practice, I usually suggested they made two, selling one of them to me. In this manner Keibi, Meya, Sekere and Yohne made bows for me. It did not matter much apparently that the wood was freshly cut. A detail of string making might be worth describing, however locally, it is an everyday household practice and also reported by England (1995: 40): sinew fibres (from the back of a cow in this instance) are soaked in water for a while.

Once soft, some two to five fibres are brought together to overlap for a good part of their length. They are divided into two threads and held at one end pointing slightly apart, and like this are placed on the lower thigh. The other hand covers both threads and moves downwards on the thigh, rolling them on one's own skin towards the foot. In this manner, both threads are rolled independently, but nearly in parallel. Then, before the sinew threads slip from the hand, the direction is reversed. The hand, held flat all the time, moves back upwards towards the knee and now joins both threads to one, rolling them together in the upward direction. Since the single threads have been rolled in the opposite direction, the resulting double thread stabilizes itself. The described procedure is repeated, adding fresh fragments of sinew in overlap to the ends of the string until the desired length is achieved (Figure 8.4). I believe this to be an old rope maker's practice known the world over.

Sekere built an unbraced music bow of *Moretlwa* wood (most likely *grewia flava*) with sinew string. On one end, a small piece of tough leather is fixed to the bow stave with a length of sinew thread onto the bow stave, which effectively permits the sounding string to be tightened or loosened by turning the string wrappings against the bow stave, effectively making

Figure 8.4 Sekere twisting and turning a bowstring from back sinew fibres of a cow. Photo: Jürgen Schöpf.

the string tuneable, almost like a tuning peg (Figure 8.5).⁹ We believe this to be the same or equivalent to the one described by England as 'skin nut' (England 1995: 40).

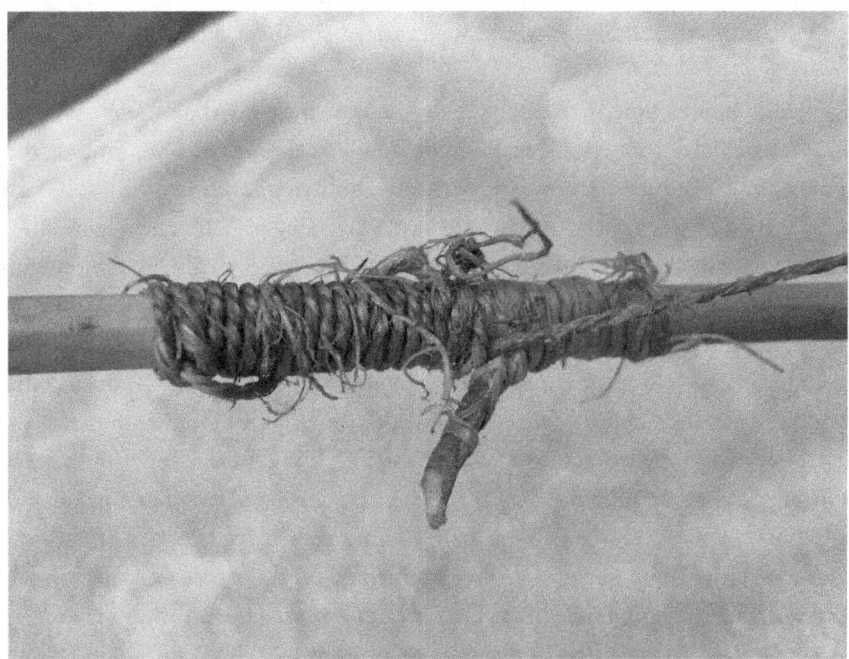

Figure 8.5 The unbraced bow Sekere built with sinew string and wrapped-in piece of leather. Photo courtesy of Klaus-Peter Brenner.

Figure 8.6a String fixation of Yohne's bow. Drawing: Jürgen Schöpf.

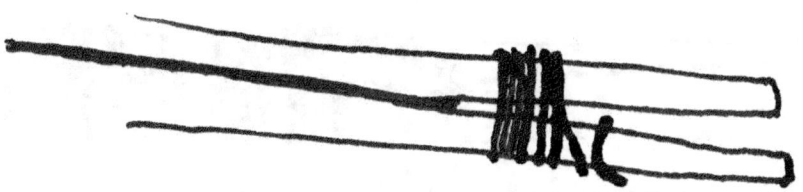

Figure 8.6b String fixation of Yohne's bow. Drawing: Jürgen Schöpf.

The bow Yohne made in Karee is a braced, wire-string mouth bow that is beaten with a grass stalk.[10] One end is conical, but without point (Figure 8.6a), the stave measures 99.5 cm along the curved bow stave. The string is fixed on one end a few centimetres before the end. This seems to facilitate the playing technique of taking the bow end into one corner of the mouth. I provided the wire that is a common standard soft iron-based 0.9 mm fence wire.

Keibi's braced bow made from the same *moretlwa* wood and fence wire as Yohne's deviates in a detail: in between some wrappings of wire around the bow stave he led it in a noose underneath the string, even two times, before finally fixing the wire end in the split bow stave (Figure 8.6b and Figure 8.7). Unfortunately, I have no detailed account of himself towards his reasons for doing so. Mechanically, however, it prevents the split bow stave of splitting down any further under the pressure of the metal string and at the same time, it improves the contact between the string and the bow stave by reducing the contact point surface. This might increase duration of the vibration noticeably.

It is worth noting that Sekere's bow is strung like a hunting bow, both ends ending pointed or at least tapered, and the string is fixed by wrapping around the bow stave (cf. England 1995: 40). In contrast to this, the wire bows have a step in their diameter or a groove at one end, and the free end of the wire string is fixed through a split at the end of the (non-tapered) bow stave. It is plausible that the hunting bow fixation does not work well for a wire string whereas a wire string does not work as a sinew for hunting. Curiously, I have in my collection an unbraced bow with sinew string that is strung to the bow stave in the exact manner as wire string mouth bows are: a noose is held by a step in diameter on one end, and at the other end the string is pulled through a split in the bow stave (Figure 8.8a and Figure 8.8b). Unfortunately, the information that made this bow is currently lost.

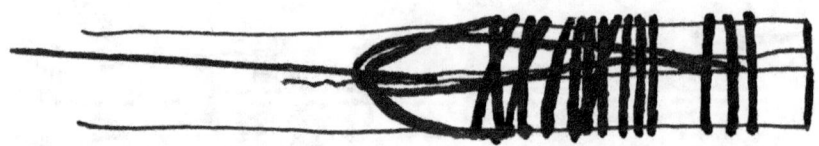

Figure 8.7 Keibi's braced wire bow (102 cm) with two nooses under the string. Drawing: Jürgen Schöpf.

Figure 8.8a An unbraced bow strung with sinew in the manner of a wire bow. Its length is rather high at 114 cm. Drawing: Jürgen Schöpf.

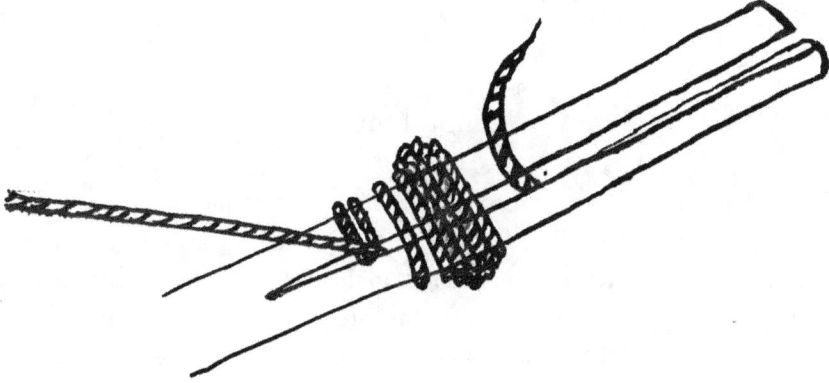

Figure 8.8b An unbraced bow strung with sinew in the manner of a wire bow. Its length is rather high at 114 cm. Drawing: Jürgen Schöpf.

The music

The most comprehensive studies of Khoisan music are Nicholas England's and Emmanuelle Olivier's dissertations. The former written in 1967 got published in 1994, Olivier has published papers and compact discs mainly about the vocal music of Namibia since the 1990s. These are the published corpora of music closest to my own data, although both were collected in Namibia. England is as part of the Harvard expeditions conducted by the Marshall family in Eastern Namibia, more than 500 km west of Khwee and thirty years earlier. Nevertheless, many of my own observations about instrumental music match those of England. For example:

Just as all Bushman music that I have encountered in the Kalahari, Zū'wa music is largely vocal. Even though there are musical instruments, they will seldom be heard without someone's singing along, joined very often by his companions or neighbours. Nevertheless, as a point of departure in this examination of Bushman counterpoint, I will cite an example of purely instrumental music with an eye toward its contrapuntal implications: a piece for the Kxi !ao (Wire Bow), a braced bow with wire string tapped with a reed or stick and resonated by mouth-harp technique. The two fundamental tones produced by the braced string are a minor third apart, a common tuning among the Zū'wasi though other intervals will be encountered from time to time.

(England 1967: 58)

England's observations above apply to the people I have met in the Eastern Kalahari.

Timbral music

Transcribing mouth bow music seems simple at first but offers unexpected challenges for a detailed analysis: The fundamental is easily measured and fixed in writing. However, when it comes to the melody of the partials, we have found conflicting opinions with different listeners. This is due to the physical composition of mouth-resonated music: the physically produced sound is – as with all natural sounds – composed of a number of partials to which we – most of the time – can assign a clear single tone experience, related to its periodicity (which is not always the same as the frequency of the lowest pitch). The literature on psycho-acoustics identifies a number of cases when our perception does not match the fundamental, but none of them is relevant here. In our case, the mouth is used as a filter to resonate certain frequencies (and at the same time suppress others). Thus, the melody of mouth-resonated music is not a melody of fundamentals as is the case with most music, but a melody of partials. However strong or 'narrow', the mouth as a filter cannot reduce the sound to a single frequency only; other frequencies of the natural string vibration remain in the sound and leave room for ambiguity. This is well attested and illustrated for example in the work of neuroscientist Peter Schneider and can be experienced in his online self-test, or in the writings of overtone singing teacher Wolfgang Saus. The latter writes:

If the volume of a single partial is increased considerably with respect to those below, our brain will suddenly take note of this partial as a tone separate from the overall sound. The threshold of this perception is not only a function of volume differences, but also one of hearing training.[11]

(Saus 2006: 69)

Therefore, while most people are likely to agree on a mouth-resonated melody, it is to some extent ambiguous and not everybody can agree on the melodic content. I have tried to accommodate alternative perceptions in my transcriptions whenever other people listening to this music have made me aware of them. Such alternative note perceptions are showing as chords in the transcription (Figure 8.11).

Wire bow acoustics

The acoustics of music bows, mouth-resonated or otherwise, has been established long ago and repeated multiple times: the string provides a natural sound in the sense that it can be described as consisting of partials that are multiples of the one with the lowest frequency. This lowest frequency is also called the fundamental, while the other partials are then called overtones or harmonics of this fundamental. This goes back to the nineteenth-century pioneers in mathematics and physics like Jean Baptiste Joseph Fourier (1768–1830) and Hermann Ludwig Ferdinand von Helmholtz (1821–94). However, when looking closely into the music of !Xhayee I noticed an odd phenomenon, for example, in measure four of transcription 1 (Figure 8.10): he first strikes the longer section of his bow, yielding the fundamental (d' -65 Cent) while his mouth resonates the second partial, the octave (d"). He continues by beating the smaller section of the string for the fundamental (f'+44Cent); however, I clearly hear the melodic note d" continue, although the fundamental has changed. While d" is the second partial to d', it does not feature in the series of harmonics of f', how come it can be heard? The reason for this is, I believe, the behaviour of the wire string of his bow. The 0.9 cm thick fence wire used on !Xhayee's bow actually has quite a noisy sound. In the language of physics this means it contains many non-linear partials. In other words, many overtones that are NOT multiples of the fundamental. I have calculated two spectrograms and related spectra with the software Sound Tools Extended (STx)[12] to illustrate this in Figures 8.9

and 8.10. Both figures have a grey top section and a coloured bottom section. The grey top section is further split into two different graphs, the left one showing the actual waveform that is not important here. The coloured display is a three-dimensional Fourier transformation. It shows time on the x-axis (seconds from the beginning of the recording), the y-axis shows frequency (linear, kHz), whereas the amplitude of any sound is represented by a colour scale, the hotter the louder, the colder the softer, thus white being the loudest, fading through yellow, orange and red to blue as the softest in the scale. Figure 8.9 has a green and a red vertical line cutting through the coloured display. These lines are marks and the top right graph in grey displays an average spectrum calculated for the sound between those red and green marks. The window for the grey spectrum is 0 Hz up to 16 kHz in this case. In both graphs we see a lot of lines, meaning a lot of partials are contained in this sound, corresponding to the sensation of a noisy sound. All efforts to find the ONE fundamental to which all these higher partials are multiples of are obviously futile. The same is true for Figure 8.10 where the second note is analysed in the same manner; however, the grey spectrum in the top right area is calculated to a maximum frequency of 1,500 Hz only. I have chosen this lower value to show the lower part of the spectrum in more detail than in the previous one. We can clearly see that there are no steep spikes, but all widely undulating hills, visualizing what our ears have told us: the sound is rather noisy and the fundamental is not very strong with respect to other partials. This means that a broad band of frequencies is actually produced by the 'noisy' string. As a consequence, a diversity of higher partials is contained and, hence, can be resonated by a player's mouth cavity. By contrast, with a single clear fundamental, we would see the orderly series of harmonics as lines at their mathematical multiples of the fundamental. For example, a sinew string, being much softer than metal wire, is a very likely candidate to have a clearer fundamental and less higher partials, and moreover is likely to have much fewer non-linear partials as well. All players I met, however, choose the bow with wire string when they performed with a mouth-resonated bow. Instances of this effect can be seen in the appended video 1 and transcriptions in cycles 4, 9, 16, 26, 38, 39 and 40.

!Xhayee Moko was the player that made most consistent use of playing overtone melodies. His title 'A'gaige' is his name for the steenbok (*Raphicerus campestris*) called *phuduhudu* in Setswana (Cole 1995: 48), and the piece is inspired by its gait. During one of our sessions with the players in Khwee, Myizer Matlhaku asked why so many pieces of bow music had animal titles and were

Eastern Kalahari Bow Music

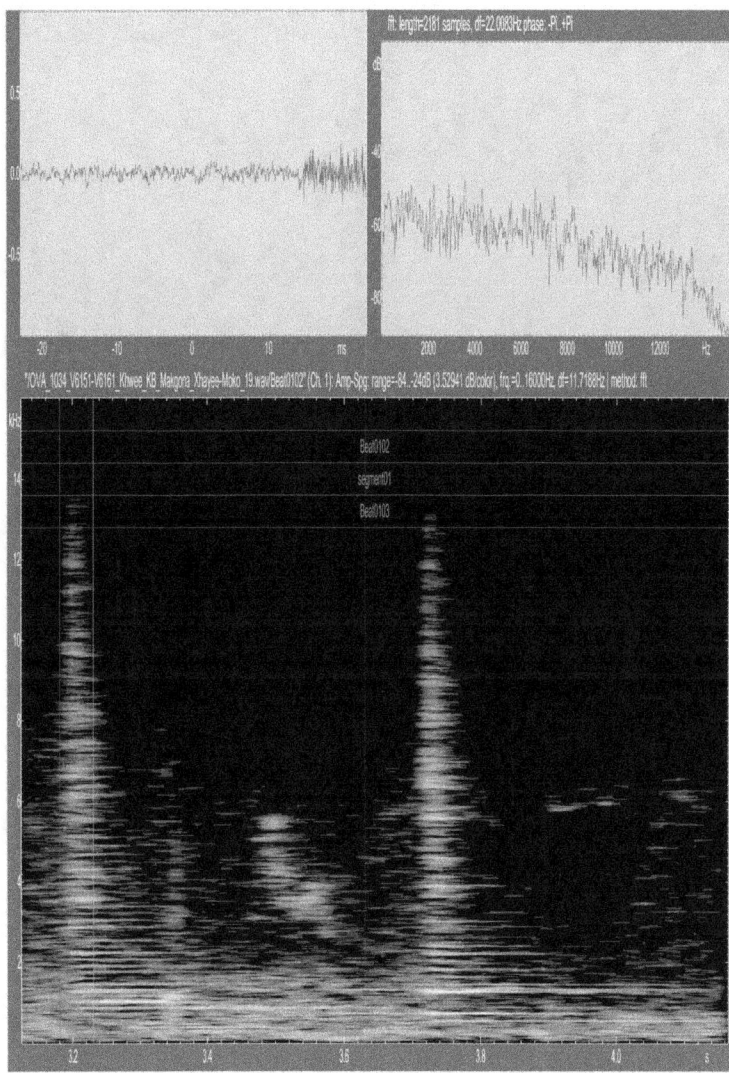

Figure 8.9 Spectrum & spectrogram of a single note stroke on f0 *c*. d'-65C. Source: Jürgen Schöpf.

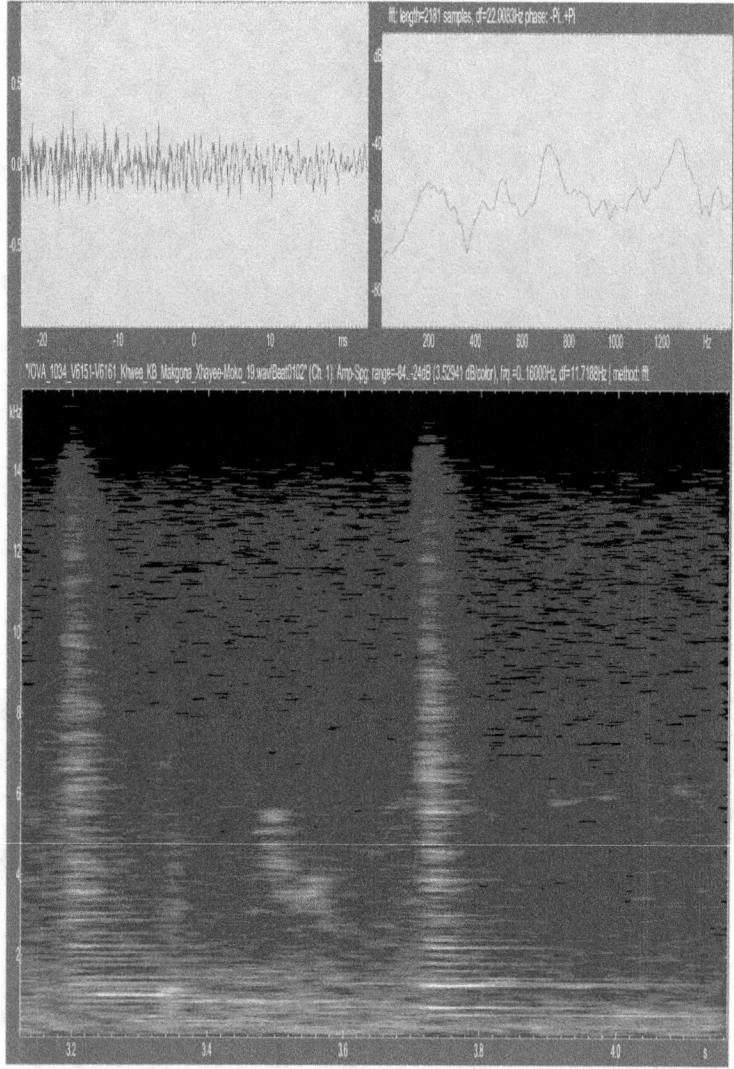

Figure 8.10 Spectrum & spectrogram of a single note stroke on f0 c. f'+44Cent. Source: Jürgen Schöpf.

played with uneven rhythms whereas the respective animals in the wild would move symmetrically and even. He got response from !Xhayee and his companions that the rhythms of the music came from times when they were still hunting with poisoned arrows and those rhythms actually depict the respective animals after they were hit with a poisoned arrow and were limping and stumbling on their flight. The hunter would then follow the animal until the poison would slow it down or even paralyse it and he could catch his prey. Meya Galotsa also played an overtone melody, but less consistent than his friend !Xhayee. All other players appeared to me to make use of the overtone resonances not for melodic use, but as timbre. Keibi had his particular way of playing mouth bow: he sang at the same time as he hit the bow in a rhythmic pattern.

Figure 8.11 Full transcription of 'A'gaige'.

N!oma jieu

Meya Galotsa in Khwee introduced me to a way to play a music bow that is called in his language *N!oma jieu* and was translated to me as 'springhare technique'. This playing technique requires more than one player and I have recorded up to three acting on the bow while even more joined with singing or clapping (Figure 8.2 and Video 3).

For this type of performance, a hollow container like a basin, bucket, can or jar is put on the ground with its opening facing downwards. One end of an unbraced bow is placed on this container with its stave firmly touching it for acoustic coupling so that the container acts as a resonator for vibrations transmitted through the bow stave. Most players put their foot onto the bow stave to ensure good mechanical contact. The other end of the bow stave rests against the chest of a player who I will call the first or principal player. His job is to excite the string. This is done by hitting it from above and pushing it down with either a small hard object or by holding a tiny twig between the hands very close together and hitting the string with this small piece of wood. In this manner, the string is pushed down a few centimetres and quickly let loose again in a brisk upward movement. This is repeated in a regular beat. The result is an excited string, but the string is also braced when it is hit, and unbraced when the object is lifted off the string. Because the string is excited in the downwards movement, the string tension rises at the same time, resulting in an upward glide of pitch. The audible result is a two-tone alternation with an upward glide between the two tones and a downward step back to the lower interval. On top of this *ostinato* a second or even third player hits the string with a tiny twig or dry stalk of grass in a contrasting rhythm. This is done as enjoyment and seems to involve a degree of improvisation and experimentation. For example, in one recording the bow stave was regularly lifted off its resonator, resulting in a sudden pause of the otherwise drone like ostinato. However playful, some of these pieces of music have titles and are composed, and in the session recorded on 2 May 1997, two younger men who did not know this music or musical game were given instructions what to do.

Mokgweba

One piece, recorded on 2 May 1997, was called 'Kamkge',[13] meaning: *mokgweba* (Setswana). Neither Matumo (1993) nor Cole (1995) discusses this word, but the former has the similar word *mokgwelea* meaning a 'bush *korhaan* or heathcock'.

A search for *korhaan* in the bird database of the website xeno-canto.org yields a species with the official name *Afrotis afraoides* (English: Northern black korhaan) which is common throughout inland Southern Africa. Recordings of this bird's call contain rhythmic beating that is easily imagined to have inspired the rhythmic pattern of the song.[14] However, the connection of both on the basis of sound content must remain speculative until further consultation with Kalahari residents can be obtained.

Another special technique inspired by an animal was shown to me by Sekere Kiema. He took a small stalk of dry grass of around 10 cm and squeezed it into the string of his unbraced sinew strung bow. He then placed the lower bow end on a resonator just as in the *N!oma jieu* technique. Now he made his fingers wet and rubbed the small stick. The resulting vibration went through the string into the resonator and made loud noises just as a friction drum. The title of this piece was translated to me as 'wild dogs', being inspired by the noises of African Wild Dogs (*Lycaon pictus*).

Summary

During a few short trips to the Eastern Kalahari region in 1997 I was able to confirm many of England's findings regarding musical bows (England 1967 and 1995). The art of using filtered partials of a mouth bow as melodic notes has been in practice still, but also obviously in decline. Only a few elderly men were still able to make and play music bows. However, there has been a variety of bow instruments and uses that point to a greater variety of styles in the past. Many songs have been inspired by animals. Notably, the rhythms have been related to the limping and stumbling of animals struck by poisoned arrows. The Kalahari residents are highly inventive in creating and re-creating sounds and expressing animal behaviour with a music bow.

Technical aspects

The recording equipment in the field consisted of a pair of Soundman OKM II original head microphones as well as two AKG Blue Line C300B/CK91 cardioid condenser microphones. My main recording machine was a Tascam DA-P1 Digital Audio Tape (DAT) recorder and backup recorder was a SONY WMD-6C professional Walkman. Transcriptions have been conducted with the help of 'Transcribe!' of Seventhstring.com (https://seventhstring.com/, accessed 3 February 2020). Spectrograms have been calculated with the STx software of the Acoustics Research Institute of the Austrian Academy of Sciences (https://www.kfs.oeaw.ac.at). Video footage was taken with a Panasonic S-VHS-C camera. All data are archived with the Phonogrammarchiv of the Austrian Academy of Sciences in Vienna (phonogrammarchiv.at).

Notes

1 My own orthography. The '!' stands for a click sound. Unfortunately, I am unable to specify the phonetic details of this click, but believe it is a post-alveolar or palatal sound, certainly not a lateral.
2 The initial 'j' is pronounced as a palato-alveolar fricative with initial stop (affricate). The following vowels are not drawn together but pronounced as three monophthongs.
3 (-21°56.609' South, 25°26.895' East).
4 A cattle post somewhat west of Mmashoro, south-east of Malatswae.
5 I recorded him while he was staying in Tlôkweng.
6 (-22°02,333' South, 25°43,948' East).
7 The orthography of his first name is mine, developed from my own hearing. It certainly starts with a click sound that is most likely alveo-dental or palatal, followed by a velar fricative and an a-to-i diphthong (uncommon in Setswana), ending in a long, closed [e] as in the English word 'mend' or a French 'é'.
8 Basarwa, San, Khoisan, or Bushmen, none of these terms is actually satisfactory. For a discussion, see Barnard (2019: 8ff).
9 Private collection of the author. This instrument is on loan to the Musical Instruments Museum of the University of Göttingen, Germany. Item no. L-101. Photo courtesy of Klaus-Peter Brenner.
10 Private collection of the author. This instrument is on loan to the Musical Instruments Museum of the University of Göttingen, Germany. Item no. L-102+a.
11 In the German original: 'Wird nun ein einzelner Oberton relativ zu den direkt darunter liegenden wesentlich lauter, dann nimmt unser Gehirn ihn plötzlich als separaten Ton neben dem Stimmklang wahr. Die Schwelle für die Wahrnehmung ist dabei nicht nur eine Funktion des Lautstärkeunterschieds, sondern auch des Hörtrainings' (Saus 2006: 69), translation by the author.
12 See https://www.kfs.oeaw.ac.at STx is free for non-commercial, scholarly and educational use.

13 As a speaker of Setswana might write it: the 'g' after the initial consonant represents a velar fricative.
14 https://www.xeno-canto.org/species/Afrotis-afraoides

References

Barnard, Alan (2019), *Bushmen. Kalahari Hunter-Gatherers and Their Descendants*, Cambridge: University Press.

Cashdan, E. (1979), Trade and Reciprocity Among the River Bushmen of Northern Botswana. PhD thesis, University of New Mexico.

Chebanne, Andy (2014), 'What Have Eastern Kalahari Khoe Languages Lost Linguistically?' *Stellenbosch Papers in Linguistics Plus* 44: 1–21. doi: 10.5842/44-0-639

Cole, Desmond T. (1995), *Setswana – Animals and Plants (Setswana – Ditshedi le ditlhare)*, Gaborone: The Botswana Society.

Dornan, S.S. (1917), 'The Tati Bushmen (Masarwas) and Their Language', *Journal of the Royal Anthropological Institute* 47: 37–112.

England, Nicholas (1967), 'Bushman Counterpoint', *Journal of the International Folk Music Council* 19 (1967): 58–66. Available online: https://www.jstor.org/stable/942188

England, Nicholas (1995), *Music among the Zũ|'wã-si and Related Peoples of Namibia, Botswana, and Angola*, New York: Garland.

Hitchcock, Robert (1979), 'A Socio-economic Survey of the Eastern Kalahari Cattle Post', *Botswana Notes & Records* 11 (1979): 137–9.

Lenssen-Erz T. and O. Vogels, (2017), 'Eine Musiklektion vom Daureb (Brandberg): Musikbögen in der Felskunst Namibias und des südlichen Afrika', in N. Rupp, G. Beck, G. Franke, and K.P. Wendt (eds.), *Winds of Change: Archaeological Contributions in Honour of Peter Breunig. Frankfurter Archäologische Schriften*, 35, 61–72, (2017),Bonn: Dr. Rudolf Habelt GmbH..

Matumo, Z. I. (1993), *Setswana English Setswana Dictionary*, Gaborone, Botswana: Macmillan Boleswa.

Morgan, Deirdre (2006), *Organs and Bodies. The Jew's Harp and the Anthropology of Musical Instruments*, The University of British Columbia, 2006 http://www.deirdremorgan.com/researchprojects (accessed 5 January 2020).

Schneider, Peter (n.d.), 'Short Test for Pitch Perception Preference', *Research Team Music and Brain*, University Hospital Heidelberg. Available online: https://www.musicandbrain.de/en/short-test.html (accessed 4 November 2019).

Saus, Wolfgang (2006), Oberton Singen [Second Edition], *Battweiler* (2006).

Saus, Wolfgang (n.d.), *Test: Are You an Overtone or Fundamental Listener?* Available online: https://www.oberton.org/en/test-are-you-overtone-or-fundamental-listener/ (accessed 4 November 2019).

Schneider, Peter., Vanessa Sluming, Neil Roberts, Michael Scherg, Rainer Goebel, Hans J. Specht, H. Günter Dosch, Stefan Bleeck, Christoph Stippich und André Rupp (2005), 'Structural and Functional Asymmetry of Lateral Heschl's Gyrus Reflects Pitch Perception Preference', *Nature Neuroscience* 8 (9): 1241–7. doi:10.1038/nn1530, http://dx.doi.org/10.1038/nn1530 (accessed 4 November 2019).

Seither-Preisler, Annemarie., Linda Johnson, Stefan Seither, and Bernd Lütkenhöner (2008), 'Exposure to Ambiguous Tone Sequences Induces Short-term Plasticity of Pitch Perception', in Frank Columbus (ed.), *Experimental Psychology Research Trends*, New York: Nova Science Publishers.

Schöpf, Jürgen (1999), 'Ethnomusikologische Feldforschung in Botswana 1997', Marianne Bröcker (ed.), *Berichte aus dem ICTM-Nationalkomitee VIII*, 155–69, Bamberg 1999: STx software of the Acoustics Research Institute of the Austrian Academy of Sciences Available online: https://www.kfs.oeaw.ac.at (accessed 3 February 2020).

Vogels, O. and Lenssen-Erz T. (2016), 'Musical Bows in Southern African Rock Art: Music-Archaeological and Ethnohistorical Observations', in M. Gutierrez, and E. Honoré (eds.), *L'art rupestre d'Afrique: Actes du congrès – Paris le 15- 16-17janvier 2014*, 217–31, Nanterre: Centre Panthéon & musée du quai Branly.

Vogels, O. and T., Lenssen-Erz (2017), 'Beyond Individual Pleasure and Rituality: Social Aspects of the Musical Bow in Southern Africa's Rock Art', *Rock Art Research* 34 (1): 9–24. Available online: http://www.uni-koeln.de/fast/people/vogels/pdf/vogels2017beyond

Wood, Elizabeth Nelbach (1975), 'A Study of the Traditional Music of Mochudi', *Botswana Notes & Records* 8 (1975): 189–221.

Wood, Elizabeth Nelbach (1983), *Traditional Music of Botswana*. Folkways Records album no. FE 4371, Compact Cassette with liner notes: 1–6.

Wood, Elizabeth Nelbach (1985), 'Traditional Music in Botswana', *The Black Perspective in Music* 13 (1): 13–30.

Xeno-Canto website, https://www.xeno-canto.org (accessed 3 February 2020).

For audio and visual examples, see https://www.bloomsbury.com/us/musical-bows-of-southern-africa-9781501346743/.

Contributor Biographies

Bernhard Bleibinger is Professor at the University of Fort Hare in South Africa. He studied at the Ludwig-Maximilians University in Munich (Germany) and the University of California Los Angeles (United States) and taught and conducted research at the Escola Superior de Música de Catalunya and the Consejo Superior de Investigaciones Científicas in Barcelona (Spain). He has conducted workshop-seminars on African musical instrument making on national and international level. Research interests: Music and Symbols, and Applied [Ethno] musicology.

Klaus-Peter Brenner is Curator of the Collection of Musical Instruments and Lecturer in Ethnomusicology at Georg-August-Universität Göttingen, Germany. He has published monographs on Turkish village music (1992), the Shona *chipendani/mbira* music of Zimbabwe (1997) and the Nzakara *kùndì/nzángu^{n}la* music of the CAR (2004). His recent articles deal with processes of improvisation and transformation in and between Shona, Venda and Sena musics. He is the editor of *Mbira Music | Musics: Structures and Processes* (2019).

Dave Dargie, born 1938 in East London, South Africa, was working to promote new isiXhosa church songs for use in the Catholic Church when he found a wonderful survival of the old traditional isiXhosa music. Since 1979 he has worked unceasingly to preserve that and other traditional music through audio and video recordings, documenting the recordings through a series of handbooks. He is the author of the book *Xhosa Music: Its Techniques and Instruments – with a Collection of Songs*, published in 1988 by David Philip, Cape Town.

Sazi Dlamini is Musicologist and Lecturer at the University of KwaZulu-Natal in Durban, South Africa. A jazz-influenced guitarist and composer in the South African township tradition, he was awarded a Doctor of Philosophy degree for his thesis *The South African Blue Notes: Bebop, Mbaqanga, Apartheid and the Exiling of a Musical Imagination*. Among his diverse research and performance interests are *ugubhu, umakhweyana, umqangala* and *uhadi* Nguni (Bantu) musical bows.

Jennifer W. Kyker is Associate Professor of Ethnomusicology at the University of Rochester. She received her PhD from the University of Pennsylvania, and is the author of *Oliver Mtukudzi: Living Tuku Music in Zimbabwe*, published by Indiana University Press. Her research has been supported by fellowships from the Fulbright and Fulbright-Hays programmes, and the American Council for Learned Societies. Jennifer also founded the nonprofit organization Tariro, which educates teenaged girls in Zimbabwean communities affected by HIV/AIDS (www.tariro.org).

Cara Stacey is a South African musician, researcher and is currently an ACLS African Humanities Programme Postdoctoral Fellow. As a Commonwealth Scholar, she completed her PhD through the University of Cape Town and SOAS (London). Her research investigated innovation in the music of the *makhweyane* bow in the Kingdom of eSwatini (formerly Swaziland). She is the International Council for Traditional Music country liaison office for eSwatini and is based between Johannesburg and Mbabane.

Vusi Sibandze is a researcher, musician and artist based in Mbabane, eSwatini. Within the country, he has been an active facilitator and manager of traditional music events and artists for many years. He has repeatedly served on the Swaziland Traditional Music Association and aided numerous recordings of *makhweyane*, *sitolotolo*, *sitontolo* and other instrument players. Vusi teaches Visual Art at a local high school just outside Mbabane.

Jürgen Schöpf studied Ethnomusicology, Music History and Linguistics at the University of Göttingen. His PhD thesis – a study of the bowed monochord Serankure in Botswana – was published in 2008. He has since worked in projects in northeast India documenting minority languages and musics for the Volkswagen Foundation and La Trobe University, Melbourne. He has further interests in Organology, Soundscape Research and Technology.

Index

Boldface locators indicate figures and tables; locators followed by "n." indicate endnotes

Abantu Baphelile (*ugubhu* song) **13**
aerophones 177 n.1
'African auriture' 168
African Musical Instruments (AMI) 30, 33 n.22
Akasangibhaleli' (*umakhweyana* song) 142, **143**, 144
Alikho la ekhaya (*umakhweyana* song) 148
Amadoda kashelani (*umakhweyana* song) 144, **145**, 153 n.40
amaXhosa 205, 226 n.3
    history in *uhadi* songs 213–16, **214** (*see also* uhadi (Xhosa))
    Kirby on musical bows of 205
andôbu (Mbuti) 75 n.4
Angas, George F. 115
Applied Ethnomusicology 33 n.18

Balfour, H. 164, 178 n.16
Basarwa 234
Bashayi Bengoma ensemble 186, 199, **199**
basic *kalimba* core (Tracey) 37, 41, 57, 61, **62**, 63
Batho 230
beehive dome (Zulu) 117, 148 n.7, 149 n.7
Bent, Theodore 163–4
berimbao 94, 110 n.5
biradical tonal organisation 133–4, **134**
Bleek, Dorothy 123
Botswana 224, 229–30, 235. *See also* Eastern Kalahari
Bow Project 226
braced bows 10, 15, 17, 18, 115, 187. *See also* unbraced bows
    with attached resonator **12**, **13**
    with bracing loop **8**, **9**
    Chipendani (*see chipendani* (mouth bow))

Keibi's wire bow 238, **238**
Kxi !ao wire bow 240
/*noukhas* (Damara) 21, 100, **101**, 109
Ondendele (OvaZimba) **102**, **109**
Sitontolo (*see sitontolo* (mouth bow))
string fixation of Yohne's bow **237**, 238
Umakhweyana (*see umakhweyana/umakhweyane* (Zulu))
xitende 20, 134, 150 n.19, 150 n.24, 152 n.29, 185
bracing 121–2, 148 n.1
Brenner, Klaus-Peter 46, 55, 59–61, 65–7, 71–2, 162–3, 167–9, 178 n.20, 180 n.29, 230
burumbumba (Cuban) 152 n.29
Buthelezi, Mangosuthu 153 n.35
Buthelezi, Mathole 140, 152 n.33, 153 n.35

calabash-resonated musical bow 10, 94, 113, 115, 117–18, 123, 126, 129–30, 137–40, 150 n.19, 151 n.28, 203. *See also ugubhu* (Zulu); *umakhweyana/umakhweyane* (Zulu)
Camp, C.M. 19, 20, 29, 178 n.16. *See also* classification (bows)
capella (*umbholoho* music) 185
Carver, Christian 33 n.22
Cavric, Gordana 230
Chawasarira, Chaka 38, 167, 178 n.18
Chebanne, Andy 235
Chemutengure (Shona *karimba* piece) 64, **64**
chidangari 158, 177 n.2
Chigamba, Brian 159, 167

Chigamba, Tute (Sekuru) 157–9, **160**, 169, 176, 178 n.14, 179 n.24, 179 n.26, 179 n.27, 180 n.28
  chipendani for older children 171–2
  cow horn plectrums 174, **174**
  early life 161
  kambuya-mbuya 158, 167, 170
  memory of father's *mukube*, recalling 173–5
  as multi-instrumentalist 167
  and Muradzikwa 161
  playing *chipendani* **162**
  playing *mukube* **163**
chijaka 40, **53**, 71–2
chimwanikoda 158, 177 n.3
chipendani (mouth bow) **8**, **9**, 17, 37, **40**, 74 n.1, 157, 161, 176, 179 n.22. See also *tshihwana* (Venda)
  analysis 41
  Chigamba playing 158, 161, **162**
  comparison 41
  construction 38
  for courtship 171–2
  intervals, fundamentals 45, **45**
  'Kwa ambuya asina keriya' 57–9, **58**
  local use, evidence 68
  mukube and 164
  one-dimensional string-divider 41–2, **43**
  physical laws 41
  players 38, **39**
  playing technique (*see* playing technique (*chipendani*))
  portrayal 162
  position and function 68
  ratios of vibrating string lengths 41, 42–3, **44**, 45
  as self-delectative 175
  tone material 61
  two-dimensional string-divider 42, **42**
chitende 152 n.29, 158, 177 n.2
classification (bows). *See also specific bows*
  with attached resonator 10, 18–19, 205–6, 211
  Camp and Nettl 19–20, **21–28**
  Dargie 20, **21–28**, 29
  Hornbostel and Sachs 18, 85, 109 n.2
  Malamusi 29
  Mukhavele 29
  without attached resonator 10, 18–19

Clegg, Johnny 29
coastal silver-oak 116
Cole, Desmond T. 248
Coplan, David 168

Damara 15, 83
  gorito 20, 84–5, 97–100, **98**, **99**, **100**, 108–9
  /*noukhas* 20, 100, **101**, 109
Dargie, Dave 1, 3, 32 n.2, 32 n.5, 32 n.7, 72, 131, 216
  banjiwe 127
  collections on bows 29
  Namibian bow songs 86
  overtones 2, 17
  recordings 72, 75 n.8
  types of bows 19–20, **21–28**, 29
Dargie 2000 to Present (the *Dave Dargie Collection*) 86, 94, 98, 110 n.9, 208, 216, 219, 226, 227 n.8, 227 n.17
dende (Venda) 115, 152 n.29
dibukandinga 158
Dima, Avhapfani Constence 68
dimbwa 158, 177 n.2
divided string 20, 42–3, 69, **120**, 129, 134–5, 137, 138, 151 n.26, 161, 232. *See also umakhweyana/umakhweyane* (Zulu)
Dlamini, Absalom Mandvulo 184
Dlamini, Sazi 30, 33 n.17, 85
Dlangamandla, Mlamli 224
Doke-Vilakazi C. 148 n.5
Dontsa, Luvuyo 224–5
drums (Zimbabwean) 167, 173, 177 n.1
Dumbu 173
Dumiso, Nosinothi 213–14, 216, **217**
Dywili, Nofinishi 204, 207–8, **210**, 211, 213, 215, 227 n.10
  Inxembula 213, **215**, 216–18
  playing *uhadi* **212**
dzikamunhenga (ground-bow) 158, 160

Eastern Cape Province 2, 32 n.2, 203, **204**
Eastern Kalahari 233, 249
  Basarwa 234
  economy 234
  instruments of 235–38
  linguistic knowledge 235
  music 239–40

EBloemfontein (*umakhweyana* song) 142, **143**, 144
elumba (otjizema) 109, **109**
end-braced bow **13**, 20, 102, **102**
England, Nicholas 236–7, 239–40, 249
Enjo 230
Erlmann, Veit 144
eSwatini, kingdom of 183–4, 199
   culture 184
   Imbokodvo National Movement 184
   music in 185–6 (*see also sitontolo* (mouth bow))

falling Shepard scale 75 n.9
Fischer, Arnold **217**
Fourier, Jean Baptiste Joseph 241
Frescura, Franco 148 n.7
fundamental notes, sounding (*umakhweyana*) 123–4, 151 n.26
   banjiwe, applicability 126–7
   method of holding 124, **124**, 126
   thiyiwe siqalo 127, 129, **129**
   ukushaya ngaphezulu 127, **128**
   ukushaya ngenzansi 127, **128**, **129**
   ukuvala uthaka 129
   vuliwe, applicability 126–7
Furniss, Suzanne 159

gabus (Korana Khoe) 163
galinga (Venda) **15**, **16**
Galotsa, Meya 230, 235, 245, 248
   playing *N!oma jieu* 232, **232**
Gandidze, John 67
Gardiner, Allen F. 115
!Gawiseb, P. **98**, 98–100, 110 n.9
gestalt effect 74
ghost notes 75 n.5
Gildenhuys, Cecilia 97
Gomba, Frank 168, 167
gora (Khoi) 20, 205
gorito (Damara) 20, 84–5, 97–100, 108–9
   !Gawiseb playing **99**, 99
   traditional song with **99**, 99–100, **100**
Grey, George 213
ground-bow 15, 157–9, 164, 176, 178 n.16, 178 n.17
   children's herding games 169–71
   as children's instrument 167
   distributions 165

dzikamunhenga 158, 160
   jacaranda leaves in resonating chamber 166, **166**
   makalapo 159
   marginalization 178 n.17
   Muradzikwa playing **165**, 165–6
   playing technique and sound 179 n.22
   with tension noose **16**
   without tension noose **15**
The Grove Dictionary of Musical Instruments 151 n.29, 152 n.29

Haididira, P. 92, **93**, 94
Hango, Eugen **90**, 90–1
harmonic parallelism 89
harmonics 10, 17, 18, 126–7, 138, 161, 241–2. *See also* overtone harmonics
harp 15, 164, 168, 177, 179 n.22, 185
Heibeb, Moses 100
Helmholtz, Hermann Ludwig Ferdinand von 241
Hitchcock, Robert 233–4
Hoffman, Carl 164
holicipation 153 n.38
Hornbostel, E.M. von 18–19, 115. *See also* classification (bows)
hugu 158, 177 n.2

Icamagu livumile (*inkinge* song) 223, **223**
idiophones 74, 177 n.1
ihadi (Xhosa) 207, 227 n.7
Ihadi liyahlabela ingoma, ndilandela ngomlomo (Xhosa song) 207
ikatari (Xhosa) 3, 20, 85, 205–6, 208, **210**, **224**
   construction 224
   as herd-boys' instrument 209
   Ngqoko Group with **211**
   Nontyolo **214**, 215
   style 224–5
Imire 160–1, 178 n.9
Impey, Angela 118, 149 n.13, 149 n.17, 159, 172
imvingo (Zulu) 113–14, 138, 148 n.4, 148 n.5, 151 n.28
   elastic potential energy 118–9
   as *izintingo* 117, **117**
   structural significance 117–18
incanco 158, 177 n.3

ingona (loop brace) 116, **116**, 149 n.11
  positional method of tuning **121**, 122
  rotatory method of tuning **122**, 122–3
  string division 119–21, **120**, 149 n.11
inkatha (support cushion) **116**, 119, **120**
inkinge (Xhosa) **5, 6**, 20, 87, 163, 205–6, 209, **223**
  Pintshana with **210, 222**
  Yakayaka – *ndemka* 222–3
inkohlisa (Zulu) 113–14, 151 n.27, 151 n.28, 152 n.32
  as performance context 137–38
  post-marital context (*umakhweyana*) 144–5, **145, 145**, 147–48
  premarital context (*umakhweyana*) 141–2, 144
  self-accompaniment of songs (Zulu women's) 138–9
  ugubhu 'love' songs (Princess Magogo) 139–40
  umakhweyana as 141
inkokha (Zulu) 113–15, 118, 121, 149 n.9
  equilibrium restoring forces 118–19
  functional forces with *ingona* 119–21
intambo/uthaka (string) 116, **116**, 118–19
International Library of African Music (ILAM) 86, 100, 180 n.30, 203. *See also* Tracey, Andrew
Inxembula (*uhadi* song) 213, **215**, 216–18
inyanga (isiZulu) 147, 153 n.41, 153 n.42
isankuni. *See ikatari* (Xhosa)
iselwa (calabash resonator) 116, **116, 120**, 123, 126, 132, 135
isicelekeshe (Zulu) 20
isigankuri. *See ikatari* (Xhosa)
isimekezo songs 140, 153 n.34
isiqomqomana (Zulu) 20, 41, 149 n.15
isiqwemqwemana (*umakhweyana*, Zulu)
  onomatopoeia and calabash resonation technique 132–3
  as synonyms 129–30
isitontolo (xiTsonga) 187
isiXhosa. *See* Xhosa

Johnston, Thomas F. 74 n.2, 179 n.26
Joseph, Rosemary 138–9, 150 n.18, 150 n.20, 180 n.29

kabarome (Mbuti) 41
kaDinizulu, C.M. 130, 149 n.16, 150 n.19, 152 n.33
  ugubhu 'love' songs 139–40, 152 n.33
Kaemmer, John 2, 32 n.5
Kahari, George 164
Kaholo (Caprivi) 90
kaleidoscopic 85
kalumbu (Ila and Tonga) 152 n.29, 177 n.2
Kariga mombe (Shona *mbira dzavadzimu* piece) 65
karimba music (Shona) 62, 167, 178 n.18
  Chemutengure 64, **64**
  lower manual 63, **63**
Karufere, P.M. 92, **93**, 94
Kauffman, Robert 161, 163–4, 178 n.13, 180 n.29
Kavango 83–4, 212
  kaworongongo 20, **90**, 90–2, **91, 92**, 108, 110 n.4
  lipuruboro 10, **14**, 20, 92–4, **93**, 108, 110 n.4
  musical bows and bow theory 86–7, **87**
  rugoma (*marugoma*) 20, 87, **88, 89**, 89–90, 108, 227 n.16
  scale usage 84
kaworongongo (Kavango) 20, **90**, 90–2, **91, 92**, 108, 110 n.4
Khoi 2–3
  gora 20, 205
Kiema, Sekere 230, 235, 249
Killick, Andrew 153 n.38
Kirby, P. R. 3, 18, 75 n.6, 87, 115, 123, 149 n.16, 150 n.26, 151 n.26, 151 n.28, 152 n.31, 179 n.26, 187, 190
  inkohlisa, categorization 137–38
  on musical bows (amaXhosa) 205, 206, 211
Kropf, A. 205
Kruger, Jaco 15, 75 n.5, 75 n.6
Kubik, Gerhard 17, 32 n.5, 74 n.3, 84, 87, 110 n.5
Kunene 84–5
  musical bows of 101–8 (*see also ombulumbumba* (otjiZimba); *outa* (otjiHimba); pluriarc (otjiZimba))
'Kwa ambuya asina keriya' (*chipendani* piece) 57–59, **58**

'Kwasenza (It happened to us)'
(*umakhweyana* song) **137**
Kyker, Jennifer 38, 68

lamellaphones/lamellophones 61–2, 230
  njari 179 n.21
  setinkane 230, 232–3, 235
lekope (Pedi/Sotho) 75 n.4, 163, 179 n.26, 187
Lenga, Luyolo 30, 33 n.23
lengope (Tswana) 163, 233
lesiba (Sotho) 10, 20
ligubhu (Swati) 133, 138, 150 n.19, 151 n.28
lipuruboro (Kavango) 10, **14**, 20, 92–4, **93**, 108, 110 n.4
List, George 180 n.29
Liyana (film) 199
Lobinger, Fritz 203
lugube (Venda) 163
Lumko 203–6, 209
  bow materials in 207
  ihadi 227 n.7
Lungisa, Nofirsti 209, **211**

Mabhiza (*chipendani* piece) 59–60
Mabuza, Sitandi 196, 201 n.8
Maezengi **102**
Magagula, Bhemani 183, 188, 190, 193
  as farmer and miner 192
  playing *sitontolo* **189**
  poetic and poignant titling 197
  sitontolo song 193–6, **196**, 198
Magagula, Cathrina 185–6, 192
Magagula, Make 192
Magagula, Thobile 'Makhoyane' 200
Mahlalela, Babe 192
Mahlalela, John 192
makalapo (ground-bow) 159
makhweyane (Swati/Swazi) 20, 152 n.29, 159, 185–6, 196
Malamusi, Moya 29
Mandela, Tandile 179 n.26
Mandumbu, Nowizine 216, 217, **217**
mangwingwindo (drumming style) 167, 173
Manisi, Mpahlolo 209, **211**
Manona, Cecil 213, 221

Manqina, Madosini 29, 225
Mans, Minette 32 n.7, 83, 85, 102, 105, 110 n.12
Marago, Makgona 230, 233
Masilela, Elias 200 n.4
matepe (*mbira*) 167, 177 n.1, 178 n.18
materials (bow)
  imvingo 117–19
  in Lumko 207
  recycled 32 n.2
  using modern materials 17, 18
Matiso, Amelia Nosilence 208
Matjatjayela (*sitontolo* song) 193
Matlhaku, Myizer 229, 230, 242
Matotiyana, Mantombi 29, 226
Matsenjwa, Elias 196
Matumo, Z. I. 248
mbira music, Shona. See Shona *mbira* music
mbulu-mbumba (Humbi) 152 n.29
Mbuti
  andôbu 75 n.4
  kabarome 41
Mchunu, Sipho 29
melodies 93, 104, 240–1
  overtone harmonics 133, 189–90, 193, 196, 207, 219, 242, 245
  parallel harmony 216
  partial tone 72, 74
  producing 17
  Sawubona magujéndlini **190**, 193
  umakhweyana polyphonic tradition 134, 137
  whistling 220
  Xhosa 207, 211–12
Mhlanga, Chris 167
Mhungu, Jacob 167, 178 n.18, 179 n.21
middle-braced bow **12**, 20, 102, **102**, 148 n.2
minor-third tuning (*tshihwana*) 69
  intervals, fundamentals 69, **70**
  mouth-filtered harmonic partials **71**, 71–2, **72**
  Nga vha mu rende Yesu 72, **73**, 75 n.8
  string length ratios 69, **70**
Moeketsane, Pae 230
mokgweba (Setswana) 248–9
Moko, !Xayee 230, **231**, 232, 235, 241

'A'gaige' 242, 245, **245–48**
overtone melodies 242
Mokwena, Evelina 206, 221, **222**
mono-heterochord musical bows 109 n.2, 113, 148 n.2
moretlwa (Setswana) 235–6, 238
Morris, Lorry Tao 230, 233, **233**
mouth resonated bows 10, 17, 19, 20, 157, 162, 187–8, 241–2. *See also* braced bows; unbraced bows
Mpayipheli, Tsolwana 208
Mphila, Gogo Khokhiwe 186
Mswati III, King 184, 197
mtangala (Nyasa) 163
Mthethwa, Bongani 144
Muchabaiwa 57–8
Muchena, Mondrek 38
   as multi-instrumentalist 167
Mugabe, Robert 178 n.9
Mugglestone, E. 3
Mujuru, Ephat 65, 167
Mukhavele, Luca 29
mukube (mouth bow) 157–58, 162, 177 n.2, 178 n.13, 179 n.27
   Chigamba playing **163**
   description 163
   memory of Chigamba's father, recalling 163, 173–5
   records 163–4
multi-bow harp-type **16**, 17
Munekamba, Metatu **106**, 107
Munyayi, P. 71–2, **73**, 75 n.8
Muradzikwa, Compound (Sekuru) 38, 59–61, 157–9, **160**, 164, 167, 168, 176
   'Buhera, Beautiful Country' 178 n.10
   and Chigamba 161
   dzikamunhenga 160
   early life 160
   ground-bow with children's herding games 170–1
   Mabhiza (*chipendani* piece) 60
   as multi-instrumentalist 167
   Ndezvemeso Muromo Chinyarara (*chipendani* piece) 59
   playing ground-bow **165**, 165–6
   Tsoko (*chipendani* piece) 61
   zvipendani 160

Murdock, George Peter 2
music composition workshop 93–4, 97, 100
musical bows 1–2, 85
   Africa and 3
   Classification (*see* classification (bows))
   events, projects and activities 29, 30, 33 n.17, 33 n.18, 33 n.20
   musicians as multi-instrumentalists 167–8
   Namibia bow music, collections 85
   resurgent interest in 158–60
   social dynamics of (Zimbabwe's) 157, 168–9
   sound production, scales and characteristics 3, 10, 17, 18, 20, 84, 94, **96**
   using modern materials 17, 18
Mususa, Green Tamanikwa 38, 167, 178 n.20, 179 n.25
   as multi-instrumentalist 167
   'Murungu' song 168–9
   as organizer of *ngoma* group 167
   playing root I **47**
   playing root II **48, 49**
   playing root III **51**
   playing root IV **52**
Muza, Cosmas 67
Mvotyo, Nopasile 219

Namibia 83, 206
   collections on bow music 85
   music of 239
   musical bows (*see specific Namibian musical bows*)
   people map **84**
Namulo, Emanuel 94, **95**, 96, 105
   song about a Kudu and a Girl **96**
   song about migrant miners 97, **97**
Ncozana, Jonathan 30, **31**, 32 n.2
Ndezvemeso Muromo Chinyarara (*chipendani* piece) 59
Ndodzungaira (Shona *mbira dzavadzimu* piece) 67, **67**
Nettl, B. 19, 20, 29, 178 n.16. *See also* classification (bows)
Nga vha mu rende Yesu (*tshihwana*-based song) 71–2, **73**, 75 n.8

Ngema, B. **147**, 148. *See also* Alikho la ekhaya (*umakhweyana* song)
Ngibambeni Ngibambeni (Zulu song) 140, 152 n.33
ngoma (drums) 167, 173, 177 n.1
Ngqoko 203
    bow as singer 207–8
    bow materials 207
    isiXhosa bows, names 205–6
    Ngqoko Group 208
    version of Ntsikana's Song 218, **218**
Ngqoko Group 208, 220, 226
    with *ikatari* **211**
    Matiso's maxim 208–9
    Nomkangaye **220**
    performers bows and purposes 209
Ngqoko Traditional Xhosa Music Ensemble. *See* Ngqoko Group
Nguni. *See* Xhosa; Zulu
Nhamo, Golden 167
njari (*mbira*) 167, 177 n.1, 178 n.18, 179 n.21
Nkambule, Sibusiso 200
N!oma 229, 230, **231**, 233
N!oma jieu ('springhare music bow') 229, 230, 248–9
    African Wild Dogs (*Lycaon pictus*) 249
    Galotsa playing 232, **232**
    Marago playing 233
Nomkangaye (*umrhubhe* song) 219, **220**
Nontyolo (Xhosa song) **214**, 215
/noukhas (Damara) 20, 100, **101**, 109
Ntsikana the Prophet 213
Ntsikana's Song 216–17, **217**, **218**, 227 n.14
Nyandoro, Sydney Musarurwa 38, **39**
    as multi-instrumentalist 167
    playing root I **47**
    playing root II **49**
    playing root III **51**
    playing root IV **53**
Nzakara *nzangu^{n}la* 75 n.9

okamburumbumbwa (Ovambo) **13**, 20, 94, **95**, 108
    hexatonic bow scale **96**
    song about a Kudu and a Girl **96**
    song about migrant miners 97, **97**
    Vashitwa va Kalunga 94

Olivier, Emmanuelle 32 n.7, 83, 85, 101, 105, 110 n.12, 239
ombulumbumba (otjiZimba) **13**, 104, 108, 110 n.5, 110 n.11
    song with 105, **105**
    Tjisura playing 104, **104**
Ondendele (OvaZimba) **102**, **109**
Orem, Eric 64
'otic illusion' 103, **103**
outa (otjiHimba) **102**, 109
    otic illusion 103, **103**
    playing method for 102
    whistling 102–4, **103**
Ovambo 83
    music composition workshop 94
    Okamburumbumbwa (*see okamburumbumbwa* (Ovambo))
    scale usage of 94
OvaZimba 84
    mouth bows **109**
    ombulumbumba **13**, **104**, 104–5, **105**, 108, 110 n.5, 110 n.11
    pluriarc 105, **106**, **107**, 107–8, **108**, 109
overtone harmonics 127
    biradical tonal organisation 133–4, **134**
    triradical tonal organization 134–5, **135–6**, 137, 150 n.24
    whistling 133, 151 n.25
overtone music (overtones) 2, 17, 32 n.10, 32 n.11, 86, 99–100, 102–3, 226, 241
    calabash-resonated bows 126
    harmonics (*see* overtone harmonics)
    Kavango bow playing 86, **87**, **88**
    sitontolo 191–2, 198, 200
    uhadi 206–7, 211–12, **212**
    of vibrating string 86, **86**

Pedi 2
    lekope 75 n.4, 163, 179 n.26, 187
    sekgapa 115, 151 n.27, 152 n.29
Peires, Jeff 214, 221
Perman, Tony 164
phuduhudu (Setswana) 242
Pintshana, Tontsi 209, **210**, **222**, 222–3
Plaatjies, Dizu 29, **224**, 226
playing technique (*chipendani*) 41, 46, 75 n.5

'Kwa ambuya asina keriya' **58**, 59
Mabhiza 60
mouth-filtered harmonic partials 54–5, **55**, **56**
Ndezvemeso Muromo Chinyarara 59
root I 46, **46**, **47**
root II 46, **48**, **49**
root III 50, **50**, **51**
root IV 50, **52**, **53**
roots, synopsis 54, **54** (*see also* root progressions)
Tsoko 60–1
pluriarc (otjiZimba) 17, 101, 105, **106**, 109
finger technique **106**
songs with **107**, 107–8, **108**
polyphonic multi-part singing 74
Princess Constance Magogo kaDinizulu. *See* kaDinizulu, C.M.
PULSES 150 n.22

Qadushe, Nomawuntini 213–14, 216, **217**
Qangi Qangi LTD. 30

Ritter, Tex 179 n.21
Rivière, Hervé 83, 85
root progressions 56–7, **57**, 59–61, 72
in abstracto 57
ostinato 74
6-step 'standard' (*see* 6-step 'standard' root progression)
12-step 'standard' (*see* 12-step 'standard' root progression)
rugoma (Kavango) 20, 87, **88**, 108, 227 n.16
overtone patterns **88**
traditional song with *marugoma* duet 87, **88**, **89**, 89–90
Rukunde, D. 87
rugoma overtone patterns 87, **88**
Rycroft, David 18, 133–4, 150 n.19, 150 n.24, 152 n.33, 197, 201 n.8

Sachs, C. 18–20, 115. *See also* classification (bows)
San 2–3, 15, 32 n.5, 87, 105, 234
scale usage 84
Thembu Xhosa 204–5
Saus, Wolfgang 240–1

Sawubona magujèndlini (*sitontolo* song) 189–90, **190**, 193
Schneider, Peter 240
Schöpf, J. 3
Sechuriti, Limphitetse 'Chibuku' 230
segankuru (Botswana) 20, 97–98
segwana (Chwana/Tswana) 151 n.27, 152 n.29
sehankule (Sotho) 20
sekatari (Sotho) 3, 206, 235
sekgapa (Sotho/Pedi) 115, 151 n.27, 152 n.29
Sekuru's Stories 161
self communication 176
self-delectative (musical bows) 159–60, 175–6, 177, 180 n.29
setinkane (lamellaphone) 230, 232–3, 235
Shandu, Cwayizile 142, 144. *See also* EBloemfontein (*umakhweyana* song)
Shepard scales 75 n.9
Shepardization 74, 75 n.9
Shona *mbira* music 37, 41, 61, 177 n.1. *See also* karimba music (Shona)
Chipendani (*see* chipendani (mouth bow))
dzavadzimu 65, 67, **67**, 157, 165, 167–68
dzaVaNdau 41, 177 n.1
harmonic progressions 64, **65**
Kariga mombe 65
Ndodzungaira 67, **67**
types 167, 177 n.1
zvipendani, dyads 65–6, **66**
Shongwe, Solomon 183, **186**, 188, 190, 198, 200 n.4
Abasanendzaba 200
as farmer and miner 192
learning experience 191, 200
making process (*sitontolo*) 187
performance 198–9, **199**
Sawubona magujèndlini 189–90, **190**, 193
Sibiya, Delisa 144, **146**, 153 n.40. *See also* Amadoda kashelani (*umakhweyana* song)
Siphum' eCancele (*ikatari* song) 224, **225**
sitontolo (mouth bow) 186

Magagula playing **189**
making process 187
Matjatjayela 193
performers of 190–2
Sawubona maguj'endlini 189–90, **190**
Shongwe with **186**
sonics and performance in 197–9, **199**
text and poeticism in 193–7, 200
tone-producing technique 188, 200
6-step 'standard' root progression 56–7, **57**, 63, 66
Chemutengure (*karimba* piece) 64, **64**
chipendani/karimba 64–5
'Kwa ambuya asina keriya' (*chipendani* piece) 58
Mabhiza (*chipendani* piece) 60
Ndezvemeso Muromo Chinyarara (*chipendani* piece) 59
Tsoko (*chipendani* piece) 60–1
typical manifestation 61–2, **62**
Sobhuza II, King 184
societies 2–3
SONY WMD-6C professional Walkman 249
Sotho 2
lekope 75 n.4, 163, 179 n.26, 187
lesiba 10, 20
sehankule 20
sekatari 3, 206, 235
sekgapa 115, 151 n.27, 152 n.29
tsorwani 99
Sound of Africa Series (Tracey) 203
Sound Tools Extended (STx) software 241–2, **243**, **244**, 250, 250 n.12
Southern Africa 2, 113. *See also specific regions*
Central African countries 2
East African countries 2
musical bows (*see* musical bows)
societies 2–3 (*see also specific societies*)
spectrograms (STx) 241, **243**, **244**, 250
'staccato' technique 124, 126, 132
Swati
ligubhu 133, 138, 150 n.19, 151 n.28
makhweyane 20, 152 n.29, 159, 185–6, 196
Swaziland. *See* eSwatini, kingdom of
Swaziland National Council of Arts and Culture 185

Tascam DA-P1 Digital Audio Tape (DAT) recorder 249
Tavasika, Chigamba 163, 167, 173
tetratonic scales 17, 61–2, 84, 86–7, 89, 91–3
Thembu Xhosa 203–5, 208, 218
timbral music 240–1
Tjisuta, Petrus 104, **104**
Tracey, Andrew 33 n.22, 37, 41, 57, 61, 63, 94, 100, 226. *See also* basic *kalimba* core (Tracey)
Tracey, Hugh 37, 57–8, 142, 175–6, 180 n.29, 203
Akasangibhaleli' 142, **143**
EBloemfontein 142, **143**
traditional music/songs 96, 98, 203
eSwatini 185
with *gorito* **99**, 99–100, **100**
with *kaworongongo* mouth bow **91**, **92**
by *lipuruboro* **93**
with *marugoma* duet 87, **88**, **89**, 89–90
Xhosa melodies 207
Zulu women, performance of 138–9
Travers, Gilly 178 n.9
Travers, Norman 178 n.9
Tree, K. B. 230, 232
Trent, Tererai 171
triradical tonal organization 134–5, **135–6**, 137, 150 n.24
tshihwana (Venda) 37, 41, 68, **73**, 187
Nga vha mu rende Yesu 71–2, **73**
one-dimensional string-divider 69, 74 n.4
string length ratios 69, **70**
tunings 68–9 (*see also* minor-third tuning (*tshihwana*))
tshipendani (Karanga) 187
tshitendole (Chopi) 152 n.29
tsijolo (Venda) 3
Tsoko (*chipendani* piece) 59–61
Tsonga 3, 115
umakhweyana bow adopted from 149 n.16, 149 n.17, 150 n.19
xitende 20, 134, 150 n.19, 150 n.24, 152 n.29, 185
tsorwani (Sotho) 99
Tswana 98
lengope 163, 233

segankuru 20, 97–8
segwana 151 n.27, 152 n.29
Tukani, Nofetyu 213, 221
tuning systems 17, 68–9. *See also* minor-third tuning (*tshihwana*)
  positional method (*ingona*) **121**, 122
  rotatory method (*ingona*) **122**, 122–3
  sitontolo 188
  umakhweyana 119, 121
Turino, Thomas 167, 178 n.18, 179 n.21
12-step 'standard' root progression 64, **65**
  Kariga mombe (*mbira dzavadzimu* piece) 65
  Ndodzungaira (*mbira dzavadzimu* piece) 67, **67**
  zvipendani, duet of 65–6, **66**

ubhaqa (grass stalk playing stick) **116**, 124, 126, 150 n.23
ugubhu (Zulu) 10, **11**, 20, 113, **116**, 152 n.31
  'Abantu Baphelile' song **135**
  biradical tonal organisation 133, **134**
  fundamental notes, sounding 123–4, **124**, **125**, 126
  imvingo 117–18
  inkohlisa 139–40
  structural features of 115–16
  terminological references to 115
  traditional performance 138
  uncertainties 151 n.28
  undivided string 119, **119**
ugwali (Xhosa) 20, 205
uhadi (Xhosa) 10, **11**, 17, 20, 94, 133, 151 n.27, 203–4, 205, 208–9, 225
  amaXhosa history in songs 213–16, **214**
  calabash as resonator 207
  description 211
  Dywili with **210**, **212**
  Inxembula **215**, 216–18
  Manisi playing **211**
  method of playing 206
  Ntsikana's Song 216, **217**, **218**
  overtone chords **212**
  overtones **212**
  and *umrhubhe* 126–7
ukuvala uthaka 129
ulizi (wood) 207
uluthi/induku (stave) **116**, 116–19, 126
ulwapes' 224
umakhweyana/umakhweyane (Zulu) 10, **12**, 17, 20, **31**, 113–15, **116**, 148 n.4, 149 n.11, 151 n.25, 151 n.29, 152 n.29, 152 n.31, 227 n.10
  borrowing 130, 149 n.16, 149 n.17, 150 n.19
  fundamental notes (*see* fundamental notes, sounding (*umakhweyana*))
  as *inkohlisa* 139, 141 (*see also inkohlisa* (Zulu))
  iselwa (calabash) as resonator **123**
  'Kwasenza (It happened to us)' **137**
  positional method of tuning (*ingona*) **121**, 122
  post-marital *inkohlisa* context 144–5, **145**, 147–8
  premarital *inkohlisa* context 141–2, 144
  rotatory method of tuning (*ingona*) **122**, 122–3
  stave (*induku/uluthi*) 117, 126
  string division (*ingona*) 119–21, **120**, 149 n.11
  structural features of 115–16
  terminological references to 115
  traditional performance 138
  triradical tonal organization 134–5, **135–6**, 137
  uncertainties 151 n.28
uqwabe/isiqwemqwemana 129–33 (*see also isiqwemqwemana* (*umakhweyana*, Zulu); *uqwabe* (*umakhweyana*, Zulu))
umbangandlala (*heteromorpha arborescens*) 116
Umbiliphi (*makhweyane* song) 197, 201 n.8
umhubhe (Zulu) 20
umngqokolo ngomqangi 226
umqangala (Zulu) 20, 163, 178 n.16
umqangi (Xhosa) 131, 205, 209, 221, **222**, 226
umqunge (isiMpondo) 205, 206
umrhubhe (Xhosa) **4**, 17, 20, 131, 133, 204, 205–6, 208–9, **210**, **219**, 221
  construction 218–19
  Nomkangaye 219, **220**
  Nontyolo **214**, 215
  uhadi and 126–7

Umrhubhe wemimangaliso 216, 219
   with whistling 226
unbraced bows 10, 17, 18, 19, 102, **102**,
   113, 248
   with attached resonator **11**, 205–6, 211
   dimbwa 177 n.2
   made of river-reed **5**
   in one piece **4**
   with sinew string 236, **237**, 238, **239**, 249
   in two pieces **6**
   Ugubhu (*see* ugubhu (Zulu))
   Uhadi (*see* uhadi (Xhosa))
   vibration/sound **7**
undivided single strings 20, **119**, 120,
   133–4, 138, 148 n.3, 151 n.28, 163.
   See also ugubhu (Zulu)
Universal Men (Juluka) 29
uqwabe (*umakhweyana*, Zulu) 115, 149
   n.17, 150 n.23
   adoption of 130
   onomatopoeia and equal-pulse rhythm
      131, 131–2
   as synonyms 129–30

Van den Berg, R. 29
Vashitwa va Kalunga (*okamburumbumbwa*
   song) 94
Venda 3, 15
   dende 115, 152 n.29
   galinga **15**, **16**
   lugube 163
   tshihwana (*see* tshihwana (Venda))
   tshikona 37, 69, 75 n.9
   tsijolo 3

Wagogo (Tanzania) 17
War of Mlanjeni (1851–3) 213–14, 216
wedsa/*wedza* 158, 177 n.2
whistling 38, 102–4, **103**, 133, 151 n.25,
   208, 219–20, **220**, 226
wire bow
   acoustics 241–2, 245
   Keibi's braced 238, **238**
   Kxi !ao 240
   Yohne's bow 233, 235, 238
Wood, Elizabeth 233

Xhosa 2, 32 n.5, 74
   amaXhosa (*see* amaXhosa)
   bow music theory (isiXhosa) 212
   dialects 126, 150 n.21, 226 n.3
   ikatari 3, 20, 85, 205–6, 208–9, **210**,
      211, **214**, 215, **224**, 224–5
   inkinge **5**, **6**, 20, 87, 163, 205–6, 209,
      210, **222**, 222–3, **223**
   names of bows 205–6
   scale and tonal shift **17**, **212**
   ugwali 20, 205
   Uhadi (*see* uhadi (Xhosa))
   Umrhubhe (*see* umrhubhe (Xhosa))
xipendana (Shangana-Tsonga) 74 n.1, 74
   n.2, 75 n.4, 179 n.26
xitende (Tsonga) 20, 134, 150 n.19, 150
   n.24, 152 n.29, 185
xizambi (Mozambique) 7, 10, 29

Yakayaka – ndemka (*uhadi* song) 213,
   221, 221–3
Yekani, Nogcinile **211**, 219
Yohne of Karee 230, 233, 235,
   238

Zimbabwean bows. *See chipendani* (mouth
   bow); ground-bow; *mukube*
   (mouth bow)
zindingwandingwa 158
zingaringi 158
Zulu 2, 151 n.27
   imvingo 113–14, **117**, 117–19, 138,
      148 n.4, 148 n.5, 151 n.28
   Inkohlisa (*see* inkohlisa (Zulu))
   isicelekeshe 20
   isiqomqomana 20, 41, 149 n.15
   map of KwaZulu-Natal **114**
   Ugubhu (*see* ugubhu (Zulu))
   Umakhweyane (*see*
      umakhweyana/umakhweyane
      (Zulu))
   umhubhe 20
   umqangala 20, 163, 178 n.16
Zungu, Nomatheku 142, 144. *See also*
   Akasangibhaleli' (*umakhweyana*
   song)

www.ingramcontent.com/pod-product-compliance
Lightning Source LLC
Chambersburg PA
CBHW072131290426
44111CB00012B/1857